NEAR DEATH EXPERIENCES

NEAR DEATH EXPERIENCES

The Science, Psychology and Anthropology Behind the Phenomenon

ANTHONY PEAKE

Foreword by Dr Pascal Michael

This edition published in 2024 by Arcturus Publishing Limited
26/27 Bickels Yard, 151–153 Bermondsey Street,
London SE1 3HA

AD011844UK

Printed in the UK

CONTENTS

Foreword

A book on the singular subject which has immeasurable implications for life – death – is a book which is forever welcomed. But another reason for this book's prescient illumination of the phenomenon of the near-death experience (NDE) is the fact that more and more people are having them. As resuscitation technologies become ever more developed and refined, more human beings, and potentially from deeper into the dying process – for a 'process' it is increasingly becoming understood as, versus mere moment – are re-emerging from the throes of death. This is echoing the so-called renaissance in psychedelic research, where, if such drugs are sanctioned in medical, legal or religious contexts (which is on the horizon for many countries and already the case for many others), the classical mystical and other 'exceptional human experiences' (EHEs) they occasion will suddenly burst into experiential possibility for countless folk for whom they might otherwise forever remain concealed. And, of course, one such EHE which may be engendered, at least in some dimensions, by psychedelics – as I and several other colleagues show – is the near-death experience. I'm especially pleased, therefore, to see a dedicated segment in this book casting light on the NDE by virtue of psychedelics, such as DMT or 5MeO-DMT.

As this nexus becomes further explored and elucidated, I would forecast that the NDE will certainly hitch a ride on the rushing winds generated by the explosion of psychedelic conversation, and become more attended to, funded and ultimately legitimized. Indeed, this mainstreaming was cleverly executed by early psychedelic researchers of this new wave, gesturing emphatically to the crisis that psychiatry finds itself in and the need to localize new methods for assuaging suffering in domains hitherto rebuked. With the paralleling upsurge in more rigorous NDE investigation, irrespective of their ontological veridicality, their occurrence in states like coma where the detection of consciousness is infamously confounding – yet critical – has prompted more young, bright neurologists and neuropsychologists to turn their sights to NDEs to help unravel their nature, and aid in the care of those with such disorders of consciousness. This book additionally includes a treatment of the UFO phenomenon, and again very happily so, owing to some obvious and other much more unexpected resonances with the NDE which I've also presented on. Even this, once an untouchable topic, is now gaining impressive momentum and official recognition. Similarly, this was via shrewd means, such as emphasizing the threat to democracy when unelected officials blockade political leaders from access to information about clandestine operations, or the threat to the safety of civilian, commercial or military pilots when unknown aerial phenomena frequently come into dangerous proximity. This is simply one way, on the level of our present social response to these exceptional experiences, that all of them are, while not yet fully explicated, a family of intimately related phenomena. As a researcher embroiled in discussing each of them – as is the author of the book you now read – I'm sure that it will be in the entangling of them together, in fact, that our confused understanding of them will become disentangled.

One of the main reasons I wanted to write the foreword to this book is that its author, Anthony Peake – who, eventually, became a friend – has had a not-insignificant influence on me ever since I was an adolescent. I read many of his books (such as *The Labyrinth of Time* and *The Infinite Mindfield*), but the first was *Is There Life After Death?*. The most affecting aspect for me was that this reading was my earliest exposure to writing which surveyed swathes of undeniably anomalous, even Fortean, phenomena, and yet also chose to incorporate and – where possible – integrate what he could garner about the mechanisms at the level of the brain. This was done with the agenda neither to shrink these phenomena down to the Laplacian level of neuromolecular determinacy nor to aggrandize them to an echelon at which they wholly superseded the relevance of the neurosciences. And within his treatment there was some tacit, and often explicit, cosmology that, even in the face of the – typically unforgiving – mechanical, could still be reconciled with the metaphysical. This approach is not abandoned in the present volume, still reverberating throughout, in sentiments from the author that (to paraphrase) the mystery of death shall not be revealed by the whimsicality of parapsychology, but by the hardness of neurology.

This feeling of mine was crystallized when, on author of esotericism Julian Vayne's YouTube series *My Magical Thing* – a sort of spiritual show-and-tell, where he invites guests to present a single chosen object which they deem magical – Peake decided to showcase the *brain* (or at least, a model thereof). Arthur C. Clarke may have famously announced that any sufficiently advanced technology will be conceived of as magic. But I submit that – while subscribers to materialism may accusatorily apply this to the perception of consciousness held by the magically-inclined – in some cases, like that of the credulity-straining mystery offered by the thinking, feeling, dreaming and loving fleshy globe that is the brain, some things may certainly be forms of technology, but may with utter simultaneity preserve a magical status. The brain is frequently heralded as the most complex object in the known universe, and as neuroscientist David Eagleman has it (in *The Brain: The Story of You*), *it is you!* This statement is usually interpreted in the light of awe and re-enchantment of the once-epitheted 'enchanted loom' which lies behind your eyes – and *ipso facto*, of your very self. As it should be! However, I think it is also very sobering, and fruitfully so, to wed this revelation with the entreaty cast above the temple of Apollo where the Delphic oracle resided: Γνῶθι σαυτόν – 'Know thyself'. That is, it is no wonder that this ancient call to the most elusive of aspirations, spiritual realization itself, is bound up with the minor task of understanding – from the inside – the most complex object ever known. Which happens to be you. It is hard to be a human being – caught in a matrix in which you identify with a mortal frame and being existentially situated such that it's tricky not to feel like a 'stranger in a strange land'. Questions of the body and of the beyond forever emerge on the plane of thought – just as this book attempts to satisfy them, even momentarily. But I've always been firmly of the position that earnest seeking into spheres encircling such phenomena as the near-death experience, given its constituting the very ricocheting from the undiscovered country back into this world, will carry with it some gifts of gnosis. Gnosis, though, importantly having the Greek denotation of knowledge of the heart, and not the type of knowledge we have, sadly, come to otherwise prize.

Peake's first book on life after death which I read may have been an example of the 'library angel' phenomenon. It was surely a serendipitous find. I simply noticed it, as I frolicked around my grandparents' sunroom as a teenager, on their bookshelf. But it was only in 2022, when I chanced upon it again in the library of my late father, Andrew, who passed away just the year prior – and rediscovered when turning to the first page that there inside also resided a very touching note from my maternal grandmother, Evelyne, herself not long deceased, to my mother, Carolyne, for whom the book was a gift in memory of her recently passed-on brother, my uncle Broderick. And parallel to this (as my dream journal notes inform me), some recent time before this finding I had a premonitory dream which conveyed as its central message the Pauline line, 'reap as you sow'. Incidentally, it also entailed the feeling of my soul spinning as a vortex, which seems apt in its evoking of reincarnatory cycles. My grandma's note read as follows:

> *We reap as we sow,*
> *and the Mystery remains –*
> *all the Whys, Ifs and Because?*
> *become a fraction of being,*
> *in the Eternity of time,*
> *that eventually develops the spirit*
> *into the Divine.*
>
> *– Evelyne Sharman, 2006*

It was a moving thing to see this book, Peake's first, on life after death occupy this small but poignant place in my family's life. And so, it's especially pleasing – after I went on in the intervening years to achieve a lectureship specializing in the near-death experience – to be able to write the foreword for what may be his last, on the very same phenomenon.

The message from beyond a multiplicity of familial graves to remind oneself that 'whatsoever one sows, they shall reap', presaged by a dream and inscribed in a book which has in its title an implicit question of ontology (what reality is, or isn't), is pivotal to realign oneself not with the quixotic quest to *know*, but with the reality of meaning. This reminds me of the discourse around Plato's allegory of the cave, in which prisoners are chained such that their only perception, and therefore model of the world, is an illusory one, one of shadow-play cast by an unwitnessed fire behind them. But this story necessitates puppet masters – those making the shadows. Religious scholar Diana Pasulka writes of her informants, in this case intelligence agents in the US, that they readily admit they operate as these very puppet masters, controlling people's assumptions about what the world consists of. But they also echo what transpires in Plato's cave, whereby the strivings of one escaped prisoner, who has laid his eyes on the fire which is the true source of their facsimile reality, to try to liberate his fellow inmates is met with not just scepticism but murderous retaliation. The intelligence operatives claimed that people do not wish to be awakened, and so they justify their continued perceptual manipulations. Whatever the truth of their own motives, an argument could still be made for how such constraining of society's cosmologies may well be for their 'own good'. That is only to say, instead of 'ruining our eyes' (as one Platonic prisoner claimed) due to the sheer brilliance of the Promethean flame, corresponding to too feverish a pursuit of the transpersonal – or to the *uberwelt* properly presided over by the 'uber-daemon', as Peake has written of it – we might do better to stay within our *umwelt*, the space of our immanent reality. After all, this space is the self-same space to which near-death experiencers are explicitly redelivered by preternatural agencies, or within which they resolve to stay despite their dissolved fear of death and ecstasy in the afterlife, perhaps due to their newfound mission in *this* life or love for those they would otherwise leave behind.

Whatever the might with which we may endeavour to end our ignorance of things of heaven and Earth, of brain and soul, it may well be that there can never be a resolution. Much like contradiction equations in simple algebra, it may be that whichever value we attempt to replace the mysterious variable with, there will never be a solution which is satisfactory or non-paradoxical. And perhaps this is a feature, rather than an error, of the matrix in which we cannot deny we find ourselves – for very similar beneficent, versus malign, reasons just expounded, but never better expressed than by one young girl after her own NDE, that 'life is for now, light is for later'. I'm reminded again of Graham Hancock, who at a private symposium we both spoke at (regarding the sentient *other* in NDEs, DMT experiences, alien abduction and other EHEs) also endorsed his suspicion that death, on account of it being a concerted design effort on the part of the divine architect, will be the one enigma never to be reconciled. I would add, however, that it may still be reconciled *with*. But these sentiments of ours are mere echoes, for instance, of the epic of King Gilgamesh, humanity's very oldest written literary text, which some (such as Gregory Shushan) speculate may have been a documentary NDE. This narrative could be compared to the story of the ancient Iranian historical figure Kartir, and his NDE-like journey associated with the magical substance *vishtasp* – a story discussed by Peake here, in the anthropological chapter which I believe was another particularly meaningful contribution to the near-death dialogue. In the case of Gilgamesh, he travelled to the ends of the Earth after the death of a loved one to find the elixir of life, but ultimately was informed by the god Utnapishtim that no one shall have dominion over death. Likewise, the story of the *Chandogya Upanishad*, the Hindu sacred text, declares that the gods had hidden the secrets of the universe not in the depths of the ocean, or vastness of the sky, but in the recesses of the mind itself.

It may well be that, however much we plumb the corpus of evidence surrounding the NDE to know the real nature of death, and thus consciousness itself, we may simply have to die ourselves. 'To conquer death...' – as Jesus in *Jesus Christ Superstar*, the font of all theological knowledge, utters in his transporting falsetto – 'you only have to die.' This of course, however, does not mean one *shouldn't* ardently ask such questions – as this book does, while deftly providing some nourishing food for thought, if it cannot arrive at exhaustive satiation. Because it is in engaging contemplatively with the nature of one's mind, as the Hindu gods were conveying, that some inner luminosity can be ignited. Turning back to Plato's allegory which is transmitted through a fictionalized *dialogos*, conducting such conversations and Socratic inquiries with others, or even with ourselves, may be the instrument towards awakening to which Plato was referring. It is the question, and discerning how to ask such questions, which is actually the point of it all.

Pascal Michael, PhD
University of Greenwich
20 April 2024

Prologue

In the mid-1960s, a young philosophy student at the University of Virginia named Raymond Avery Moody attended a seminar by Professor John Marshall. The subject of the symposium was the philosophical issues related to death. Marshall told the group of a locally based psychiatrist who had been pronounced dead with a case of double pneumonia and then successfully resuscitated. While he was 'dead', the psychiatrist had the remarkable experience of finding himself outside his body. Marshall asked the students what this experience implied about the subjective nature of death.

A few months later, Moody had the opportunity to hear the psychiatrist, Dr George Ritchie, explain in detail what had happened to him in 1943 when he had been in hospital in Texas with a respiratory infection. What Ritchie then described was to fire in the young philosophy student a fascination to discover in detail what happens to human consciousness at the point of death. He began an intensive programme of research into the subject. He interviewed more than 150 individuals who, in life-threatening scenarios, had experienced a series of perceptions suggesting that death was not the end of life but the beginning of another existence. He called this the near-death experience, or NDE.

Although the circumstances surrounding each reported near-death experience may have been different, Moody noted that several similar traits could be identified, suggesting that the experience was more than simply a personal dream sequence. This was significant evidence for Moody that he was dealing with a universal, rather than a subjective, phenomenon. Typically, then, an NDE involves the following sequence of events. Firstly, the person would experience a powerful buzzing sensation, followed by the perception that they were leaving their body, usually by being drawn upwards. From this position outside the body, they might perceive the circumstances of their death, for example, in an operating theatre or at a car crash scene. They would then feel that they were being drawn down a long, dark tunnel. At the end of the tunnel would be a powerful source of light. This light might be coming from all directions, or it might have as its source a radiant figure, a literal 'being of light' which might or might not be accompanied by other similar beings who seem to be there to assist in some way. At this time, the person might see or hear spiritual versions of dead relatives or friends. They then would be given a review of their life and the choice of crossing a border or a boundary to a beautiful, other-worldly environment, from which there would be no return, or to go back to the world of the living and an abrupt return to the body.

In 1975, Moody published a book discussing his findings. It was an immediate bestseller, with the intriguing title *Life After Life*. Like most effective book titles, its name precisely defined its findings: that, after we die, we enter another life and that self-aware consciousness does not need the physical body to continue.

Life After Life has sold more than 13 million copies worldwide and has stimulated many other authors, laypersons and professionals to investigate what happens to human consciousness at the point of death.

A year after Moody's book, a poll by Gallup concluded that 69 per cent of Americans believed in life after death. This was followed in 1982 by another Gallup survey which suggested that 23 million Americans 'have, by prevailing medical definitions, died briefly or . . . come close to death' and that about 8 million of these persons 'have experienced some sort of mystical encounter along with the death event'. (Gallup & Proctor, 1982, p. 6)

Of those responding to the questionnaire, 26 per cent reported an out-of-body sensation, 32 per cent had a life review and 23 per cent sensed the presence of another being, with the tunnel experience reported by 9 per cent. What is particularly interesting – but was not part of Moody's nine traits – was that 23 per cent of the responders described experiencing heightened visual perceptions; 6 per cent claimed precognition.

Since 1975, scores of books, hundreds of academic papers and any number of mass-media articles have been written on the subject. In 1978, the International Association of Near-Death Studies (IANDS) was founded to investigate the science of the phenomenon.

My intention with this book is not to revisit material already written but to bring together some of the more neglected areas of the NDE into the public domain, specifically the anthropological aspects of the phenomenon, and to attempt a linkage between the NDE and other experiences such as alien abductions and the neurology of altered-states of consciousness, including those facilitated by mind-altering substances such as the hallucinogenic drug dimethyltryptamine (DMT) and the anaesthetic ketamine. This book will not be an extensive list of 'it happened to me' anecdotes and wild speculation regarding the mystical aspects of the experience. I have kept the number of NDE narratives to the absolute minimum. I will discuss only a handful of the classic cases as examples of the subjective nature of the experience.

I have written extensively about the NDE in several of my previous books and contributed my explanatory model to the mix, which I call 'Cheating the Ferryman'. However, I will only mention this in passing; my advocacy of this model is not the aim of this book. I make no apology for the few sections where I have lifted my own work from previous books. I feel it is a waste of time to re-word a narrative that has already worked effectively. This will allow you, the reader, to decide if you wish to investigate the source material further.

I have also included an extensive bibliography and reference section. I highly recommend reading some, if not all, of these important academic papers and books. They will enrich your experience and allow you to dig deeper into this fascinating topic.

PART 1

Classic Modern Cases

Introduction

In this chapter, I review a handful of much-reported cases regularly cited in books, articles and websites that wish to prove that the near-death experience is evidence of life after death. However, as with all biased reporting, the truth is far more complex than the often sensationalist 'gee-whiz it happened to me' accounts would have you believe. Each case cited has created a welter of controversy, with claims and counter-claims made by the two warring factions who accept and deny the stories being told. I will describe both arguments and leave you to make up your own mind. But please at all times bear in mind the famous injunction of Danish sociologist Marcello Truzzi: 'An extraordinary claim requires extraordinary proof.' (Truzzi, 1978).

Classic Modern Case – 1943 – George Ritchie

As mentioned in the Prologue, Dr George Ritchie's case from 1943 started the modern fascination with the near-death experience by stimulating Raymond Moody's interest in the subject.

On 20 December 1943, Ritchie, then a 20-year-old US Army private, was rushed into an Army hospital in Abilene, Texas, suffering from a severe respiratory infection. The illness had come on him suddenly and had somewhat compromised his plans to enrol at medical college in Richmond, Virginia, the following day. In fact the diagnosis was not good: he had a case of double pneumonia. As he lay in bed, Ritchie became aware that his temperature had suddenly increased; he leaned forward and began coughing up blood. Then, for a few seconds, everything went black. When he regained consciousness, Ritchie looked around the hospital room. It had changed. This surprised him. It dawned on him that he may have slept through the night, in which case it was the day of his enrolment at college. He felt much better and decided to get up and try to catch the train to Richmond. He jumped out of bed and went to where he had left his uniform, folded over a chair. To his surprise, it wasn't there. He looked for his duffel bag and that too had disappeared. He turned around to look under the bed and froze with horror. (Ritchie & Sherrill, 1978, p. 78) Lying in bed was the body of a young man: a young man that George immediately recognized as himself. Confused, and not a little disturbed, he walked out of the room into the corridor. Approaching him was one of the ward assistants. The man continued walking towards Ritchie as if he could not see him. Ritchie braced himself for a collision but nothing happened; the ward assistant passed through him.

The next thing George Ritchie knew, he was running down the corridor towards the metal door at the end. He went straight through it and found himself outside the hospital, flying through the air. He had no sensation of cold, even though he could see that he was only wearing his pyjamas. But he did have a feeling of travelling at great speed through the air. He knew he was flying east because the North Star was to his left. This was precisely the direction he needed to go from Abilene to Richmond. Ritchie's determination to get to the enrolment centre knew no bounds, it seemed. However, he was also aware that he needed to get specific directions if he was to fly to Virginia. He managed to slow himself down and, after flying over a bridge across a river, spotted a large city. Ritchie decided to stop and ask for directions. He descended to around 15 m (50 ft) and hovered above a white, single-storey building with a red roof. He noticed a blue light, which he quickly realized was coming from a neon sign advertising a beer called Pabst Blue Ribbon. On getting closer, he saw that the building was an all-night café with a neon sign shining through a right-hand window next to the entrance. On the other side of the door was a second window. (Ritchie, 1998, p. 29) Ritchie spotted a man walking towards the café and decided to try to speak to him and find out the city's name. He landed and attempted to engage the stranger in conversation. Just like earlier in the hospital, he was ignored and, again, the man walked straight through him. In shock, Ritchie approached a telephone pole with a guy wire. He tried to lean against it, only to see his hand go straight through. 'In some unimaginable way, I had lost my firmness of flesh, the body that other people saw,' he would later write. (Ritchie, 1998, p. 29)

It was at this point that Ritchie realized that he needed to get back to his body at the Army hospital in Abilene. He rose into the air and, at rapid speed, flew back in the direction he had come. After arriving at the hospital he found his body in an isolation cubicle with a sheet drawn over its face. He knew it was his body from the college fraternity ring on his left hand. Suddenly, Ritchie understood that he was dead. At this point, the whole room became illuminated with a powerful white light, the source being what Ritchie later described as a 'man made of light' that had entered the room. The being told Ritchie, 'You are in the presence of the Son of God.' Ritchie, a Christian, immediately assumed that the being meant Jesus. He then found himself experiencing every single episode of his life to that date, all of it happening simultaneously.

Ritchie then experienced himself high above the Earth and moving towards a pin-pick of light that eventually resolved itself into a city. There, he witnessed other dead people trying desperately to attract the attention of the living. He was informed by the Being of Light that those people were suicides and were trapped between worlds, not aware that they had died and, as such, unable to move on. He was also shown others who had died under normal circumstances and who, again, were trapped in this world without being able to engage with it physically.

Ritchie was then shown a vision of Heaven and a vision of Hell that seemed to be so clichéd as to suggest that at least some of his experience was being created by his own religious beliefs. He was given a vision of the future in which wars and natural disasters were commonplace.

He saw armies invading the US from the south, involving the extensive destruction of lives and property.

The Being of Light then told Ritchie that he had to return to the human plane and informed him that he had another 45 years left to live. Instantaneously, he found himself back in his body, lying under the sheet that he had seen earlier. An orderly who had been preparing the body for the morgue noticed feeble signs of life in the corpse and called the doctor. The worried medic hastily injected adrenaline into Ritchie's heart. This jolted the young man into life; a second life. Although Ritchie had not taken a breath for nine minutes, he showed no symptoms of brain damage. The commanding officer at the hospital would call the Ritchie case 'the most amazing circumstance of my career' and would later sign an affidavit stating that George Ritchie had indeed made a miraculous return from virtual death on that fateful night of 21 December 1943.

Ritchie made a full recovery. Ten months later, in October 1944, he and three soldier friends drove from Camp Barkeley, the hospital where his experience took place, to Cincinnati and on through Memphis and along the Mississippi River to Vicksburg. They were trying to find the city George had landed in during his out-of-body experience (OBE). Ritchie started to feel intense sensations of recognition as they drove through the streets. He saw a white all-night café with a red roof, and over the door was the Pabst neon sign that he had seen in his OBE, together with the telephone pole and guy wire.

This proved to Ritchie that what happened to him was a real experience. He had, in some way or other, travelled to a place he had never been to before and returned with information he could not have known about. Such was the power of his experience that he was happy to share it with others.

And so it was that, many years later, he told his story to a young Raymond Moody, and the world discovered the phenomenon of the near-death experience.

It is not at all surprising that many NDE cases occur in a hospital setting. This is the place where so many people end their lives. But one case, among all others, has been cited as irrefutable proof of the true and verifiable – 'veridical', in the terminology used in this field – aspect of the NDE, one in which a person was deliberately taken to the point of death as part of a surgical procedure. It is to the famous and somewhat controversial case of Pam Reynolds that we now turn our attention.

Classic Modern Case – 1991 – Pam Reynolds

Probably the most famous near-death case was reported in August 1991. This time, not only were the circumstances surrounding the NDE witnessed by medical professionals, they were deliberately created by them.

Pam Reynolds was a 35-year-old woman who had suffered a basilar artery aneurysm. In effect, a very large artery at the base of her brain had developed a blockage, causing it to fill with blood and expand like a balloon. It was in danger of bursting, which would have resulted in her death. Immediate action had to be taken. But the location of the aneurysm was highly problematic. To surgically clear the blockage, the blood supply to the artery had to be stopped. The surgeons would then be able to open Pam's skull, clear the blockage, and do any necessary repair work to the artery and surrounding tissue. This process would need at least an hour to be completed successfully. However, it was also known that any disruption of the blood supply to the brain longer than a few minutes would be fatal. How, then, could Pam be operated on and survive?

Fortunately, in modern medicine, anaesthetists are able to conduct a process known as a 'standby'. This involves giving the patient a general anaesthetic then, when this takes effect, cooling the patient's bodily temperature down to 15°C (60°F) and placing them in a form of suspended animation. The patient's heart is then stopped, and the blood drains out of the head. In effect, when this happens, all brain activity stops as well. The patient has 'flatlined', in that no measurable electrical activity will show up on an electroencephalogram (EEG). The patient is, in effect, brain-dead.

The operation on Pam Reynolds was completed by one of the leading experts in his field, neurosurgeon Robert Spetzler, and Pam survived to live another 19 years. However, something strange occurred while she was in a state of zero brain activity. When she awoke, she discussed in detail what had taken place in the operating theatre, including a description of what music was played ('Hotel California' by The Eagles). She also described a series of conversations that took place. She explained how she had watched the opening of her skull by the surgeon from a position above him. She described in detail the bone-cutting device and the distinct sound it made. What is strange about this is that in each of her ears were specially designed ear speakers that shut out all external sounds. In turn, the speakers were broadcasting audible clicks, which were used to confirm that her brain stem had ceased activity. This means that, even in normal circumstances, she would not have been able to hear anything; indeed, as she had also been given a general anaesthetic, she should have been fully unconscious.

It is important here to clarify precisely what the hypothermic cardiac arrest process involves and how it is monitored. It had been developed in the 1950s and Reynolds was not the first person to have it applied to a basilar artery aneurism. Her surgeon Robert Spetzler had followed an identical procedure with seven earlier patients. (Spetzler et al., 1988). By this methodology, the patient is given a general anaesthetic involving several different drugs (see below), the effects of which on the recipient's consciousness are monitored through what are known as Brainstem Auditory Evoked Potentials (BAEPs).

Auditory evoked potentials (AEPs) are microscopic electrical voltage signals generated by a sound through the auditory pathway. The evoked potential is generated in the cochlea, goes through the cochlear nerve, through the cochlear nucleus, superior olivary complex, lateral lemniscus, to the inferior colliculus in the midbrain, on to the medial geniculate body, and finally to the auditory cortex. To monitor the signals, a pair of moulded earphones is placed in the patient's left and right ear canals and taped in position. The earphones broadcast 100-decibel clicking sounds at 11.3 clicks per second. One hundred decibels is the equivalent of a power tool operated a few feet away from your ears, so it is very loud.

While Spetzler was opening Pam's head, a female cardiac surgeon located the femoral artery and vein in Pam's right groin; these vessels turned out to be too small to handle the large flow of blood needed to feed the cardiopulmonary bypass machine. Thus the left femoral artery and vein were prepared for use.

As she heard the bone saw activate, about 90 minutes into the process, Pam began a full near-death experience. She saw her body from outside and felt herself pulled down a tunnel of light. She saw her grandmother and other relatives at the end of the tunnel. She was then told by an uncle that she had to return. She felt him push her back into her body and, on entering it, she described it as like 'diving into a pool of ice-cold water. . . . It hurt.' (van Lommel, P., 2010, p. 173)

Contrary to many reports regarding this case, there is no evidence that any of Pam's NDE took place when she was 'flatlined'. In other words, there would have been measurable brain activity when she had experienced the NDE. For example, when the surgeon began the procedure to open Pam's skull, the standby process, the stimulus for the NDE, had not yet been started. Indeed, Pam described how she heard the nurses discussing the difficulty they were having finding suitable veins in her groin to commence the standby process. However, this does not explain how Pam could hear the conversations that were happening while under full general anaesthetic and with moulded earplugs in her ears. It would have been impossible for her to hear anything. She also described in detail the 'Midas Rex' bone saw, something again she could not have possibly seen.

So, whatever Pam did see and hear while on the operating table can only have been via some paranormal means.

Adding to the details of Pam's experience is the testimony of the man who conducted the operation, a highly skilled surgeon and director of the Barrow Neurological Institute. In a 2002 TV interview, Robert Spetzler stated that:

> *At that stage in the operation, nobody can observe or hear in that state. And I find it inconceivable that your normal senses, such as hearing, let alone the fact that she had clicking modules in each ear, that there was any way to hear [what she heard] through normal auditory pathways. I don't have an explanation for it.*[1]

In 2011, the anaesthesiologist Dr Gerald Woerlee took a more sceptical position. Citing information on BAEPs from a journal article written by Robert Spetzler himself, he showed that there was more than enough time between the clicks produced by the modules that Pam wore during the operation for her to hear and process the sounds.

What this means is that there was more than enough silence in the intervals between the clicks for Pam's brain to process the sounds in the operating theatre. But, of course, if Pam was totally unconscious at the time, then she could not have heard anything. Or perhaps she could: there is in fact evidence that anaesthetized patients can sometimes perceive, assimilate and recall what is taking place around them during medical procedures. (Cherkin & Harroun, 1971)

Woerlee, in his paper, then discussed several potential explanations for how Pam may have been aware of the information she claimed she perceived in her OBE state while under anaesthetic. He specifically focused on the issue of what Reynolds could actually hear whilst in such a deep state of unconsciousness. He stated that, since the early

---

1 Broome, K. (producer). 2002. *The day I died: The mind, the brain and near-death experiences* (motion picture). Glasgow, Scotland: BBC. Available for purchase at http://ffh.films.com/id/11685.

1970s, it has been known that people under general anaesthesia respond to sensations such as touch, movements, sound and pain. (Thornton & Sharpe, 1998) The issue is that these perceptions are rarely remembered when the person regains consciousness.

The question of Pam's encounter with the tunnel of light and her deceased relatives is also significant. It is improbable that this would have taken place, as many critics have argued, as she was coming out of the general anaesthetic, simply because people are incapable of any form of coherent thought at that stage, particularly not the kind of thought that can create complex and, more importantly, fully recalled dreams. This leaves us with the possibility that the NDE aspects (rather than the OBE aspects) took place during the standby process. This fact alone makes this case of profound importance to any serious researcher looking into evidence of the survival of consciousness after death.

The central issue of contention in this case is whether Pam was clinically 'dead' during the standby procedure, for how long and whether this coincided with her OBE perceptions.

In his much-discussed IANDS journal article from 2007, sceptic Keith Augustine of Internet Infidels drew up a timeline of Pam's operation. He claimed that she had no cerebral cortical activity for around half an hour. Indeed, his chart suggests that her OBE began a full two hours and five minutes before cooling her blood began. He argues that we know this from her account because she specifically recalled that the OBE started when there was an issue with the failure by the cardiovascular surgeon, Dr Murray, to insert tubing into her femoral blood vessels located in her right groin:

> *Someone said something about my veins and arteries being very small. I believe it was a female voice and that it was Dr Murray but I'm not sure. She was the cardiologist [sic]. I remember thinking that I should have told her about that. (Sabom, 1982, p. 42)*

Augustine used two sources to isolate the correct timings: Robert Spetzler's 'Head Surgeons Report' and Dr Murray's 'Operative Report'. (Augustine, 2007, pp. 219–220)

In his report, Spetzler recorded that, while he was cutting open Pam's skull using the Midas Rex, he saw 'Dr Murray performing bilateral femoral cut-downs for cannulation for cardiac bypass'. (Sabom, 1998, p. 185) In her report, Murray described the difficulties she encountered in accessing Pam's femoral artery.

Augustine then moved on to the actual accuracy of Pam's OBE perceptions. Pam claimed she could see from a location behind the surgeon's shoulder, looking in the direction of her body. She noted how strangely her head had been shaved and that she could see what looked like an electric toothbrush with a dent. She noticed that it had interchangeable blades. (Sabom, 1982, p. 41)

Augustine makes the point that, on waking from the procedure, Pam would have been aware of the peculiar way her head had been shaved. This is not an unreasonable assumption, but it does not invalidate the possibility that Pam may have seen this in her out-of-body state.

However, in a book published in 2010, Oxford University neurophysicist Professor Michael Marsh made a far more critical observation about Pam's OBE perceptions:

> *She neither saw her head being opened, nor did she competently report the most crucial detail of the operative technique employed: that is, her head was turned sharply to her left and held there rigidly by a robust, mechanical three-point pin head-holder, in order to allow the surgeon to proceed. (Marsh, 2010, p. 24)*

So, she was able to describe in detail the unusual way her head had been shaved but missed seeing the three-point head holder that surely would have obscured parts of the shaving areas? Indeed, to see her shaved head, she must have seen the head holder. This supports Augustine's observation that this element of her OBE was embroidered by future knowledge acquired when she regained consciousness.

Of course, all these scenarios can be used to explain what could have happened, but they do not tell us what actually happened. Various alternative explanations for any set of circumstances can be posited, but these do not prove that those circumstances did not occur. Alternative explanations are not proof. To quote Marcello Truzzi again, extraordinary claims demand extraordinary proofs.

The real question has to be, why was Pam Reynolds adamant that she was floating outside her body? Why would she make such claims if they did not happen? We cannot overlook Pam's claim that, during her experience, she was 'the most aware I think I have ever been in my life'.

All the arguments above were given within the context of our modern, scientific understanding of how the universe works. But, as I have stated, they do not prove or disprove in any way that the experience could have been precisely as Pam Reynolds described it. Indeed, a few years later, in 1998, another case was reported involving a person undergoing an emergency quadruple bypass operation. The patient, Al Sullivan, subsequently reported that he watched the surgery taking place and witnessed from a location outside of his body the surgeon making a strange gesture in which he waved his arms as if trying to fly. When the psychiatrist and author Bruce Greyson investigated this case, after discussing it with both the surgeon in question and Sullivan's cardiologist, who was also in the operating theatre at the time, he confirmed that this was precisely what took place.

After this, Al Sullivan experienced many of the features described by Pam Reynolds and, of course, many other people who claim to have had a NDE, including travelling through a dark space, seeing a tunnel, perceiving an unusually bright light, and meeting deceased loved ones.

The Pam Reynolds case is justifiably one of the most famous NDE cases. Clearly, there are elements of it that can be questioned, but all the alternative explanations for it do not prove that it did not happen as Pam Reynolds and Michael Sabom described it.

Another much-cited hospital-based case was to present itself six years later in the Pacific Northwest. Again, this has proven to be controversial. Central to it was, of all things, a shoe.

Classic Modern Case – 1997 – Marie's Shoe

One of the all-time classic examples of a 'veridical' NDE/OBE is the much-quoted and much-analysed case known as 'Maria's Shoe'. (Ring & Lawrence, 1993)

In April 1977, a female migrant worker was admitted into Seattle's Harborview Medical Center in Washington State. She had suffered a heart attack, so she was quickly rushed to the coronary care unit. She was in a very bad way and, three days later, suffered a second, massive heart attack. Fortunately, specialist staff were on hand and she was successfully resuscitated. Later that day, a social worker called Kimberly Clark called in to check on Maria. Although still ill, Maria was very excited and was keen to tell Clark that she had experienced a strange series of sensations while unconscious. She described how she witnessed her resuscitation from a position outside and above her body, noting printouts flowing from the monitoring machines measuring her vital signs. She then said that she became distracted by something over the area surrounding the emergency room entrance and 'willed herself' outside the hospital. She accurately described the area surrounding the emergency room entrance, which Clark found curious since a canopy over the entrance would have obstructed Maria's view if she had looked out of her hospital room window.

Floating in the air outside the window, Maria spotted something strange on a third-floor window ledge at the far side of the hospital. Again, she realized she could 'will' herself to another location as she suddenly found herself right next to the object that had caught her attention. It was a man's tennis shoe, specifically a dark blue left-foot shoe with a worn-out patch over the little toe and a single shoelace tucked under its heel. With this image in her mind, she found herself back in her body as the crash team seemingly saved her life.

Clark was fascinated by this and agreed to try to see if Maria had actually seen something that existed outside of her imagination. She walked outside the hospital but could see nothing from ground level. She then re-entered the building and began a room-to-room search of the floor above where Maria's resuscitation took place. Clark could see nothing, even when pressing her head against the window to get a better view. Eventually, and to her great surprise, on entering a room on the third floor of the north wing, she spotted the shoe. From her vantage point, she could only see a part of it and could not, for example, verify if it had a worn-out toe or a tucked-in shoelace.

The major problem with this case is that there is no confirmative information from any source other than Maria herself, and Clark reported the case seven years after her discussions with Maria. Indeed, by that time Maria had disappeared and was untraceable.

But just how much of this fascinating story can be taken as evidence of a veridical OBE during an NDE?

Because of this case's huge popularity, several in-depth investigations occurred. Seventeen years later, in 1994, Hayden Ebbern and Sean Mulligan visited Harborview to survey the sites where a number of the incidents occurred. They argued that as Maria had been in the hospital for three days, she would have become quite familiar with the monitoring equipment to which she was attached. Indeed, for that time, her hospital room was directly above the emergency room where her OBE took place. They then moved on to the central and most-discussed element of her NDE, the shoe.

Clark stated that the only way that Maria would have been able to see the shoe from her room would have been if she had pressed her face flat against the glass.

Ebbern and Mulligan placed a similar shoe in the location reported by Clark and then went outside the main reception area to test whether it could be seen. Even though considerable construction work was happening outside the building, the investigators claimed they could easily see the shoe. They concluded that people near Maria might have discussed this within Maria's hearing.

Of course, this is not evidence that Maria's experience was not real or reported accurately. However, we must acknowledge these issues rather than just repeating the story without any supporting information, as many writers have done.

Classic Modern Cases – 1997 – Vicky Umipeg and blind NDEs

The OBE cases discussed above involve sensory perception supplied by an unknown process. How can a person 'see' and 'hear' things when they have no eyes to see or ears to hear? Indeed, the mystery of how this process works deepens when one considers that there is no physical brain to present this information to consciousness. If veridical OBEs are real and not simply a hallucinatory state, then our understanding of how the brain works is in error. This is not a minor error but something that would demand a radical re-assessment of everything we have learned from neurology and physiology. In this scenario, the brain is not the location of consciousness. Even more amazing is the idea that consciousness does not need the physical body to continue existing.

As such, it will take more than the evidence presented by subjective experiences to change modern scientific thinking. However, there is one specific area of veridical OBE research that is very difficult to dismiss as hallucination. This involves the near-death experiences of blind people who, in the OBE state, claim that they can see.

The NDE researcher Kenneth Ring identified 21 blind individuals who had experienced an NDE. Of these, ten had been born blind, nine had lost their sight before the age of five and two were severely visually handicapped. Interestingly, ten of the subjects claimed that they 'saw' their body below them during the NDE. These ten all reported the usual Moody traits, including flying down the tunnel towards a bright light and encountering a being of light. One of the most interesting subjects was Vicki Umipeg, who when she revealed her story was a 43-year-old married mother of three children.

Vicki had been born extremely premature, and too much oxygen had been given to her after her birth. This destroyed her optic nerve and left her blind. During her life, Vicki had suffered two NDEs. The first was when she was 20 and was brought about by an attack of appendicitis. However, it was the second NDE that excited a great deal of interest. She was involved in a car crash when she was 22. In her NDE, she 'saw' herself as she hovered above the hospital bed. She noticed that a section of her long hair had been shaved off. After this, she felt herself float through the roof, and saw streetlights and houses below her. She then found herself in a field covered with flowers. In this field were people she had once known who were long dead. Suddenly, a radiant figure walked towards her. She considered this figure to be Jesus, although he never identified himself as such. This Being of Light gave her a full 'life review' that she saw in full colour and in great detail. After this, the being told her she had to return, to 'bear her children'. With this, she found herself slammed back into her body and experiencing once more the heavy dullness and intense pain of her physical being.

This case, and the others presented by Kenneth Ring and his co-writer Evelyn Elsaesser-Valarino in their book *Lessons from the Light*, suggests another way in which the mind can process sensory stimulation that does not involve an embodied brain or an eye. But the real question we must ask here is how can anyone see during an out-of-body state, not just blind people? Sight is a very complex process whereby light (electromagnetic energy) of a specific wavelength and/or a stream of photons enters the eye through the pupil and lands at the back of the eye on a light-sensitive area known as the retina. This then converts the image contained in the light into an electrical signal, which is carried by the optic nerve to the visual cortex at the back of the brain. Here, the image is re-converted and, in some magical process, is perceived by consciousness. For it to be possible for a person to see, all of these processes need to work at the same time

(I have simplified the explanation greatly here, but have written about it in greater detail in some of my other books). In an OBE state, there is no pupil, retina, optic nerve or visual cortex to process the image. So, how can a point of non-physical consciousness see anything? Indeed, the whole reason why blind individuals like Vickie Umipeg cannot see anything is that one or more of the visual processes do not work. This problem can be applied to all sensory perceptions. We hear through air vibrating the eardrum; we smell through molecules reacting with sense nerves in the nose and mouth. Again, in a disembodied state, there are no sensory organs to process the sound waves or molecules. There is only one psychological state in which sight, sound, smell and taste are processed without any sensory input, and this is in dreams. So, could an NDE not be another form of dream? We will return to this topic later when we discuss entheogens, the mind-altering substances such as DMT (Dimethyltryptamine).

Classic Modern Case – 2001 – The Dentures

One of the most celebrated and much-discussed cases of a veridical near-death experience took place in the Netherlands in 1979. It featured a 44-year-old Dutchman who had been found unconscious in a field by a group of walkers. An ambulance was called, and he was rushed to a local hospital. On arrival, medical checks showed that he had no pupillary reflexes, he was not breathing, and he had no pulse. He was also extremely cold to the extent that his skin had a blue colouration. To all intents and purposes, he was clinically dead. Further examination showed that he had suffered a massive heart attack and had probably collapsed in the field while walking. The medical staff started immediate resuscitation using artificial respiration, heart massage and a defibrillator. There was also a need to place a tube down his throat to facilitate breathing. To do this, his dentures had to be removed. A nurse took them out and placed them on a cart. After an intense 90 minutes of attention, he started to respond and his heart rhythm and blood pressure returned to such an extent that he could be moved to the intensive care unit (ICU).

Over the next week, the patient showed significant improvement. He regained consciousness and soon engaged the medical staff in conversation. It was at this time that the male nurse who removed the dentures was on the ward for the first time after the incident. The patient immediately recognized him and announced that he would know where his missing dentures might be. He explained that he had watched his dentures being removed from a position near the ceiling. He then went on to describe how worried he was at that time that the resuscitation team would give up on him and he would die. He had desperately tried to communicate with them but had found it impossible. He also described how he felt the pain in his chest caused by the extreme impact suffered to his ribcage as part of the ICU process.

In a subsequent paper on this case published in the Journal of Near-Death Studies, Dutch researchers Rudolph H. Smit and Titus Rivas discuss in great detail how this is a classic case of veridical perception during an NDE-induced OBE. (Smit & Rivas, 2010) The nurse's account was recorded on 2 February 1994 by a member of the Merkawah Foundation, a Dutch NDE research organization. The nurse gave a detailed account of what happened that night in twelve closely typed pages. In fact, the male nurse found that the patient not only remembered the dentures being placed on the cart but also recounted, in great detail, conversations that had taken place between the nursing staff. In a very curious comment, the patient stated that while he was floating outside his body, he was also very aware of the pressure that his body was feeling as the crash nurse sat on top of it. He described how he felt 'enormous pain' when the heart massage machine was turned on. Indeed, although this sense of bi-location should have felt very odd to the patient, the nurse reported that the patient 'told it so matter-of-factly, so down-to-earth', adding, 'He certainly was not a woolly thinking person, whose fantasy had run wild.'

In April 2008, many years after the event, Rivas managed to trace the nurse and asked for further information regarding the incident. The nurse confirmed all the details of the case. He confirmed that the night had been extremely cold and, on arrival at the hospital, it was reported that the patient had no heartbeat, no breathing, no blood pressure and that his body was 'as cold as ice'. It was at this point that his dentures were removed, not later when he had started to recover.

However, in the Summer 2010 edition of the *Journal of Near-Death Studies*, Australian anaesthesiologist Gerald M. Woerlee published an article that proposed an alternative explanation for this much-cited case. (Woerlee, 2010)

Woerlee first pointed out the issue of exactly how long the patient ('Mr B') was in the field before the medical team assisted him. The original transcript states it was 11 minutes, but Woerlee argues it would have been considerably longer as nobody saw him fall in the first place. Research has shown that neurological damage occurs after 6–8 minutes of cardiac arrest at 28–32°C (82–89°F) and after 30–60 minutes of cardiac arrest at 10–20°C (50–68°F). (Sealy, 1989) According to the medical records, when Mr B was found the ambulance team attached electrocardiogram (ECG) electrodes to his chest and discovered that his heart was beating in a very dangerous rhythm known as ventricular fibrillation. His heart was twitching uncontrollably rather than following a regular beat. Because of this, it was failing to pump the blood around his body. It is known that at average body temperature, ventricular fibrillation brings about a loss of consciousness in about 20 seconds, with brain damage starting after 4 minutes. If it continues for longer than 12 minutes, the person will die.

The ambulance team failed to stop the ventricular fibrillation, so by the time the patient arrived at the hospital he was showing all the signs of extreme oxygen starvation. In order to get his heart back to a regular beat, the medical staff used a mechanical heart massager. It was at this point that Mr B's dentures were removed. His pupils were regularly checked, and he continued to show signs of oxygen starvation. After 90 minutes, the fibrillation stopped and a regular heartbeat was restored.

Mr B, still unconscious, was transferred to the intensive care unit, where he eventually began to breathe unaided and regained consciousness. At this stage, he described his OBE and commented about his dentures.

Woerlee focused on the fact that even though Mr B was in a state of ventricular fibrillation for an extended period, he was discharged from the hospital with absolutely no signs of brain damage. How could this be? Woerlee suggested that the crucial element in this incident was Mr B's body temperature in the field and the hospital. He argued that because the patient's body was hypothermic, it was consuming far less oxygen than a normal, warm body. For this reason, the patient could survive a long period of little, if any, blood flow.

Woerlee then moved on to the patient's pupils' non-reaction to light. This is usually a vital sign of brain oxygen starvation. However, hypothermia invalidated this for the reasons mentioned above. Indeed, all the observed signs of death that were reported by the clinical staff in the patient's case can be brought about by hypothermia. Another interesting point is that, while in a hypothermic state, the damage to the brain brought about by cardiac arrest is also minimized.

But how could somebody in such a deep state of body coldness be aware of anything, let alone the removal of the dentures and 'seeing' who had removed them? Woerlee cited several academic papers in which it has been shown that consciousness can be maintained in body temperatures as low as 21°C (70°F). (Mallet, 2002; Moser et al., 2005; Oberhammer et al., 2008)

Although technical in nature, Woerlee's argument is simple: that the patient could have been conscious during the resuscitation procedures, in which case all the information he shared regarding what went on at that time could have been through hearing what was happening around him. Indeed, as a final point, Woerlee states that the patient distinctly described how he felt extreme pain in his chest when the cardiac massage was taking place. This would be precisely what he would have felt had he been conscious during the CPU process but paralysed due to the effects of oxygen starvation and hypothermia.

However it is important to again focus in on precisely what the experiencer describes. In this case, the patient never stated that he 'heard' any discussion about his dentures but that he saw the nurse take them out of his mouth and place them on a tray. Of course, he could have confabulated the visual scene from tactile cues and sounds at the time (particularly if he was, as Woerlee argues, conscious and aware). But this is not what he described afterwards. He believed he was viewing the events from a position outside his body, as was Pam Reynolds, whose circumstances were totally different. Just because a series of assumptions can explain something does not mean these explanations are correct. Let us assume for a second that the OBE state is real. This means coming up with tortuous and convoluted explanations to shoe-horn the experience into the modern materialist-reductionist model of reality. I am reminded here of the epicycles, or orbits within orbits, invented by medieval schoolmen to describe the observed retrograde motion of the solar system's outer planets to support the geocentric universe of Aristotelian science. Of course, they were wrong, but it took the courage of Copernicus to go against the medieval equivalent of 'scientism' to show the objective proof of heliocentrism. The advice, as always, is to follow where the evidence points rather than clinging to your prejudices.

Classic Modern Case – 2006 – Anita Moorjani

In February 2006, Anita Moorjani, a Hong Kong-based Sindhi businesswoman, was dying of lymphoma, a particularly aggressive form of cancer. The illness had taken total control of her body and she was moving into the terminal phase. One morning, she took a turn for the worse; she could not open her eyes, and her face was grossly swollen. Her husband Danny phoned the family doctor and Anita, in a seemingly unconscious state, was rushed to hospital. However, from the viewpoint of Anita herself, everything was fine. She was observing everything from a curiously enjoyable semi-dream state. At the same time, she felt amazingly awake. She was hyper-aware of everything that was going on around her. In her book *Dying To Be Me*, she explained that she was perceiving but in a way that didn't involve her usual five senses. She was simply aware. This suggests that she was attuning to another form of sensory processing. She was not 'hearing' or 'seeing' things because neither her eyes nor her ears were involved. She was gleaning information from a 'field' of information that surrounded her and was part of her. She described it like this:

> It was as though I'd been a prisoner in my own body for the past four years as the cancer ravaged my physical form, and at last I was being released. I was tasting freedom for the first time! I began to feel weightless and to become aware that I was able to be anywhere at any time . . . and this didn't seem unusual. It felt normal, as though this were the real way to perceive things. I didn't even think it odd that I was aware of my husband and the doctor speaking to each other outside the ICU, some 40 feet down a hallway. (Moorjani, 2012, p. 63)

She recognized the doctor explaining that there was nothing they could do. Her body was full of tumours. She noted her husband's reaction to this terrible news, and she was desperate to take away his grief by telling him that she was okay. However, she felt herself being pulled away. It was then that she began to undergo what is generally known as the 'oceanic experience':

> As my emotions were being drawn away from my surroundings, I started to notice how I was continuing to expand to fill every space until there was no separation between me and everything else. I encompassed – no, became – everything and everyone. (Moorjani, 2012, p. 63)

Anita then became aware of her brother, thousands of miles away, on an aeroplane on his way to see her. She noted his worried look and again tried to communicate that she was okay.

As her 'expansion into the other realm', as she described it, took place, she made a fascinating observation: she felt that she had not so much physically gone somewhere else but that she had *awakened* as if roused from a bad dream. Then something strange happened. She became aware of the presence of her father, who had died ten years earlier. He communicated with her by 'emotion' rather than words. They were then joined by her friend Soni, who had died of cancer three years ago.

She realized that her new sensory awareness was total. She had 360-degree vision and a total awareness of her surroundings. She also felt that time had changed:

> *I was aware of everything that pertained to me – past, present and future – simultaneously. I became conscious of what seemed to be simultaneous lives playing out. I seemed to have a younger brother in one incarnation, and I was protective of him. But I knew that this sibling's essence was the same as Anoop's, only in that existence, he was younger instead of older than I was. This life I was now perceiving with Anoop seemed to take place in an under-developed rural setting, in a time and location I could not identify. We were living in a sparsely furnished mud hut, and I looked after Anoop while our parents went out to work in the fields. (Moorjani, 2012, p. 66)*

This suggests a perception of alternative timelines in which she has lived, or will live, a very different one to that which she had just experienced. Here, we have evidence of a 'many-worlds'-like scenario reminiscent of the 'cheating the ferryman' concept. This also suggests that she perceived a life in another time but still as herself. However, she stressed that it did not feel like a *past life* but something that was happening now. She makes a fascinating point:

> *Our five senses limit us to focusing only on one point in time at any given moment, and we string these together to create an illusion of linear reality. Our physicality also limits our perception of the space around us, confining us to only what our eyes and ears can see and hear or to what we can touch, smell, or taste. However, without the limitations of my body, I took in all points of time and space as they pertained to me, all at once. (Moorjani, 2012, p. 67)*

She initially wondered what was giving her this information. She then realized that God is not a being but a state of being . . . and she was now that state of being. That is, she was 'God'.

She was then 'told' by her father that it was not her time and that she must go back. At this stage, she decided that she wanted to stay in this new state of being. But like countless other NDErs before her, she encountered an invisible barrier she could not cross. She knew that if she crossed it, she would be dead within consensual 'reality'. She perceived what effect this decision to cross the boundary would have on her loved ones. She saw her distraught husband holding her frail hand and his head buried in her lifeless chest.

Anita then understood that, if she went back with this new awareness of the power of her true self, she would be able to cure her cancer and continue living. Indeed, she also sensed that she had a greater purpose to fulfil on earth: to heal others.

Around 4.00 pm on the afternoon of 3 February 2006, Anita came back. Standing next to her bed were her husband and her brother, Anoop. She also recognized the doctor and called him by name, Dr Chan. She explained that during the night she had seen him draw fluid from her lungs. Dr Chan was surprised by this revelation, stating that this was impossible as Anita had been, at that time, in a deep coma.

Three days later, it was found that Anita's tumours had shrunk considerably, as had the swelling of all her glands. Six days later, the doctors did a bone marrow extraction and were stunned to find that there was no evidence of cancer in the biopsy. This was thought to be impossible. The sample was sent to another laboratory and, four days later, came back as testing negative for cancer cells. A few days later, a lymph node biopsy was taken, which entailed minor surgery. As the scans took place, Anita later recorded what she heard the specialist say: 'I don't understand. I have scans that show this patient's lymphatic system was ridden with cancer just two weeks ago, but now I can't find a lymph node on her body large enough to even suggest cancer!' (Moorjani, 2012, p. 85)

On 9 March 2006, Anita was released from hospital. She had been given a full-body positron-emission tomography scan, and this confirmed that her body was, indeed, cancer-free.

At this time, she had never heard of the near-death experience. Her brother spotted the website of the Near-Death Experience Research Foundation (NDERF), the organization established by the oncologist Dr Jeffrey Long. On the site was a request for individuals who had experienced an NDE to send in their stories, which Anita duly did. The following day, she received an email from Dr Long. As a cancer specialist, Long was fascinated by Anita's case, which he considered one of the most exceptional he had ever read. In the summer of 2006, another oncologist, Dr Peter Ko, contacted Anita. Ko was particularly interested in spontaneous remissions. He requested from her copies of her medical reports. On reading them, he responded: 'Lady, whichever way I look at it, you should be dead!'

Since then, Anita has given up her career and now travels the world telling others about the redemptive effects of near-death experiences. She is not alone in having a huge life change facilitated by an NDE. Indeed, another case has proved to be even more famous than that of Anita Moorjani, and that is because it happened to a sceptic – and one who was more than qualified to interpret his experience.

Classic Modern Case – 2008 – Eben Alexander

One of the most famous NDE cases took place in the autumn of 2008, when Dr Eben Alexander, a neurosurgeon at the Lynchburg General Hospital in Virginia, awoke with an extremely intense headache. He was rushed to the hospital in a state known as 'status epilepticus': in effect, he was going from one epileptic seizure to another. A bacterial meningitis infection brought about this state after seeping through his cerebral spinal fluid and into his brain, attacking his neocortex, hippocampus and other parts of the limbic system. Within a few hours, his cerebral cortex was shut down, and he fell into a deep coma. He was in this state for six days. His neurological examinations revealed deeply pathological cortical reflexes, and scans revealed cortical disruption throughout his neocortex. Much to the surprise of the physicians caring for him, on the seventh day, Alexander came out of the coma state. What was even more surprising was that he had experienced something extraordinary while in his deep coma state – a state in which no such experience should have been possible. His cortex had not just been malfunctioning; it had been switched off. On his initial awakening, the physician's brain function was devastated – he had no memories of the life of Eben Alexander before the coma; even his language had been deleted. He did not even recognize beloved family members at his bedside – at least not at first. Words came back to him over hours, personal memories over weeks, and all his knowledge from decades working as a neurosurgeon returned completely over a few months. Alexander's rich and ultra-real memories from deep within his coma, which completely violated all neuroscientific principles about the relationship of the neocortex to consciousness, became an increasingly haunting mystery that demanded a better explanation. Over a period of months, it became clear that his near-death experience had been far more than a simple hallucination.

Alexander claimed that after he had lost consciousness within this world he found himself in another. He was aware that he was submerged in a kind of transparent mud with tree roots all around him. A deep, rhythmic pounding surrounded him. He pulled himself out of the underground state to be confronted with a series of grotesque faces that screeched at him. He then heard a complex melody playing around him, and a white-gold rotating light hovered before him. He rose up into the air and hovered over a beautiful landscape. While in this state, he realized that he was not alone. He turned around to see an attractive young woman with high cheekbones, long golden-brown hair and piercing blue eyes. He looked around to see millions of beautiful butterflies surrounding him as far as he could see; furthermore, he and his enigmatic companion were sitting on a stunningly patterned butterfly's wing.

He then found himself moving ever higher into a realm he called 'the Core', an unending, inky blackness that had at its centre a light source that Alexander immediately associated with the sound that also permeated, or more accurately, resonated, everywhere within the Core. The sound was the vocalization 'Om'. He identified the light as being the source of everything there is. A source of infinite love, which he identified as 'God'. He understood that he and God were one, a singular unity, and he felt that he now knew everything. Alexander then found himself falling through the various realms and back to the place of mud. Now, though, he was able to manifest the 'Om' melody, knowing that each time he did it, he would rise again. But after what seemed like many lifetimes, Alexander's ability to create the melody suddenly ceased and he became aware of another realm; he saw faces in the mist. At that point, he came out of the coma and was back in this world as Dr Eben Alexander, a human being with a great story to tell.

Which is precisely what he did. Published in 2012, his book *Proof of Heaven: A Neurosurgeon's Journey into the Afterlife* was an immediate bestseller.

There have been several criticisms of Alexander's narrative, including a reasonably damning article that appeared in *Esquire* magazine in 2013. For this piece, journalist Luke Dittrich interviewed Dr Laura Potter, the emergency physician who treated Alexander during his illness. Dittrich discovered several inconsistencies regarding Alexander's account and Potter's recollections. For example, Alexander claimed that a rare case of *E. coli* bacterial meningitis had caused his coma. However, it seems that Potter and her associates induced the coma. (Dittrich, 'The Prophet', *Esquire*, July 2013)

This is a relatively minor discrepancy of detail and had no bearing on Alexander's experience and its interpretation. But the next thing that Potter described to Dittrich was far more significant. Alexander argued that during his week in ICU his brain was 'all but destroyed'. (Alexander, 2012, p. 9) A crucial argument for the idea that consciousness can exist outside the brain is that the memories that record what is experienced during an NDE occur in a non-functioning brain. If awareness exists during these times, then it must be located in a place other than the brain. Or, as Alexander himself wrote, 'If you don't have a working brain, you can't be conscious.' (Alexander, 2012, p. 9) So, if the NDE is simply a brain-generated 'hallucination', how can a non-functioning brain generate such hallucinations?

But in her interview with Dittrich, Potter stated that, during the time Alexander was in the induced coma state, he had been 'conscious but delirious'. (Dittrich, 2013) If this is correct, Alexander's NDE did take place in a functioning brain, a scenario that invalidates his arguments against the brain-generation of hallucinations.

In response, NDE researcher Robert Mays published a commentary on the Dittrich article on the International Association of Near-Death Studies website. In this, he presented an alternative explanation for the embellishments Dittrich cited. Another witness to the events at that time was Alexander's wife, Holley. In 2013, Mays spoke to Holley, who stated that she and a neighbour, Michael Sullivan, witnessed the events her husband described, and distinctly heard him call out 'God help me' from the other side of the curtain where he was being worked on:

> She said this incident occurred about an hour after arriving in the ER with Eben. 'It happened before they sedated him while the doctors were trying to get vital signs and spinal fluid and all that. I said to Michael [Sullivan], "He spoke!"

and Eben kept writhing. Dr Potter might not have heard
it. She was in and out, checking scans, spinal fluid, so it's
very likely that she wasn't there.' (Mays, R., 2013)

This does give a possible explanation as to why Dr Potter did not hear Alexander call out. It was after this evidence of seeming consciousness that Alexander slipped into a coma state and perceived his NDE.

In his article, Mays explains how coma is defined as a period of unconsciousness lasting more than six hours. During that period the person does not respond to the infliction of pain, react to bright lights or have any voluntary actions. From this definition it is clear that Alexander's plea for God to help him proved that, in his pre-intubation stage, he was not in a coma state. Mays adds that according to the Glasgow Coma Scale (the standard measurement of the depth of coma) applied to Alexander on his admission to the hospital, it was recorded as a level 8. This is defined as suffering 'severe brain injury' and a state of coma.

Alexander released his medical records, which were given a formal objective review. The published conclusions were:

Three physicians not associated with Lynchburg General
Hospital completed an independent review of the complete
medical record of Dr Alexander's hospitalization and
spoke with the hospital's two consulting neurologists to
gather additional information. The records indicated that
Dr Alexander was brought to the emergency department
unresponsive, with evidence of a bacterial infection, and he
was assessed to have moderate brain injury, which rapidly
progressed to severe brain injury over the next few hours.
Brain scans showed that the membranes covering the brain
as well as the grooves in his cerebral cortex were swollen
with pus-filled liquid, compressing the cortical tissue.
Laboratory examination showed evidence of a bacterial

infection in his cerebrospinal fluid, due to an organism that very rarely causes meningitis in adults, and, when it does, is almost always fatal or resulting in permanent neurological deficits. Nevertheless, after a profound near-death experience, Dr Alexander eventually awoke from his coma and, within a few months, had made what his surprised neurologists called a 'complete and remarkable recovery' from an illness they agreed might well have been fatal, without any residual neurological deficit. (Alexander, n.d.)

This seems to have put to bed most of the significant criticisms cited by Dittrich's article. However, a more interesting and quite relevant observation with regard to our enquiry was made by neuroscientist Sam Harris, who, in an article published in *Newsweek* in October 2012, argued that Alexander's experience could have been facilitated by the psychedelic substance N, N-dimethyltryptamine (N, N-DMT). I find it interesting that, in defence of his case, renowned sceptic Harris states quite categorically that 'DMT already exists in the brain as a neurotransmitter,' adding, 'Did [Alexander's] brain experience a surge of DMT release during his coma?' (Harris, 2012)

Harris's observation was very perceptive in that in June 2023, a paper was published in the academic journal *Frontiers in Psychology* in which Pascal Michael, Oliver Robinson and David Luke of the Centre for Mental Health at the University of Greenwich interviewed a person identified as 'Nikoli', an individual considered ideally qualified to comment on the similarities (and differences) between a near-death experience and a DMT 'trip', having encountered both. A careful reading of the paper identifies 'Nikoli' as being none other than Eben Alexander.

It is essential to clarify here that there is a very similar hallucinogenic substance known as 5-Methoxy-N, N-Dimethyltryptamine, or 5-MEO-DMT, which is not as widely found in plants and animals as standard

N, N-DMT. It brings about similar altered states but is described as being more 'spiritual' and 'mystical' with regards to the imagery it evokes.

Alexander/'Nikoli' revealed to Michael and Luke that he had had previous experience of 5-MEO DMT. Drawing on this experience, he was able to explain to Michael and Luke that, in his opinion, the effects of DMT were not the same as those of an NDE. In their article, Michael and Luke concluded that:

> *Despite the similarities in phenomenology, the participant was insistent that his NDE and psychedelic experiences were insufficiently similar, and thus, endogenous psychedelics did not play a role in the induction of his NDE. This is reflected in his very low quantitative appraisal of 2/10 for both similarity and likely psychedelic induction. (Michael, Luke & Robinson, 2023, p. 14)*

But they also added that these conclusions on the part of Alexander were based on his experience of the 5-MEO variant of DMT (which he had taken three times), rather than his rather more limited knowledge of the N, N-DMT, which, if he had encountered it all (which he did not accept), had been while experiencing his NDE. 'Thus,' they wrote,

> *he may be less equipped to draw the extant and extensive parallels in the same way that the subculture of the psychedelic community is, which has developed a nuanced vocabulary to parse these transcendent states. (Michael, Luke & Robinson, 2023)*

Later, we will discuss in detail something known as the 'perinatal' theory of the tunnel experience, as advocated by Carl Sagan and Susan Blackmore, among others. In this regard, I was intrigued by the suggestion of Pascal Michael and his associate authors when they pointed out the similarities between Eben Alexander's NDE and the effects of

5-MEO DMT. Michael et al. present a number of parallels with possible perinatal memories found in Alexander's narrative. For example, in his NDE, Alexander finds himself in an 'Underworld':

> . . . *which he later characterizes as the 'Earthworm's Eye-view', composed of 'visible darkness . . . transparent. . . blurry, claustrophobic, suffocating'. A 'deep, rhythmic pounding' also accompanied him, which was* 'like a heart-beat . . . *as if a giant, subterranean blacksmith is pounding an anvil'. This space was primitive in nature,* 'as if I had regressed to . . . the very beginnings of life'. *[Italics added by the authors.] (Michael, Luke & Robinson, 2023, p. 10)*

Adding:

> *After elucidating his Core experience, encompassing darkness suffused with light, he continues: 'My situation was* . . . akin to that of a fetus in a womb . . . with the silent partner of a placenta, which nourishes it and mediates its relationship to the everywhere present, yet . . . invisible mother. [Italics added.] In this case, the "mother" was God, the Creator, the Source. . . . This Being was so close, there seemed to be no difference between God and myself.' (Michael, Luke, & Robinson, 2023, p. 10)*

I find it particularly important that the authors relate this to a form of 'shamanic re-birth' a theme we will discuss in much greater detail in the next chapter.

We have now finished our review of a handful of the most famous near-death cases in the literature. This has given us a reasonable picture of what it must be like to experience such a state of altered consciousness. What we need to do next is look at whether these cases are simply a modern cultural phenomenon unique to those who have read about or seen TV programmes on the near-death experience or something that has been encountered across history and geography. We will now embark on an in-depth review of the history and anthropology of this fascinating subject.

PART 2

The History and Anthropology of the Near-Death Experience

Anthropology – Introduction

We know from archaeological remains that human beings have long believed in a form of life after death. For example, in 1934, French archaeologist René Neuville discovered the graves of seven adults and nine children in a small cave near the Wadi el Hadj in Israel. All had been carefully buried, and with them had been placed a small selection of tools to be used in the afterlife. In 1988, radioactive dating showed that the remains were at least 100,000 years old. There is strong evidence that the Neanderthals followed similar burial customs. We also know from later written records worldwide that the idea of an existence beyond the grave has long been a universal human belief. However, and quite surprisingly, all the myths that surround death describe the 'arrival' in the afterlife, as it were, rather than the journey to it. The actual manner of expiration seemed to be a taboo subject, probably because it was associated with the horrors of a painful, unpleasant and traumatic dying process.

The question that must be asked regarding the near-death experience is whether it is a product of cultural influences and expectations. If it is a universal human trait, it should be found across all cultures and reported throughout history. Therefore, cross-cultural comparisons must be applied.

In the late 1970s, anthropologist Dean Shiels studied 67 traditional cultures worldwide, focusing on a belief in out-of-the-body states, a crucial element of then near-death experience. Shiels found that at least 64 cultures believed such states to be real. He argued that these beliefs came about because of genuine events witnessed and recorded within each society. He concluded that:

> *When different cultures at different times and in different places arrive at the same or a very similar out-of-the-body belief we begin to wonder if this results from a common experience of this happening. (Shiels, 1978)*

This stimulated a great deal of research, and according to near-death researcher Dr Sam Parnia, among most cultures and across history the most common features were: having an out-of-body experience; reuniting with dead loved ones; experiencing a vision of light accompanied by joy and peace; and witnessing a border or dividing line between the living and the dead. (Parnia, 2013, p. 152)

It is also important to acknowledge that although the general themes may be similar across all cultures, the details seem culturally determined. This is not a new consideration. In the late 1920s, the great American anthropologist Walter Evans-Wentz made the following observation in his commentary on his translation of *The Tibetan Book of the Dead*:

> *Accordingly, for a Buddhist of some other School, as for a Hindu, or a Moslem, or a Christian, the Bardo experiences would be appropriately different: the Buddhist's or the Hindu's thought-forms, as in a dream state, would give rise to corresponding visions of the deities of the Buddhist or Hindu pantheon; a Moslem's to visions of the Moslem Paradise; a Christian's, to visions of the Christian Heaven, or an American Indian's to visions of the Happy Hunting*

> *Ground. And similarly, the materialist will experience*
> *after-death visions as negative and as empty and as*
> *deityless as any he ever dreamt while in the human body.*
> *In other words, as explained above, the after-death state*
> *is very much like a dream state, and its dreams are the*
> *children of the dreamer's mentality. (Evans-Wentz, 1957,*
> *pp. 33–34)*

Is this a reasonable position to take? To come to any conclusion, we need to review the cultural and historical aspects of the near-death experience in greater detail. We will do this by conducting a more in-depth analysis of such beliefs across time. I intend to focus on non-Abrahamic experiences as there is extensive material on Christian, Jewish and Islamic near-death experiences available in numerous books. Because of a lack of space, I will only focus on examples from Asia and Oceania in both ancient and modern times. In future work, I intend to expand upon my research into the anthropology of the near-death experiences in the American indigenous cultures, ancient Greece, Africa and the Abrahamic religions.

SHAMANIC NDEs

It is usually stated, with a great degree of assuredness, that the word 'shaman' has its origins in the Siberian Tungusic language word *samān*, from the Tungusic *sā-*, meaning 'to know'. This is why most writings on shamanism focus in on the Northeast Asian roots of this intriguing belief system.

One such writer was the great Finnish linguist and explorer Kai Donner. Between 1911 and 1914, he travelled extensively in Siberia and interviewed many shamans. In 1954, his notes on these interviews were published. One such interview is particularly relevant to our enquiry into the anthropology of near-death experiences. The interview opened with

Donner asking a member of the Samoyed tribe what he knew about the underworld, to which he received a surprising reply: 'Why should I not know about it? I have been there myself.' The man went on to describe how, when suffering from a severe illness, he had been prematurely pronounced dead. While the funeral ceremony was underway, he travelled to the underworld and finally returned to his body. (Donner, 1954, p. 69)

However, in 1923, Russian anthropologist Sergei Shirokogorov argued that the word *samān* appears to be a foreign addition to the Tungusic language, which has no similar words in its lexicon. (Shirokogoroff, 1923, pp. 246–249). None other than the world-recognized expert on shamanism, the Romanian anthropologist Mircea Eliade, agreed, arguing that, for him, 'the phenomenon of shamanism itself displays elements of southern origin, specifically Buddhist (Lamaist) elements.' (Eliade, 1989, p. 496) Indeed, Eliade then focuses on the Indo-Aryan Vedic word *śramana*, which denotes a wandering holy person.

As we shall soon discover, the Vedic language and its later variation, Sanskrit, is evidence that three great ancient belief systems, Hinduism, Zoroastrianism and the chronologically later Tibetan Buddhism, came from the same shared belief system of shamanism.

It is believed that at around 5000 BCE, Indian and Iranian tribes lived together in one place, the legendary Airyanem Vaejah. The two groups were thought to be split along linguistic lines, using mutually intelligible languages based upon Vedic: Avesta and proto-Sanskrit. From this, it is fair to conclude that they shared similar religious beliefs. It was sometime in the 3rd millennium BCE that the groups went their separate ways, one going southwest to Iran and the other south to India. Indeed, I would suggest that the differential between the two groups was simply the choice of emigration direction and that, at that time, the two cultures were effectively identical.

They also inherited a heritage from their shamanic roots, using a mysterious drink called *soma* by the Indian Sanskrit speakers and *haoma* by the Iranian Avesta speakers. We shall discuss this drink in greater detail below as we explore what the two great belief systems of Iranian Zoroastrianism and Indian Hinduism tell us about the near-death experience.

ZOROASTRIAN NDEs

If its own narratives can be believed, Zoroastrianism, the belief system of the original Aryans, is probably one of the oldest religions in the world. It started in the country now known as Iran, a name derived from the root 'Aryan'. In fact, 'Iran' is the country's original name, though it was known as Persia for centuries. The Zoroastrians believe that their original homeland was Airyanem Vaejahi and that they spread across India, Iran, Russia and Europe. They further believed that their religion was a pure version of the beliefs held during the 'Golden Age', when man was far more advanced than he is now.

This is fascinating because, as we have discovered, the historical evidence suggests that both Hinduism and Zoroastrianism came from the same earlier, more advanced belief system. This system was effectively shamanistic in content, and what it can tell us about what happens at death may be of great importance.

This shamanic heritage may be more familiar than it first seems. In 1938, Swedish anthropologist Hendrik Samuel Nyberg, a recognized world expert on the history and culture of Iran, made a series of intriguing claims regarding the roots of Zoroastrian beliefs. He argued that they may have been influenced by communities of ecstatic warriors who performed shamanic ecstasies and otherworldly journeys to a heavenly place while intoxicated with hallucinogenic substances.

French historian Gherardo Gnoli drew a similar conclusion. Gnoli noted that the Gâthas, a collection of songs or hymns contained within the Avesta, the sacred book of Zoroastrianism, mention a psychological state called *maga*. This was a condition of visionary union with entities known as the *amesha spentas* ('beneficent immortals'). While in this state, the Zoroastrian shaman gains mystical knowledge known as *cisti*. Interestingly, in the Gâthas there is also a subtle distinction between a general physical vision, something projected into the visual world (known as a *getig*) and these powerful internal altered states of consciousness that in the Middle Iranian language were called *menog*. (Gnoli, 1965)

The Gâthas are believed to be the words of the religion's founder, Zarathustra, who lived between 1000 and 600 BCE. These written precepts concerning the afterlife are generally thought to be the oldest existing religious documents. Indeed, they contain several afterlife motifs that appear in several later religions; these include judgment at death, a balance in which the deeds of all deceased are weighed, and a bridge over hell that narrows for the wicked and widens for the righteous, which they have to negotiate to enter heaven.

In the Avesta it states that after death the soul splits into two separate entities. This is intriguing. In my book *The Daemon – A Guide to Your Extraordinary Secret Self*, I discuss the similarities between my own Daemon-Eidolon Dyad and the Zoroastrian concept of soul duality. (Peake, 2008, p. 138). In life, there is the physical body (the *tanū*), which is animated by the soul (the *urvan*). But there is, according to Zoroastrian beliefs, another element, an immortal being known as the *fravashi*. This acts as a protective spirit for the *urvan*, watching and guiding it through life. The *fravashi* is also an ancestor spirit in that it embodies the essence of all the ancestors who contributed to creating the living *urvan*. I describe this as the *UberDaemon* in my 2022 book *Cheating the Ferryman*. (Peake, 2022, pp. 245–246)

As well as the soul (*urvan*), there is also the spiritual double known as the *daēnā*. At death, the dead person's personality is divided into two sources of consciousness: the *urvan* and the *daēnā*. The *daēnā* manifests as either a beautiful maiden or an ugly hag. She embodies all the deeds done in life and presents these to the *urvan*. The *urvan* is held accountable for these deeds, which are weighed. Depending upon the outcome of this evaluation, the *urvan* either successfully crosses what the Zoroastrians call the Činvat Bridge to the other world or falls into the abyss.

This complex model means that the Zoroastrians have a form of reincarnation somewhat different from that found in Hinduism and Buddhism, whose reincarnations occur so that the soul may learn and develop. Within Hinduism and Buddhism, the incarnating soul has no recollection of its past life; it starts the new life with a clean slate. The Zoroastrians' model is slightly different. They believe that the life lessons of one life are carried forward into the next. These recordings are encoded in a location close to the pineal gland in the brain's centre.

This post-mortem encounter with the *daēnā* is described on a stone inscription discovered in 1924 at the Sar Mashhad archaeological site in the Iranian province of Fars, the location of several Sasanian rock carvings. The inscription is dated around 290 CE. In it, somebody called Kartīr describes what seems like a near-death experience.

There has been a long debate among Iranologists as to the identity of Kartīr. The fact that he had such an impressive stone inscription created to tell his story suggests high rank. The discoverer of the inscription, Ernst Herzfeld, identified him with Tansar, the legendary high priest of King Ardašīr I, the founder of the Sasanian Empire that controlled much of Persia and the Near East for several centuries.

In the inscription, Kartīr describes how he embarked upon the journey to heaven to regain his confidence in the traditional Zoroastrian practices and beliefs. The inscriptions tell how he was given wine and a substance called *mang of Vishtasp*, which put him to sleep.

So what is this mysterious *mang of Vishtasp*, the hallucinogenic substance that the Zoroastrian shamans and Kartīr used to create their NDEs? Well-respected ethnobiologist R. Gordon Wasson has suggested that when the proto-Iranians had emigrated west from their homelands in the mysterious Airyanem Vaejahi, they had taken with them a tradition of using a hallucinogen known as *soma*, thought to be dried fly agaric mushroom. A substitute was needed when they settled in their eventual homeland as fly agaric did not grow in Persia. The Avestan drug *banqha*, probably henbane (*Hyoscyamus niger*), was one such substitute. (Wasson, 1986)

Gherardo Gnoli backed up this idea, and described *mang of Vishtasp* as a mixture of henbane and wine. (Gnoli, pp. 437–438) This is precisely what the inscription states that Kartīr used to facilitate his journey.

Indeed, to put Kartīr's experience into perspective, we must reference a later story that appears in the *Denkird* (also known as *The Book of Arda Wirāz*), a text dating from the 10th century CE and written in Middle Persian but believed to be based on very ancient material, probably from before the inscriptions were made at Sar Mashhad. It involves King Vishtasp, whose name is used with regard to *mang*. Although not as elaborate as the experience of Kartīr, King Vishtasp's story contains several parallels to it. Specifically, to facilitate his near-death experience, King Vishtasp is given the same mixture of wine and henbane, but this time it is administered on the orders of God (*Ohrmazd*) himself. According to the *Denkird*:

> *To enlighten Vishtasp (and teach him) . . . and that he would attain a high post, permanent power, riches and food, Ohrmazd the Creator sent at the same time to the house of Vishtasp the yazat [a lesser divine being] Neryosang with a message urging . . . Arthavist to give to drink to Vishtasp the lightened drink that would grant the eye of whoever took it a glimpse at the spiritual world. . . . And speak to Arthavist: 'Lord Arthavist! Take the nice plate, the nicest of all that have been made . . . to take, from us, Hom [Haoma] and mang. . .* (Denkird 7.4.84–86)

The *Denkird* is a critical work regarding our enquiry into ancient near-death experiences because it explicitly references the life review. According to it, only those who have lived a wicked life suffer the review because it relives all of the horrible things that they have done. (Masumian, F., 2002). This precisely echoes the contents of many modern near-death-experience-facilitated life reviews.

Returning to the experience of Kartīr, he takes *mang of Vishtasp* and finds himself walking along a bright road. He is joined by a beautiful young woman who joins him from the east. Kartīr is delighted to see this lovely young *daēnā* as evidence that he is one of the righteous. If he had not been, his new companion would have been an ugly old hag. Then something extraordinary happens. The narrative describes how Kartīr's consciousness is split into two, and standing next to him is his double, his *fravashi*. While one part of his awareness stays on the road, the other, located within the sensory perceptions of the *fravashi*, is taken by his *daēnā* to meet one of the lesser gods seated on a golden throne and has, in front of him, a balance. Then the *daēnā* and the *fravashi* walk together to the east, where they encounter a throne of gold, a hell full of vermin, a bridge 'more wide than long' and, eventually, paradise, where Kartīr (still in the guise of his own double) stops to eat bread and meat.

Is it possible that the shamanic ecstasy facilitated by *haoma* was another avenue by which the near-death experience could be facilitated?

As we have already discovered, historians have long argued that the people of Southern Iran and Northern India, collectively known as the Aryans, have shared roots. Indeed, the term Hinduism, the name of the major religion of the Indian subcontinent, is Persian in origin. The border river between the areas of Iranian influence and Indian influence, the Indus, was known as the Sindhu by the ancient Indians and the Hindu by the Iranians. The people who settled on the banks of the Indus were described as being 'Hindus'. Over time, this word also became synonymous with the belief system of these people, a religion that was quickly to spread across the whole subcontinent.

Therefore, it is no surprise that the after-life experiences described by Zoroastrianism and the wonderfully complex Indian religion Hinduism have significant similarities. We now focus on the near-death experience described within the Hindu scriptures.

HINDU NDEs

One popular theory suggests that the Aryans invaded India from Iran at some time between 2000 and 1500 BCE and that their culture merged with that of the Dravidian tribes living south of the Indus. This has been contested by those who argue that, according to the ancient Hindu texts known as the Vedas, India was the original home of the Aryans. This is supported by the writings and silvercraft found by archaeologists, suggesting that India had a very advanced civilization before 7000 BCE. It is, therefore, possible that Indian Aryans influenced Iranian Zoroastrianism, and that this is the source of the similarities in their belief systems. As regards our enquiry into near-death experiences within these two cultures, this matters little. The similarities are important, suggesting that they are actual descriptions of experiences rather than simply a reflection of beliefs.

The theology and philosophy underpinning Hinduism were laid down thousands of years ago in the sacred writings of Hinduism, the Shruti ('that which is heard') and Smriti ('that which is remembered'). The Shruti consists of the four Vedas, the oldest books in the world. These are the Rigveda, the Samaveda, the Yajurveda and the Atharvaveda. With regards to eschatology, the part of theology concerned with death and judgement, the Rigveda is of significance to our enquiry.

Although it is generally believed that Hindus have thousands, if not millions, of 'gods', this is a misinterpretation of the philosophy; everything, including the gods, is simply manifestations of a singular being called Brahman, the Absolute. The Absolute controls the universe through three primary qualities known as the Trimurti – Brahma, the Creator; Vishnu, the Preserver; and Shiva, the Destroyer. The Absolute also has a female aspect, the Divine Mother. But everything is Brahman, and we are all aspects of Brahman's dream. Indeed, each of us is a personified aspect of the Absolute. This is known as the Ātman and is trapped within the illusion of reality created by the senses, a concept known as Maya. In this way, our journey through many lives is to discover the god within and realize our own divinity.

Central to the eschatological beliefs of Hinduism are the twin concepts of karma and samsara. Karma is how the individuated Ātman's actions throughout their life affect their afterlife, and samsara is the belief that the Ātman is reborn again. So, karma has a direct influence on samsara.

This is of significance with regard to NDEs because the concept of re-birth, in other words reincarnation, seems, at first evaluation, to conflict with the NDE motif that, at death, the personality continues in an after-life world where the already dead are met and a judgement takes place. Reincarnation (samsara), on the other hand, suggests a rebirth into another body in another location or time. But this also conflicts with the Hindu concept of Yamaloka, the place of the dead, presided over by Yama, the Lord of the Dead.

In the Rigveda, the oldest of the Vedas, the realm of the dead is located in the 'spheres above which firmly support the heavens' and is a place of 'inextinguishable light' where the dead are 'fed and satisfied' by Yama. Historian Gregory Shushan observes that:

> Yamaloka itself is 'adorned by days, waters and nights', suggesting that it follows earthly cycles and is an idealized mirror-image of earth, with horses and pastures, grass and trees (X.14.1–9, 10.56). Upon arrival there, the deceased will join Yama, Varuna (god of justice, and moral and cosmic order) and various other gods and ancestors in feasting and drinking soma. Soma was both an intoxicating, life-giving ritual drink, and a deity associated with the drink. (Shushan, 2011, p. 203)

This association of Yama with *soma* is of great significance. As Shushan states, Yama is also personified as 'King Soma' and it is he who decides if a recently dead person is reincarnated or is awarded true immortality by becoming a god. According to both the Rigveda and the later post-Vedic Sanskrit texts known as the Upanishads, this process of deification is facilitated directly by the drinking of *soma*. He quotes a section from the Upanishads:

> *'We have drunk* soma; *we have become immortal; we have gone to the light; we have found the gods.'* Soma *enables the deceased to see the light of heaven and to find the sun (IX.104, 14). This is done by sailing on a boat on the primaeval ocean. (Shushan, 2011)*

Shushan also points out that according to the Upanishads, Yamaloka is the realm of the sun, associating it with both light and cyclical rebirth. He notes that another concept known as 'redeath' (*punarmrtyu*) should be avoided. He suggests that this may be an intermediary disembodied state. This seems very similar to the Bardo state of Tibetan Buddhism, which we shall discuss later.

Hindu NDEs – Research

There have been several surveys of Indians who have described NDE-like experiences. For example, in 1995, Satwant Pasricha of the National Institute of Mental Health and Neurosciences in Bangalore discovered 26 individuals who were reported to have died and been revived, of whom 16 (62 per cent) reported an NDE. (Pasricha, 1995) From the original number surveyed, this suggests a prevalence rate of one in a thousand. Of the 16 who experienced an NDE, 14 (71 per cent) reported visiting an unearthly realm where their life deeds were reviewed and judged by Yama. Of these, 10 encountered deceased relatives. This is of significance to me. Unfortunately, Pasricha does not disclose the religious beliefs of those surveyed. Still, it is reasonable to conclude from the location (a district of Karnataka State in southern India) that most, if not all, of the respondents were Hindus. If this were the case, they would believe in samsara and reincarnation. So, the question must be asked as to how Indian NDErs met dead relatives. If all people reincarnate after death, how could such encounters take place? This suggests to me that these NDEs are only in part culturally determined.

Some of the cases described several of Moody's NDE 'traits', such as going towards the light, an unearthly realm, a form of past-life review involving judgement and crossing a barrier or bridge. However, it must be noted that these are interpretations rather than accurate parallels.

It is of possible significance that several of Pasricha's cases describe how the dying person is sent back because of a clerical error. Is this a reflection on the much-discussed bureaucratic nature of Indian society? Indeed, this was the opinion of Pasricha in an earlier 1986 paper describing the results of a survey she and Ian Stevenson conducted of reported Indian NDE cases. A major theme in the 16 cases was mistaken identity, and it was the discovery of this error that brought about the person's return to life. (Pasricha & Stevenson, 1986) This contrasts with American instances in which the dying person usually returned because of the love they had for the people they were leaving behind. However, there is also the regularly reported motif of the person being told by the 'beings of light' that their 'time had not yet come'. This could be interpreted as an administrative error.

Alan Kellehear also noted this strongly administrative and bureaucratic element in a 1993 paper, where he observed that both American and Hindu NDE accounts included life reviews. Yet, unlike Hindu subjects brought up in the United States, they had reported a life review during which the beings of light read a record of the NDEr's life to them. He states that the reading of one's life record is part of the Hindu traditional belief system. (Kellehear, A., 1993)

To expand on this, in his contributory chapter to the essential book *The Handbook of Near-Death Experiences: Thirty Years of Investigation*, Farnaz Masumian points out several similarities between Hindu beliefs and reports of near-death experience survivors. For example, in the Rigveda, there is a reference to a place of light:

. . . Place me in that deathless, undecaying world Wherein
the light of heaven is set. (Griffiths, 1926, p. 399)

In this place of perpetual light, beautiful music can be heard. Masumian cites how 'the sound of singing and the flute is also among the delights available'. (Keith, 1971). In this regard, I would like to reference a description of the NDE environment described to researcher Kenneth Ring by one of his correspondents:

There were no sounds of any earthly thing. Only the sounds
of serenity, of a strange music like I had never heard. A
soothing symphony of indescribable beauty blended with
the light I was approaching. (Ring, K., 1984, p. 54)

In Western NDEs, one of the most commonly reported 'traits' is an initiating autoscopic out-of-body experience. Interestingly, this was not featured in any of Pasricha's 1995 cases. However, in an earlier survey undertaken in 1993, she discovered one OBE description.

However, this is not what psychologist Susan Blackmore discovered. In 1991, she undertook a small survey of Indian NDEs by placing an advertisement in *The Times of India*. She asked if anybody who had experienced a close brush with death could write to her. She subsequently sent out a questionnaire based on Kenneth Ring's Weighted Core Experience Index (WCEI) to those who responded, and received 19 replies. Three of the cases specifically described the dying person leaving their body and rising up. One described 'floating in a dark space'. (Blackmore, S. J., 1993, p. 211), another 'being flown away by two winged creatures toward the higher skies'. (Blackmore, S. J., 1993, p. 212) And a third, a pop star who was electrocuted on stage, described how:

I felt 'myself' light as a feather, shooting upwards at an
indescribable speed – which can never be measured by the
words 'speed' or 'time' – and there, below me, above me,

surrounding me on all sides were lights of all colours –
shining spots which were not moving with me. (Blackmore,
S. J., 1993, p. 212)

As we shall discover later, this rushing out of the body at great speed is a much-reported sensation facilitated by the powerful hallucinogenic dimethyltryptamine (DMT).

A more recent study of Indian NDEs was published in 2012 in the journal *Annals of Neurosciences*. It was written by psychiatrist Moushumi Purkayastha and neurosurgeon Kanchan Kumar Mukherjee of the Institute of Medical and Education in Chandigarh, northern India. ('Three cases of near death experience: Is it physiology, physics of philosophy?' Purkayastha & Mukherjee, 2012) As the paper's title suggests, the authors were keen to understand if the near-death experience could be explained by physiology, physics or philosophy. In the paper, they discussed three cases of Indian nationals who experienced NDEs.

The first one was a 30-year-old postgraduate Hindu woman who had been badly injured with a severe head injury. She was in a deep coma state and needed an emergency operation. She was on a ventilator for three days and subsequently unconscious for around two months. On regaining consciousness, she described how she had been floating in a brilliant light where she could hear the doctors discussing the technical matters regarding her operation. She then felt herself rise up to 'heaven', where she encountered the Hindu gods Brahma, Vishnu and Shiva. But deep within the light, possibly its source, was an entity that called itself 'Om'. It was Om who decided that she needed to go back and return to her earthly existence.

Again, it is essential to note that the 'gods' did not discuss her being reincarnated, just that she needed to go back. She also describes a veridical perception while in an out-of-body state. None of these are part of traditional Hindu beliefs.

The second case concerned a 22-year-old Hindu male suffering from a cardiac arrest caused by complications of peritonitis. He was resuscitated from the cardiac arrest and remained unconscious for 36 hours. On recovery, he described how he had travelled through a tunnel of white light at immense speed. In a similar way to the first case, he also observed from an out-of-body state the medics trying to resuscitate him. Unfortunately, the paper does not describe whether the OBE happened before, during or after his tunnel experience.

The third case is particularly intriguing because it involves a three-year-old Hindu child who was near death from gastroenteritis. On his recovery, the child described how he had been in a 'silvery white cloud' for what he felt was many months. This 'time dilation', another of the NDE 'traits', is intriguing as he was unconscious for about a week.

So, what can we make of these cases? It is evident that some cultural artefacts are used to structure the experience, but these are part of a core experience that overrides any personal beliefs and is universal. In these three cases, we have tunnels, veridical OBEs, brilliant light sources, meetings with entities and time dilation.

But what has been happening since 2012? India is a rapidly changing society with a vast modernization project. The culture is changing, melding the best of its Hindu, Islamic, Sikh and Jain cultures with extreme modernity. I was keen to find an up-to-date case and, earlier this year, I found what I was looking for.

In January 2023, Indian travel writer Murli Menon wrote an article for the online Hackwriters.com website. In this, he described two near-death encounters he experienced, the first when he was 13 years old in January 1980 and the second in 1994.

It is important to note that Menon describes himself as a devout Hindu. Here is what he wrote regarding his understanding of what happens to consciousness at death. It is important to quote this in full, as he directly references several important Hindu concepts within the structure of a classical NDE. For example, the role of the primal sound of 'Aum' (or 'Om') which is, according to the Vedanta, the background vibration of the universe, all-pervading and resonating in each human being from the right hemisphere of the brain:

The first thing one realizes, when you die or slip into a coma, is that though the body is mortal, the atman is immortal. The atman leaves the body through the agnya chakra, and consciousness remains after death. Post death consciousness is more vivid than in real life. One can see colours unseen during earthly life. One can hear the holy sound OM and the Gayatri mantra in the afterlife . . . .

Before reaching the light, one gets a chance to review one's life from a 360 degree perspective and one realizes how other souls felt during your earthly interactions. You get the chance to experience emotions other souls experienced during your earthly interactions.

Here, he describes in detail a number of the standard traits outlined during Western NDEs. Admittedly, he puts his cultural interpretation on to the traits, but it is impossible to avoid the conclusion that his experiences and those described by Western NDErs are virtually identical.[2] Is this because Western culture is now part of the Indian psyche, or is it simply that modern Indians are being given the language and structure to describe their NDEs more accurately?

As we have already discussed regarding Zoroastrianism and Hinduism, both these belief systems had shamanism as their primary influence. This moved down from Siberia and added to the Central and South Asian cultures a definite model of the afterlife. Zoroastrianism and Hinduism brought forth another philosophy that was also to have at its source the particular forms of shamanism it encountered as it spread east to China, Japan and Korea and back north into the mountainous vastness of the

2 https://www.hackwriters.com/Menon-23.htm
ceo@tips4ceos.com

Himalayas, where several other isolated shamanic belief systems had developed, with both cultural encounters generating a powerful feedback mechanism that enriched all the cultures involved.

We now move our narrative to Buddhism in its Japanese, Korean and Tibetan variations.

BUDDHIST NDEs

As we have discovered, Hinduism and Zoroastrianism probably had a common ancestor culture that existed in the distant past in north Central Asia and Siberia. This was shamanic and perhaps the driving belief system that inspired the 'Aryans' to move south, west and east. In this cultural exchange, shamanism may have been introduced into the Tibetan Plateau, which created the mystical tradition and spread further east into China and Japan. Indeed, this cultural mixing was made more complex and interesting when a young Hindu Indian prince, Siddhartha Gautama, living in what is now Nepal, took his birth religion and created a new philosophy known as Buddhism. This spread across India and Asia and melded with the Bön tradition of Tibet to create a model of the afterlife that echoes many elements of the modern near-death experience. It is to this philosophy that we now turn our attention.

You will recall that the central belief of Zoroastrianism is that the world presented to us by our senses is a corrupted representation of how its creator planned it to be. This is not a permanent state of affairs; the universe will develop into the planned perfection.

This belief is also reflected in the Vedanta, a sacred system of the early Hindus. Humans can escape this distorted, corrupted world by focusing on the inner Divine nature that resides in all life.

In contrast, Buddhism argues that not only is the physical world a corrupt reflection of the actual reality that lies behind it, but also that the universe is an illusion, or, more accurately, a delusion and the objective of all consciousnesses is to dissolve into the actual reality and merge into a blissful state of non-ego.

Buddhism has many sects within it, and it is a religion that has been incredibly syncretic in its approach. This means that believers are happy to incorporate local beliefs into their greater philosophy and are not restricted by dogma. A classic example of this came when Buddhism encountered the older shamanic beliefs of the inhabitants of Tibet. By amalgamating the two systems, a fascinating belief system was created known as Bön, which contains numerous references to near-death experiences and the environment encountered after death.

The Tibetan Bön Tradition

Although part of the greater school of Tibetan Buddhism, Bön takes many of its techniques of spiritual enlightenment from the much older shamanic tradition of the Tibetan Plateau. (Kvaerne, 2001) Central to this tradition is the primacy of light in spiritual development. For the Bön, the source of all consciousness is a multi-coloured sphere of light that exists outside of space and time. This source of 'enlightenment' can be accessed by deep meditation and entering dream states where the 'Clear Light of Death' can be encountered.

In effect, this Clear Light is the meditator's 'true self'. In merging with this light, the meditator's soul can avoid the compulsory rebirth forced upon those who remain in the Bardo state, ignorant of their true purpose. In becoming a literal 'enlightened being', the soul remembers all its previous lives and can decide if it wishes to return to follow the cycle of birth and death again. Such enlightened beings are called Tulkas.

This primacy of light can also be found in the shamanic practices of another great Buddhist culture, Japan.

Buddhism and the Far East

In her 1975 book *The Catalpa Bow*, British anthropologist Carmen Blacker studied shamanistic practices in Japan and described how the concept of the Tama is present in Japanese shamanistic culture. The Tama is the life force that can depart from the body at certain times during life or permanently at death.

> *The Tama can detach itself from its host and wander about the country unanchored, occasionally revealing itself as a large shining jewel or ball to which its name proclaims its association. (Blacker, 1975, p. 25)*

Again, we have the concept of light relating to disembodied existence. When actual death occurs, the Tama remains an individuated source of self-awareness for 33 years (49 in some areas of Japan). Then, it merges into the collective consciousness known as the Ancestor, 'in which all past forebears of the family are believed to be encapsulated'. (Blacker, 1975, p. 25) This state of permanent rest is known as *jōbutsu*.

In a 1997 article that appeared in the periodical *Mortality*, theologian Paul Badham discussed the beliefs of the Buddhist sect known as the 'Pure Land'. Primarily found in China and Japan, Pure Land has as its central concept an entity known as the Amida which appears to a dying person at the point of death. The Amida then leads the person to the Pure Land paradise. (Badham, 1997). This paradise consists of a beautiful landscape with wonderful gardens, shimmering lakes and refreshing fountains. In this place, there is no pain or suffering.

Indeed, Badham also makes a fascinating link between modern reports of near-death experiences and the Pure Land religious tradition concerning the Ushiku Daibutsu statue of Buddha, located in the town of Ushiku, in Ibaraki Prefecture north of Tokyo, and also known by the acronym ARCADIA (Amida's Radiance and Compassion Developing and Illuminating Area). The statue was completed in December 1992 by Higashi Honganji temple and stands in the heart of the traditional burial ground of the Pure Land Sect. Visitors enter it via the ground-floor lobby, which is entirely dark except for the centre of the room, where a single shaft of light shines from above onto a cauldron of smoking incense. This level is called 'Infinite Light and Infinite Life'. Past the cauldron is an elevator. As the visitor enters the elevator, the lights are turned out, and they experience the sensation of rising rapidly upwards through a tunnel. The elevator doors open, and they see again the pillar of radiant white light reaching upwards. In front is a narrow window where the twin peaks of Mount Tsukuba can be viewed in the distance. The intention here is to re-create an image of Buddha's 'Pure Land' perceived after a near-death experience.

In South Korea, it is believed that, after death, the departed soul is confronted with a gate guarded by a judge. This judge questions the soul about particular aspects of their life and, depending upon the answers, will rebuke or praise them. They then move on to negotiate nine more gates and judgements. At the eleventh gate, they are met by an entity that has elements of the classic 'being of light' of Western NDEs. It is the role of this being to act as a mentor and to assist the soul in responding to questions that arise as their lifetime of good and bad deeds are weighed against each other. At the twelfth gate, the being of light argues on behalf of the soul for any mitigating circumstances that may have brought about a balance between bad deeds and good ones. This has echoes of a life-review scenario.

Buddhist neuroscientist Todd Murphy reported near-death experiences from Thailand (although he admitted that he had not collected them from subjects himself but rather from published accounts), and they differed significantly from the American near-death experience. Thai near-death experiences involved messengers from the Lord of the Dead (Yama) taking the person on a tour of hell, meeting Yama or his assistants, being told that the subject was the wrong person, and being ordered back. Of significance here is that both tunnels and panoramic life reviews were absent. (Murphy, 2001)

We have now completed our Eurasian review of the anthropology of near-death experiences. It is evident that all these cultures and belief systems describe an experiential phenomenon that cultural expectations do not create and have an independent existence. However, the NDE is interpreted in different ways by the perceivers. But we must admit that cultures cross-fertilize their ideas, and it is clear that there have been considerable overlaps between shamanism, Zoroastrianism, Buddhism and Hinduism. To an extent, this must undermine the argument that the NDE is a real rather than a psychologically determined perception.

Fortunately, we have a part of the world that has, for centuries, developed in isolation from the major monolithic cultures of both Asia and Europe, and that is the vast expanse of water dotted with isolated islands known as Oceania. Some of the most isolated cultures on the planet are found there. We need to examine their belief systems and see if their models of the afterlife and the transition zones between life and death have similarities with the traits reported elsewhere.

OCEANIAN/AUSTRALASIAN NDEs
Oceanian/Australasian NDEs – Introduction
Of all the human civilizations spread around the globe, it is generally believed that the most isolated are those ranging across the vast South Pacific. Over huge distances are islands, some in extended archipelagos and others in small clustered groups. These cultures developed in isolation. It is, therefore, interesting and significant to examine the NDE accounts of people there, to see if they share any of the 'traits' with NDE stories told by people in the West – a culture with which they have presumably had had little or no contact.

Oceanian/Australasian NDEs – Cargo Cults in Melanesia
In the last 80 years or so, anthropologists have been able to observe the development of modern-day shamanic-like sects within an indigenous

culture. These are the so-called 'cargo cults' of Melanesia and New Guinea. As with all religions, these new belief systems also involve complex models of the afterlife. Professor Dorothy Ellen Counts of Canada's Waterloo University spent 50 years studying these groups, doing extensive fieldwork in the West New Britain Province of Papua New Guinea. She was particularly interested in the interpretations of near-death experiences within Melanesian communities. In 1983, she published a paper in *Anabiosis*, the journal of the International Association of Near-Death Studies, in which she analysed three near-death experiences described by Melanesian Kaliai people and compared them to NDEs described in North America and India. (Counts, D. A., 1983)

The first experience studied by Counts involved 'Frank', a Kaliain-educated and cultured ex-headmaster, who described how he 'died' while suffering from extreme pains across his body:

> *I think I died for about five minutes. I saw a group of* aulu *[ancestor spirits] who showed me a road. I followed it and saw a man with white skin, long white robes, a beard and long hair. He was bright, as though there was a flashlight focused on him, and although he did not light up the area around him, his light seemed to be directed at me. He had large hands which he held up, palms toward me, blocking the road. He moved his middle fingers, motioning me to stop, and stared at me. Then he motioned to me to turn around and come back. Then Alois [a fellow villager who had died sometime before] cut my leg and spat ginger on it. It was as though I were asleep, but my eyes were open.* (Counts, D. A., 1983, p. 119)

Counts's second case involved a young man she calls 'Andrew'. He was 'dead' for around six hours, and during that time, the villagers had dug his grave and prepared a funeral feast. Sadly, one of the women who had been assisting with the preparations died suddenly in the village square a few miles away. News of this reached the mourners as they were preparing Andrew's body for burial. It was then that Andrew recovered consciousness and, no doubt, surprised the mourners further by announcing that he knew the woman in question had died. In Counts's interview with him, he stated:

> At the time I died, there was a woman who hadn't died. She cooked food and distributed it. But when I died, my spirit met hers on the road. (Counts, D. A., 1983, p. 119)

This is intriguing. It seems that he was in some form of out-of-body state whereby he witnessed the woman distributing food to the mourners, but, later, it appears in his vision that he met her in the land of the dead. Of course, there is another possible explanation for this. As we shall discover later, there is evidence that individuals showing all the medical signs of clinical death may be aware of things taking place around them. Indeed, in her footnote, Counts points out that:

> … while Andrew lay dead, the news of her death came to Vuvu and the villagers attending his body began to mourn and to discuss this second tragic event. If we interpret Andrew's death as a comatose state rather than as a clinical death, it is possible that in that state, he continued to receive and process information that affected his vision, including details about the death of the woman in the nearby village. This rests on the supposition that Andrew's attendants confused a comatose state with death. Not having been present at the event, I am unwilling to assert unequivocally that this was the case. Kaliai are ordinarily very clear about the signs of physical death. (Counts, D. A., 1983, p. 134)

Of course, even though, as Counts states, the 'Kaliai are ordinarily very clear about the signs of physical death', they will not have had, especially in the early 1980s, the in-depth medical knowledge available to modern neurologists, anaesthesiologists and physicians – a group of specialists who themselves continue to debate what the the actual signs of physical death are.

Whatever the source of Andrew's knowledge regarding the woman's death, the other elements of his NDE are, yet again, evidence that whatever the actual explanation of the experience may be, it had a number of 'traits' that seem to be consistent across cultures and widely dispersed geographical locations.

For Counts and several others researching the anthropological aspects of the near-death experience, what he perceived next was of great significance:

> There were all kinds of things inside this house, and I wanted to see them all. There were some men working with steel, and some men building ships, and another group of men building cars. (Counts, D. A., 1983, p. 120)

This is intriguing. Why are ships and cars needed in the afterlife? Indeed, where is the steel sourced for such an enterprise? An answer may be found in a social phenomenon unique to Melanesian societies: the 'cargo cult'. Of significance is that this belief system was, and still is, found in the Central Highlands of Papua New Guinea. On encountering white men for the first time, the indigenous Melanesian peoples of New Guinea, the Solomon Islands and the New Hebrides were astonished by their visitors' technology and where the objects of their technology were fabricated. The Melanesians observed that white men wrote secret signs on scraps of paper for which they were given shiploads of goods ('cargo'). It was then said that the dead ancestors made the cargo in the Land of the Dead and that it was meant for the local inhabitants, not the white interlopers. With the outbreak of the Second World War and conflict in the South Pacific after the attack on Pearl Harbor in December 1941, thousands of US and ANZAC (Australian and New Zealand Army Corps) troops arrived in the area, bringing with them even more evidence of the 'cargo'. Is this belief the one that fuelled Andrew's vision? This would make sense. If the Land of the Dead is where the cargo cults believe the cargo is made, and the ancestors make this cargo, then this is precisely what would be expected to occur there.

Andrew next encountered a 'beam of light', which he followed:

> *I was to come back, but there was no road for me to follow, so the voice said, 'Let him go down'. Then there was a beam of light, and I walked along it. I walked down the steps, and when I turned to look, there was nothing but forest. . . . So I walked along the beam of light, through the forest and along a narrow path. I came back to my house and re-entered my body and was alive again. (Counts, D. A., 1983, p. 120)*

So, the 'beam of light' led him back to his body and he became alive again. I cannot help but draw parallels here to classic out-of-body experiences that are not directly related to NDEs and also to ayahuasca and entheogenic experiences that will be discussed later in this book.

We know that light is one of Moody's traits, and this should be acknowledged. But this encounter is far more intriguing for me. I will, again, expand on this later in Part Five of this book.

Here is an account of one of the NDEs as described to Counts by one of the Melanesian villagers:

> *When I died everything was dark, but I went through a field of flowers and when I came out everything was clear. I walked on along the road and came to a fork where there were two men standing, one on either road. Each of them told me to come that way. I didn't have time to think about*

it, so I followed one of them. . . . The man took my hand
and we entered a village. There we found a long ladder
that led up to a house. We climbed the ladder but when we
got to the top I heard a voice saying, 'It isn't time for you
to come. Stay there. I'll send a group of people to take you
back.' (Counts, D. A., 1983, pp. 119–120).

In her conclusion, Counts listed the major differences between New
Britain/Melanesian near-death experiences and those described by the
people Raymond Moody interviewed. (Moody, R., 1975) She pointed
out that in none of the cases did her respondent describe looking down
at their sleeping or dead body or floating in a disembodied state. This
suggests that the out-of-body aspects of the NDE may not feature in
Papua New Guinea experiences. Also, there were no reports of buzzing
noises, music or ringing sounds, nor any sensations of hurtling through a
tunnel. What was reported was walking along a wide path or road. This
is reminiscent of the Iranian experiences discussed earlier, and suggests
a strong cultural aspect. As does the following observation she made that
is very suggestive of cargo cult beliefs:

People apparently experience the land of the dead as
having desirable aspects that are unobtainable or at least
not ordinarily encountered in this life. North Americans
and Europeans see a beautiful garden, while Kaliai
find an industrialized world of factories, highways and
urban sprawl.

Significantly, the Melanesian cargo-cult NDEs are preoccupied with
technology and its societal advantages. They see 'heaven' as a place full
of mechanical and electronic wonders, with flying machines and flashing
lights. What is particularly intriguing is how these NDEs contain many
elements of another experience that I will focus on later in much greater
detail: UFO encounters and abductions.

We have now come to the end of our review of the NDE across history and cultures. Whatever is taking place is a genuine psychological state. The handful of standard 'traits' consistently described by NDErs over time are of particular interest. Can these traits be explained scientifically? A great deal of important work has been done in this area, and we need to explore this in greater detail.

PART 3

The Categories

NDE Categorization – Introduction

As we've already seen, in his 1975 book *Life After Life* Raymond Moody identified a sequence of events experienced by NDErs. He later was to isolate 15 commonly reported 'traits' found in the reports. These were: ineffability, hearing oneself pronounced dead, feelings of peace, hearing unusual noises, seeing a dark tunnel, being 'out of the body', meeting 'spiritual beings', a bright light often experienced as a 'being of light', panoramic life review, a realm in which all knowledge exists, cities of light, a realm of bewildered spirits, a 'supernatural rescue', sensing an uncrossable border or limit, and returning to the body.

Later, in the early 1980s, psychiatrist Bruce Greyson reduced these to four core elements, which were: (a) cognitive features of time distortion, thought acceleration, a life review and revelation; (b) affective features of peace, joy, cosmic unity and an encounter with a loving 'being of light'; (c) seemingly paranormal features of unnaturally vivid sensory experiences, putative extrasensory experiences and precognitive visions, and out-of-body experiences; and (d) transcendental features of otherworldly encounters with mystical beings, visible spirits and an uncrossable border to an unearthly realm. He used these as the basis of his much-applied Near-Death Experience Scale Questionnaire (NDESQ), which he presented in 1985 (Greyson, 1985, pp. 967–968).

In our review of the cultural, anthropological and historical aspects of the near-death experience, we have discovered that these traits are not confined to Western cultures, nor are they in any way influenced by mass media or social pressure. They have been reported throughout history and appear in the NDEs of individuals living in total isolation from Western media exposure.

It is therefore crucial that we understand the phenomenology of these NDE elements. To do this, we need to review several of the main 'traits' in detail and discuss the science behind them. Sadly, space does not allow a complete discussion of each one, so I have isolated what I believe to be the most important. These will be: the out-of-body experience; the tunnel and the light; the panoramic life review; time distortion; and encounters with entities.

THE CATEGORIES – THE OUT-OF-BODY EXPERIENCE
OBEs – Introduction

The out-of-body experience (OBE) is one of the most common traits reported by individuals who have experienced an NDE.

The presence of three perceptual characteristics has defined the OBE. The first is a feeling of disembodiment, that perceptual awareness is located somewhere in space other than in the body looking out. As an aspect of this, the second characteristic is viewing the external environment from an elevated and distanced visuo-spatial perspective and, finally, the impression of seeing one's own body from this perspective. (Bünning & Blanke, 2005)

It is important to note that the out-of-body state has been reported regularly throughout history and many, many years before Moody's book brought it to the general public's attention as an NDE factor. For example, in his 2021 book After, Bruce Greyson cites an intriguing example of an out-of-body experience described by the Scottish military surgeon Sir Alexander Ogston, who discovered the staphylococcus bacteria. (Greyson, 2021, p. 81)

In 1901, Ogston was seriously ill with typhoid fever when he found himself outside of his own body:

Mind and body seemed to be dual and, to some extent, separate. I was conscious of the body as an inert tumbled mass near a door; it belonged to me, but it was not I. I was conscious that my mental self used regularly to leave the body . . . until something produced a consciousness that the chilly mass, which I then recalled was my body, was being stirred as it lay by the door. I was then drawn rapidly back into it, joined it with disgust, and it became I and was fed, spoken to, and cared for. When it was again left, I seemed to wander off as before . . . and though I knew that death was hovering about, having no thought of religion nor dread of the end, and roamed on beneath the murky skies apathetic and contented until something again disturbed the body where it lay, when I was drawn back to it afresh, and entered it with ever-growing repulsion. (Ogston, 1919, pp. 22–23)

He later describes how he could see through the walls of the building, how he witnessed in detail the death of another patient and what the medical staff had subsequently done with the body. During his recovery, the nurses confirmed to him that he had seen precisely what had taken place.

Ogston's experience is of great importance because here we have somebody many decades before Moody's book describing details regarding his OBE state that are uncannily similar to those described by modern accounts. Can this be dismissed as simply anecdotal evidence? It is proof that whatever the actual explanation for the out-of-body state may be, it cannot be denied that it is real for the person experiencing it. The question, then, is what we mean by 'real' in this context. Yes, it is a real experience in the sense that it is felt, but during an NDE is the person truly outside their body? Have such perceptions been verified under controlled conditions? A series of experiments in Canada in the middle of the 20th century suggest that they have been – and that whatever the

OBE sensation may be, it is in many important respects objectively real. Let us now discuss these in greater detail.

OBEs – Science – The Discoveries of Wilder Penfield

One of the most extraordinary breakthroughs of modern neurosurgery took place in 1941 in an operating theatre at the Montreal Neurological Institute in Canada. The surgeon was Wilder Penfield, and what he discovered that day was to have profound implications for our understanding of how the human brain processes reality.

Wilder Graves Penfield was born in Spokane, Washington State, in 1891, the son of a physician. He moved with his family to Hudson, Wisconsin in 1899. After graduating from Princeton in 1913, Penfield was awarded a Rhodes Scholarship to study medicine at Merton College, Oxford.

It was while at Oxford that he met Charles Scott Sherrington, a brilliant neurophysiologist who, in 1932, would receive the Nobel Prize in Medicine for his work. The two men became close friends and continued to share their thoughts on medicine and the workings of the human brain even after Penfield moved back to the US, where, after completing his medical doctorate at Johns Hopkins University, he became a surgeon at the New York Presbyterian Hospital.

In 1928, Penfield visited Breslau in Germany to learn more about the pioneering work of neurosurgeon Otfried Foerster. Foerster had been working on removing scar tissue (lesions) in the cerebral cortex of epileptic patients. It was known that lesions were responsible for epileptic seizures and that by removing them the epilepsy could be relieved. It is of great significance to note that Foerster was greatly influenced by the pioneering work of Hans Berger, whose work we will soon review in great detail.

From this, Foerster wondered if gentle electrical stimulation of the cerebral cortex could cause epileptic-like reactions in non-epileptic individuals. For the previous six years, Penfield had worked as a neurosurgeon in New York, hoping to understand the causes of epilepsy. To do this, he had worked on brain wounds. Foerster needed a pathologist to work on his collection of excised brain material from his operations. He had a collection of 12 brain sections contained in glass containers of preservative (formalin). Penfield was the ideal person for this task. The two worked together and, in 1930, published a paper on their findings in two versions, one in German and one in English. (Foerster & Penfield, 1930)

In this paper, they argued that charts and surface markings were unreliable in localizing the tissue to be removed, which should be mapped using a much more reliable electrical stimulation performed with electrodes. They also made some fascinating points about how the stimulation of specific areas of the brain could be used to create hallucinations, writing, for example, that the 'stimulation of Area 17, the occipital pole, yields light, flames, and stars in the contralateral visual field. In contrast, stimulation nearby produces a hallucination of formed figures and gaze to the opposite side'. (Foerster & Penfield, 1930, p. 101)

Foerster and Penfield went on to explain that, when a section of the brain is surgically removed, there is no subsequent joining together of brain tissue and that it creates different type of scar tissue, known as a cicatrix, from that which results from a lesion. Interestingly, they found that surgically-created scars do not induce epilepsy, whereas lesions do (though not always). From this, they concluded that the original lesion brought about by brain injury could be surgically removed, thus curing the epilepsy.

Soon after arriving in Germany, Penfield realized that another use could be made for Foerster's electrode in addition to mapping the brain. He explained his logic in a lecture delivered in 1972:

> *It was clear that the electrode had a new use here. It could be employed during operations under local anaesthesia on cooperative, conscious patients for two practical purposes: 1. to discover the epileptogenic focus and 2. to map out*

the brain's anatomy, thus making surgical removal safer
and more effective. We believed there was a great future
for this method of radical treatment of epilepsy. Thus,
Foerster showed the way to a further field in neurosurgery.
(Penfield, 1972, p. 300)

Penfield realized that to continue this promising line of enquiry he needed a much larger facility than that at Breslau. So, in September 1934, he moved to the Montreal Neurological Institute, which had a financial endowment from the Rockefeller Foundation in New York. With his new colleagues, he could use his electrode technique to map out the human brain's motor, sensory and speech areas.

After applying local anaesthetic to the scalp, Penfield was able to remove an area of a patient's skull to reveal the surface of the cerebral cortex. As the brain itself feels no pain, he was then able to apply an electrode pen to its surface and ask the patient what they were experiencing as he probed different parts of it.

And this is how the circumstances described at the start of this chapter came about. The patient, identified as 'G.A.', suffered habitual epileptic attacks that never evoked any form of hallucinations. However, as soon as Penfield applied electrical stimulation of her right superior temporal gyrus, she spontaneously exclaimed: 'I have a queer sensation as if I am not here. . . . As though I were half here and half not here,' later confirming that she had never experienced anything similar in the past. Penfield re-applied the electrode pen, and she stated that she again felt strange and that she was floating away. The sensation of being out of her body continued as the Penfield electrode stimulated the area of the brain now known as the temporoparietal junction. What was of particular interest concerning our enquiry into the near-death experience was that Penfield stated that the patient had what he described as 'mental diplopia'. By this, he meant she was fully aware that she was in an operating theatre in Montreal, but she was also aware that underlying that reality was another location she could sense. In effect, she was in two places at the same time. In a later stimulation, she reported that she felt that she was floating above the bed, close to the ceiling of the operating theatre. (Penfield & Erickson, 1941, pp. 261–265)

OBEs – The TPJ link

Many critics have argued that Penfield's experiments have yet to be reproduced. This is not correct. In 2005, Swiss-German neuroscientist Olaf Blanke and his team designed an experiment in which they stimulated the brain's TPJ (the temporo-parietal junction). It is crucially important here to realize that the TPJ is also the area where Penfield was able to create what he called mental diplopia in his patient G.A.. It is of even more importance to know that the TPJ is the area of the brain that it is believed generates gamma oscillation-induced dream states.

Blanke and his team were keen to understand the mechanisms whereby the brain generates illusory body sensations during an out-of-body experience. They were particularly intrigued by the fact that these sensations are not confined to clinical populations but are also reported by 10 per cent of neurologically 'healthy' individuals, an extraordinarily high number. (Faguet, 1979)

Blanke et al. argue that OBEs may result from a deficient multisensory integration in the TPJ. They first suspected this to be the case when, in 2002, they reported the results of an attempt to find the brain location of seizures experienced by a 43-year-old woman. To do this, they placed electrodes on the surface of her brain and administered mild electrical shocks to various locations of her cerebral cortex. (Blanke O., Ortigue, Landis & Seeck, 2002)

When they stimulated an area known as the right angular gyrus, located behind the right ear, she reported floating above the bed and looking down on her body. Again, this was the area of the brain where Penfield created a similar OBE sensation in his patient G.A.. It is crucial here to note that Blanke's patient felt her consciousness was located in the body floating above the bed, not that she saw a version of herself floating above. These are two different psychological states. To look at one's body from a location outside of it is known as autoscopy. To see a version of oneself in front or above is to be experiencing heautoscopy or 'Doppelganger Syndrome'. She was, in a genuine sense, disembodied. Blanke believed, and still feels, as far as I know, that he could explain this. In a paper published two years later, he wrote that out-of-body experiences were simply a:

> . . . *disintegration within personal space (multisensory dysfunction) and disintegration between personal space (vestibular) and Extrapersonal (visual) due to interference with the temporo-parietal junction. (Blanke, O., 2004)*

Further support for the TPJ model appeared in 2011 with a fascinating paper published in the *New England Journal of Medicine*. The lead author, Dirk De Ridder, a neurosurgeon based at the University Hospital Antwerpen, in Belgium, described how a patient suffering from intractable tinnitus had a paddle electrode implanted over his right temporoparietal junction. Unfortunately, the electrode failed to deal with the tinnitus, but it facilitated several powerful out-of-body experiences when activated. The researchers realized that as they could create an OBE state at will – and that it was one whereby they could not only monitor what was taking place in the brain when the OBE state was evoked but also ask the patient what they were subjectively perceiving at that time.

The patient described how, as soon as the stimulation began, he sensed that he was in a state of disembodiment, located about 50 cm (20 in) behind his body and off to the left. Of importance was that there was no sensation of autoscopy and, at all times, the patient's visual field was from his actual, not OBE-perceived, location. These experiences lasted, on average, around 17 seconds.

A positron emission tomography (PET) scanner monitored the patient's brain activity. When an OBE began, he was asked to press a button. This confirmed that brain activity was increased specifically within his right temporoparietal junction when an OBE state was perceived. The team stated that:

> Our PET data suggest that the experience of disembodiment is mediated by the coactivation of a small area at the junction of the angular and supramarginal gyrus and the superior temporal gyrus-sulcus. Activation of the angular and supramarginal gyrus junction alters vestibular–somatosensory integration of body orientation in space. Coactivation of the posterior part of the superior temporal cortex, with its internal map of self-perception, results in altered spatial self-perception. (De Ridder, Van Laere, Dupont, Menovsky & Van Der Heyning, 2007, pp. 1832–1833)

Ending with the hypothetical question (and response):

> Whether these regions are activated in patients who report disembodiment as part of a near-death experience – and if so, how – is a provocative but unresolved issue. (De Ridder, Van Laere, Dupont, Menovsky & Van Der Heyning, 2007, p. 1833)

I think the case has been strongly made for the role of the TPJ regarding the facilitation of the out-of-body state. What is less clear, in my mind, is how this part of the brain generates such a powerful 'hallucination'. Indeed, one could counter-argue that the TPJ facilitates the exit of consciousness from the confines of the skull and allows it to wander within the external environment. The TPJ model no more invalidates the OBE as a real perception than anything else does. An issue to me is that it seems that, in all cases that have been cited, the subject genuinely believes that they are outside of their body and not that they perceive a hallucination that they are outside of their body. For me, the defining factor of which variation of this TPJ-facilitated perception is correct is a simple one: how powerful and convincing is the evidence for veridical perceptions in such circumstances? For example, how did Sir Alexander Ogston know of the circumstances of the death of his fellow patient back in 1901? Indeed, if this was an isolated case, it could be dismissed, but people have regularly reported seeing and hearing events that they could not have possibly known.

But before we do this, we need to discuss a series of experiments that took place at a similar time to the research and discoveries regarding the TPJ, and sleep transitions, an area that also relates to this part of the brain.

OBEs – Sleep Transitions

It has been noted many times that the out-of-body state, whether in relation to a near-death experience or in other ways, has phenomenological links with dreaming. Indeed, OBEs have been associated with a number of sleep-related conditions, including narcolepsy and sleep paralysis. (Nelson, Mattingly & Schmitt, 2007) According to Nelson et al., near-death experience OBEs are simply a response to a life-threatening set of circumstances which involves a combination of 'dissociation from the physical body, euphoria, and transcendental or mystical elements'. (Nelson, Mattingly & Schmitt, 2007, p. 794). This is supported by the research of Owen et al., which showed that an NDE with all its associated traits can be experienced even when the patient is not actually in danger of death. (Owens, Cook & Stevenson, 1990) All they have to do is believe that their death may be imminent. In a subsequent paper, Ian Stevenson et al. suggested that in recognition of this discovery, the term 'fear death experience' was a more accurate descriptor than 'near' death experience. (Stevenson, Cook & McClean-Rice. 'Are persons reporting "near-death experiences" really near death? A study of medical records', 1990, p. 53)

In 2006, Kevin Nelson and his team at the Department of Neurology at the University of Kentucky published a short article in the academic journal *Neurology*, in which they suggested that such experiences may be related to an experience known as REM-Intrusion. (Nelson, Mattingly & Schmitt, 2007)

The physiologists Eugene Aserinsky and Nathaniel Kleitman first discovered REM, or 'Rapid Eye Movement', in the early 1950s. (Aserinsky & Kleitman, 1953) Later that decade, French neuroscientist Michel Jouvet linked muscle atonia to REM, which is now the standard explanation of sleep paralysis during REM-intrusion phases. (Jouvet & Michael, 1959) This is when the dream scenario overlaps with an internally-generated schematic of the external environment surrounding the dreamer. The atonia paralyses the dreamer, leaving them in a state of subjective vulnerability. What is of possible significance with regard to the areas of enquiry we will pursue later is that REM is significantly overrepresented in immature mammals and birds and even more significant in premature mammals. (Dreyfus-Brisac, 1964) It has been estimated that, at 30 weeks of gestation, the embryo is in a continual REM sleep mode. (Birnholz, 1981) They are dreaming all the time. What can they possibly be dreaming about? Modern neurologists suggest from this that REM has a crucial role in developing the embryo brain. Indeed, this model indicates that REM awareness occurs before we ever encounter the waking sensorium. It is the testing ground by which we ultimately encounter and react to consensual reality.

However, to understand more fully the possible relationship between REM activity and NDEs, we need to know more about this curious state of consciousness. It has been discovered that REM experiences usually commence at around 90 minutes after the onset of sleep and recur regularly throughout the night, the last time being about an hour before the person wakes up. It is generally agreed that there are two related forms of REM. We have already discussed REM intrusion, but the second form may be of greater significance for our enquiry. This is known by two names, depending upon when in the sleep cycle it is experienced. If the person is falling asleep, it is called hypnagogia, and when they awake, hypnopompia. In both cases, the person feels that they are fully awake. In this state, dream imagery is experienced as part of the everyday sensory world surrounding the dreamer. These experiences can last for a few seconds to a few minutes and can be terrifying.

Nelson and his team suggest the link may involve the brain's arousal system. This system is comprised of brainstem structures that control or influence sleep–wake states, alertness and attention.

To make the links between NDEs and REM intrusion and sleep paralysis, Nelson and his colleagues interviewed 55 individuals who reported having an NDE incident. It was discovered that those who had an out-of-body experience along with near-death were more likely also to have had some REM intrusion in their lifetime. This meant that instead of passing directly between the REM sleep state and wakefulness, the brain switch blends these states into one another. When in this state, another somewhat disturbing sensation is perceived, something known as sleep paralysis. This is a common variation of REM intrusion, which causes temporary paralysis along with visual or auditory hallucinations immediately after waking up or before falling asleep.

Nelson et al. argue that an out-of-body experience is statistically as likely to occur during a near-death experience as it is during the transition between wakefulness and sleep. This suggests that phenomena in the brain's arousal system, which regulates different states of consciousness, including REM sleep and wakefulness, may cause these types of out-of-body displays.

However, the team found this relationship both 'curious and unexplained', adding:

> *Atonia with OBE during medical danger would reinforce a sense of death with subjective features characteristic of many NDE narratives. Why OBE should have a relationship with arousal is speculative. OBE could arise from the amygdala, which is vigorously activated during the REM*

state. OBE is elicited by the temporo-parietal cortex, whose stimulation also produces vestibular sensations and complex somatosensory distortions. (Nelson, K., 2015)

So, let's dig deeper into this mystery. Sleep transitions are the term for those liminal states between being awake and asleep. As we go to sleep, we can enter what is known as a hypnogogic state as we drop off and a hypnapompic state as we wake up. Sleep paralysis usually takes place during hypnapompia and is believed to be quite common.

In these 'hallucinations', dream imagery becomes incorporated into the external world, similar to how augmented reality is perceived when wearing a virtual-reality headset. Similarly, dream-generated sounds appear to be located in the external environment. This can be highly terrifying because the hallucinations seem real. These perceptions can last for anything from a few seconds to a few minutes. However, as subjective time can be dilated within the dream world, it is impossible to say how long they actually last. What adds to the sense of horror is that, usually, the person feels that they are paralysed as if they are dead – hence the 'sleep paralysis' designation.

In a critical study published in 2009, psychologists Allan Cheyne and Todd Girard described the results of extensive research in which they received completed questionnaires from over 13,000 people who had experienced sleep paralysis. (Cheyne & Girard, 2009) Almost 40 per cent also had OBEs during the episode. What is difficult to explain here is how nearly half of the respondents who experienced the OBE also experienced a phenomenon known as autoscopy, where they could see their body while in an out-of-body state. (Cheyne & Girard, 2009, p. 205) It is important to analyse in greater detail what is taking place here. It is easy to dismiss a vague sensation of poking out of one's body, but to see one's body located in space is a wholly different set of perceptions. How does the brain create this supposed hallucination? And, more importantly, why does it do so? Is this simply a variation of a lucid dream state?

What makes this an even more significant challenge to those wedded to the simplistic 'hallucination hypothesis' of the NDE is that autoscopy is not only found in clinical populations but also appears in around 10 per cent of the 'healthy' population. (Faguet, 1979; Bünning & Blanke, 2005)

So what does modern material-reductionist science make of hallucinations? Well, the word gives several clues as to how far back in time these glimpses of other realities reach and how enigmatic they are. The word 'hallucinatory' has its roots in the Latin *allucinari*, which means 'to wander in mind'. The first written reference in the English language dates from 1569 when Swiss Protestant theologian Ludwig Lavater used the term in his book *De spectris, lemuribus et magnis atque insolitis fragoribus* (*Of Ghostes and Spirites*). Its first use with regards to modern understanding was by the French physician Jean Etienne Esquirol in 1837. (Ohayon, 2000, p. 154)

Research undertaken in 1991 for Baltimore's National Institute of Mental Health Epidemiologic Catchment Area Program suggested that visual hallucinations in males were around 20 per 1,000 per year and in females about 13 per 1,000 per year. Intriguingly, the number increased to 40 per 1,000 per year for females over 80 years of age. The paper did not mention the figures for men in the same age group. This was a significant exercise with a cohort of around 20,000 subjects. (Tien, 1991)

In early 2000, Dr Maurice M. Ohayon of the Stanford University Sleep Disorder Center in California organized an important survey on the prevalence of hallucinations in the general population. His sample was taken from the non-institutionalized general population of the United Kingdom, Germany and Italy. This involved 13,057 individuals. Just under 39 per cent of the sample reported hallucinatory experiences, 19.6 per cent less than once a month, 6.4 per cent monthly, 2.7 per cent once a week, and 2.4 per cent more than once a week. This shows that hallucinations are very common. The most reported hallucinations were hypnagogic and hypnopompic, 24.8 per cent and 6.6 per cent respectively. (Ohayon, 2000, p. 153) As with REM sleep, hypnagogic hallucinations take place as we drift into sleep and hypnopompic ones when we awaken.

These results are intriguing. But, to reiterate a question I asked earlier, all these brain-facilitated states no more explain OBE perceptions than attempts to explain consciousness as simply a byproduct of brain function. They are just another aspect of Chalmer's 'Hard Problem' (see Part Four). Suppose the OBE is merely a hallucination, a position that many philosophers, known as eliminative materialists, believe is also the case with self-aware consciousness. In that case, veridical OBE perceptions should be impossible. But are they?

In 1968, a much-cited experiment took place under controlled conditions that suggested that information could be acquired in an out-of-body state. We now need to turn our attention to the work of psychologist Charles Tart and the enigmatic case of 'Miss Z'.

OBEs – Miss Z

Ever since he was an electrical engineering student at the Massachusetts Institute of Technology in the 1950s, Charles Tart had been keen to discover if information could be brought back from another location while in an out-of-body state. From 1959 onwards, he attempted a series of unsuccessful tests. But 22 years later, in 1981, he was to claim a much-discussed success with a young woman he identified as 'Miss Z'.

Miss Z was his children's babysitter. In a general conversation with Tart one day, she mentioned that ever since childhood she had experienced sleeping dream sequences in which she felt she was floating near the ceiling, looking down at her body.

She explained that, although not as regular as in her younger years, these perceptions still occurred occasionally. This interested Tart and he suggested that a way of proving she was really outside her body was to test herself. He proposed that she write the numbers one to ten on slips of paper and then randomly select one, without looking at it, and place it in a box on her bedside table. She subsequently informed Tart that she had tried the experiment seven times and correctly saw the number in her OBE each time.

Tart invited Miss Z to his sleep laboratory, where she spent four nights. Each night, he recorded her electroencephalogram (EEG) using his knowledge to identify when she was awake, drowsy or asleep. He also used a miniature strain gauge to monitor rapid eye movements, and electrodes were placed on her body to measure skin resistance. In the room, but out of sight of the subject, Tart placed a five-digit number in a location that could only be seen if the subject was outside her body. Curiously, he informed her that the number would be on a card propped upright against the wall on the shelf near the ceiling. I can only assume that Miss Z knowing where to look when in her OBE state would prevent her from wasting time trying to find the number card.

Miss Z claimed she managed an out-of-body state during these four nights, but for the first three she failed to identify the number. However, on waking after the fourth night, she loudly announced that she had seen the number and its sequence was 25132. What was of even greater significance was that she noted that the card was lying flat, not upright, on the shelf. This was, indeed, how the card was subsequently found to be. In his paper, Tart stated that the odds of a correct guess would be 1 in 100,000.

But, of course, there could be another explanation. It seems that Miss Z was never observed directly by any of the researchers when she was in the sleeping room. She had already been told where the number was, so what stopped her from simply detaching the various measuring devices and looking for herself? I am not stating that I believe this is what happened, but, applying Occam's Razor, it is more likely that she was not actually out of her body – and I suspect that this is the approach most sceptics take to this case.

But there are other cases that cannot be so easily dismissed, incidents that seem to prove that OBEs are genuine perceptions. We will now review a handful of them.

OBE – Penny Sartori's 'Patient 10' (2004)

In 1997 Dr Penny Sartori, then a nurse based at the Morriston Hospital in Swansea, began a five-year prospective hospital study in South Wales. In the first year, she interviewed every patient who survived admission to the intensive therapy unit, followed by four years of interviewing patients who had survived cardiac arrest.

One particular case that Sartori witnessed personally involved a 60-year-old man who was recovering from complications following surgery for bowel cancer. Soon after the operation, he developed blood poisoning and multiorgan failure, but it seemed that he was on the road to recovery. He was sitting in a chair beside his bed when a nurse noticed he was distressed. It was at this stage that Sartori was called in to assist. She manually ventilated the patient, but his condition deteriorated and he fell into a deep state of unconsciousness where he was unable to respond to verbal commands or deep, painful stimuli. (Sartori, Badham & Fenwick, 2006, p. 72)

This was of great concern to the physiotherapist, who had persuaded the patient to get out of bed and sit in the chair. Sartori later wrote that the therapist stood outside the bedside screens, nervously and intermittently poking her head around to check on the patient. (Sartori, Badham & Fenwick, 2006, p. 73) When the patient's condition had been stabilized, it was noticed that he had been drooling. A nurse cleaned this using a long suction catheter and then a pink oral sponge soaked in water. The patient showed no signs of alertness for 30 minutes; it took three hours for him to fully regain consciousness.

When he did, however, he was in a state of excitement. He was unable to speak as he was still attached to the ventilator, and was given a letter board by the physiotherapist. What he spelt out stunned all present, including the doctors and nurses. 'I died, and I watched it all from above,' he wrote. Later, when the patient had recovered, Penny Sartori interviewed him. He told her:

All I can remember is looking up in the air and I was

floating in a bright pink room. I couldn't see anything; I was just going up and there was no pain at all. . . .

I could see everybody panicking around me. The blonde lady therapist boss, she was panicking; she looked nervous because she was the one who got me out in the chair. She hid behind the curtains, but kept poking her head around to check on me. I could also see Penny, who was a nurse. She was drawing something out of my mouth, which looked to me like a long, pink lollipop, like a long, pink thing on a stick – I didn't even know what that was. (Sartori, Badham & Fenwick, 2006, p. 73)

According to Sartori, everything that the patient stated he 'saw' while he was in a state of deep unconsciousness actually took place. Recall that his eyes were permanently closed, so there was no chance that he experienced a subliminal memory of the events.

OBE Turning into an NDE – Tony Cicoria

It is occasionally reported that what begins as a standard out-of-body experience can develop into what appears to be a classic NDE. One such example was the case of orthopaedic surgeon Dr Tony Cicoria as described by Dr Oliver Sacks, a New York-based British neurologist, in his 2007 book *Musicophilia: Tales of Music and the Brain*.

In 1994, Cicoria was 42 years old and living and working in a small town in upstate New York. He was attending a family gathering one stormy autumn afternoon when he left the group to call his mother from a nearby public phone box.

As the call ended, a bolt of lightning struck the kiosk. A flash of light came from the phone and hit Cicoria in the face. He was violently flung backwards and, after struggling to his feet, watched as his mother-in-law came running towards him, screaming. He called out to her, but she didn't respond. Instead, she ran straight past him. Cicoria then found himself surrounded by what he later described as a bluish-white light, which gave him a tremendous feeling of well-being. He then found himself floating through a wall to see an image of his children having their faces painted, and he knew that, whatever happened, they would be okay. He then saw a series of images:

> *The highest and lowest points of my life raced by me. No emotion associated with these . . . pure thought, pure ecstasy. I had the perception of accelerating, being drawn up . . . there was speed and direction. (Sacks, O., 2007, p. 4)*

But all these wonderful images began to fade as he felt a sharp series of thumps on his chest. A nurse, who happened to be waiting outside the phone kiosk when the lightning strike had taken place, was giving him CPR and pumping his chest.

Cicoria then felt pain from the burns caused by the lightning strike. It was at this point that he said to himself that 'only bodies feel pain' and he realized that the woman's CPR efforts had been successful and that he was being drawn back into his body. He was in such a state of bliss that this was the last thing he wanted. When the police arrived they wanted to call an ambulance. Cicoria refused, even though he was in considerable discomfort, and was taken home. On arrival, he phoned his doctor, a cardiologist, who gave him a medical examination and confirmed that he must have experienced a brief cardiac arrest. For a few seconds, he had been clinically dead.

What is important here is not just the classic panoramic life review that Cicoria experienced but also his initial state immediately after the lightning strike, which was an out-of-body experience. I am particularly interested in how he described how he 'floated up the stairs – my consciousness came with me'. This was a perception within the reality of the party and the lake house. He was seeing the actual real world from a location outside of his body. But then there is a sudden transition, and he sees his children, who were not present in the area but elsewhere at the party, having their faces painted. He perceived this not from his vision as his body was floating up the stairs but as a form of internally-generated vision. And then, in a cloud of bluish-white light, he experienced the panoramic life review. He was no longer by an upstate New York lake on a stormy autumnal afternoon but entirely within a powerful, timeless NDE state. The transition was immediate, something that is regularly reported in OBE and lucid-dreaming states.

Within the usual chronology of the NDE, the sensation of being out of the body usually turns into a rapidly increasing sense of forward motion in which the dying person enters the most iconic NDE trait, the tunnel.

THE CATEGORIES – THE TUNNEL AND THE LIGHT
The Tunnel – Introduction

Of all the perceptions described by NDErs, it is probably the 'tunnel' that resonates most with the general public and the media. Indeed, the tunnel features in a famous painting by late medieval Flemish artist Hieronymus Bosch. Around 1490, Bosch painted a series of four panels that are now individually known as *The Terrestrial Paradise*, *Ascent of the Blessed*, *Fall of the Damned into Hell* and *Hell*. It is believed that a fifth panel, depicting the Last Judgement, was part of the series but has now been lost. For those interested in the NDE, the depiction of the souls of the newly dead ascending into a tunnel of light with silhouettes of mysterious humanoid figures in the light beyond the tunnel exit is powerful evidence that Bosch had either experienced an NDE himself or had been told of such visions from others. We shall never know what Bosch's inspiration was, but his imagery is undoubtedly an accurate image of hundreds of modern reports of NDE survivors.

According to research done by the NDE researcher Pim van Lommel and his associates, 31 per cent of 344 Dutch heart attack survivors interviewed in their 2001 study perceived a tunnel during their brush with death. (Van Lommel, P., van Wees, Meyers & Elfferich) This is much higher than the 8.7 per cent and 5.7 per cent recorded respectively by Sri Lankan and Chinese researchers on patients in their countries for studies they conducted. (Lai et al., 2007) This strongly suggests that the tunnel experience is generally more of a Western perception. However, it must be acknowledged that if it was simply a cultural issue, then why did any of the Chinese or Sinhalese NDErs report a tunnel? None of them should have experienced it. Could it be a question of culturally influenced attention? Westerners look for a tunnel and see it, whereas others see the effect but identify it differently.

In *The Handbook of Near-Death Experiences* (Holden, Greyson & James, 2009) Alan Kellehear has an article on the cultural aspects of the near-death experience and a section on the tunnel. He agrees that the tunnel does not appear as a theme in non-Western NDE accounts. However, he does point out that he has discovered several references to darkness or a void. This may be evidence of cultural programming in that Westerners and non-Westerners interpret more profound sensory stimuli according to sociologically determined expectations. Westerners expect a tunnel and see it; other cultures expect darkness and see it.

Of all the experiences reported by NDErs over the years, the tunnel has most interested scientists. We will now review some of the attempted explanations, including a topic we shall return to in much greater detail later: the role of oxygen starvation in circumstances of near-death, a process known technically as anoxia.

The Tunnel – Carl Sagan and Birth Memories

In 1979, astronomer Carl Sagan suggested tunnel perception was simply a birth memory. (Sagan, 1979) In his book *Broca's Brain – Reflections on the Romance of Science*, Sagan focused on the research of Stanislav Grof, the well-known Czech-American psychiatrist. Grof has used psychedelic drugs in his psychotherapy practice for over half a century. From this, he has concluded that many psychedelic experiences can be related to two key phases in a person's life: the perinatal and the perithanatic. The first of these is the period around birth; the second the time around death. Grof's perinatal argument is based upon the fact that a large number of his patients, after a suitable number of sessions, begin to recall, and in some cases re-experience, profound and long-forgotten memories of their pre-birth state, actual birth and early years of life. Initial pre-birth memories are of an idyllic womb-existence of a small, dark, warm universe contained within the amniotic sac. However, this is ultimately brought to an end when the birth process begins, terminating abruptly with the infant being pushed out into a harsh, terrifying new environment.

Sagan describes this as being hugely traumatic, as the child perceives:

> ... a tunnel illuminated at one end and senses the brilliant radiance of the extrauterine world. The discovery of light for a creature that has lived in darkness must be a profound and, on some level, an unforgettable experience. And there, dimly made out by the low resolution of the newborn's eyes, is some godlike figure surrounded by a halo of light – the Midwife, the Obstetrician, or the Father. At the end of a monstrous travail, the baby flies away from the uterine universe and rises toward the lights and the gods. (Sagan, 1979, p. 353)

Could this be an explanation for the much-discussed NDE tunnel experience? Psychologist Susan Blackmore was not so sure. In an article published in *New Scientist* in May 1988, she observed that the birth canal is nothing like a tunnel and questioned how any memory of such an experience would make sense to an adult many years later. (Blackmore, S., 1988, p. 44) To test the validity of this idea, Blackmore gave a questionnaire to 254 people, of whom 36 had been born by

Caesarean section. Interestingly, she discovered that there was no difference between the two groups. Both reported the same proportion of tunnel experiences and out-of-body experiences. This suggested to her that the tunnel experience was based upon 'the idea of birth in general'. (Blackmore, S., 'Visions from the dying brain', *New Scientist*, May 1988, p. 44).

However, there is also a straightforward argument against the birth-memory model that had already been proposed by Carl Becker in 1982. He pointed out that newborn infants' brains and visual systems are not developed enough to store such memories. He also argued that the birth canal is hardly like a wide tunnel from the viewpoint of the baby:

> *The birth is more analogous to breaking through a membrane from a dark room into a lighter room, or to surfacing from a muddy swimming hole, than to peering down a long tunnel with a glowing light at the other end. Moreover, even if the opening did let light in, the baby is unable to tilt either his head or his eyes upwards to see it (Jones, 1926). If the light registered at all on the untrained brains of the infants, it should be remembered as light streaming in from cracks at the top of their visual field, and not as images in which the recipient is looking forward down a long tunnel. (Becker, 1982, p. 107)*

Psychiatrist Stanislav Grof avoided those objections, as well as the reductionistic implications of a literal birth-memory model, by conceptualizing NDEs as products of a Jungian archetype of a birth experience rather than as memories of actual birth events. (Grof, 1975)

In a similar vein, parapsychologist Michael Grosso describes what he calls 'the archetype of death and enlightenment', a psychic template of rebirth experience that he saw reflected in NDEs, dreams, mythology, ancient mystery rites and psychedelic experiences. While that framework does place NDEs within a larger context, its proponents have not described how it leads either to testable hypotheses or to therapeutic interventions.

In support of the birth-memory hypothesis, William Serdahely, a professor of Health Science at Montana State University, and Barbara Walker, a psychologist at Eastern Illinois, published a paper describing a near-death experience that seemingly took place at birth. (Serdahely & Walker, 1990) In this, the authors argued that, up until then, the earliest remembered NDE was recorded by Harvard Medical School psychiatrists David Herzog and John Herrin, who discussed the recollections of a three-year-old girl who had an NDE when she was six months old.

At the time Serdahely and Walker interviewed her, the subject was 23 years old. During her birth on 31 December 1965 in the Philippines, her mother's umbilical cord had wrapped around the subject's neck, causing her clinical death due to lack of oxygen. This state continued for five minutes until a physician was able to revive her. She clearly remembered what she perceived during that time. She remembered being frightened and uncomfortable. She was in an almost black space with a cone-like narrowing at the far end. In an extraordinary statement, she said that the light at the end 'reminded her of an eclipse'. (Serdahely & Walker, 1990) With regards to her birth-related NDE, she described how she remembered aggressively fighting to return to her body, which she subsequently did. While it is important to acknowledge that these 'memories' actually came to her in a series of dreams she experienced as a child, it is also important to recognize how, in his book *Babies Remember Birth*, psychologist Dr David Chamberlain gives examples of a number of his correspondents who remembered their births through dreams. (Chamberlain, D. B., 1990)

It is worth noting here that the perception of a 'tunnel' during altered states of consciousness is not just confined to near-death experiences. In a fascinating paper published in the medical journal *Brain* in 1998, clinical neurologists Mark Manford and Fred Anderman presented a series of cases involving complex visual hallucinations. In one of these, they describe a 50-year-old woman suffering from mild right hemiparesis with dysphasia. In simple language, this means weakness on one side of the body and an inability to speak or understand language fully. Neither of these are usually related to the generation of extraordinary hallucinations, but that is what happened. She experienced vivid and powerful visions involving four tall men in pinstriped suits trying to push her into a pit full of snakes. From the description by Manford and Anderman, it seems these hallucinatory encounters occurred on a number of occasions with the same entities. In one of these, the men managed to get her into the pit, which turned into 'a tunnel with a golden gate at the end'. (Manford & Anderman, 1998, p. 1822)

However, a 'birth memory' scenario, although popular with those who wish to explain the tunnel motif as a psychological issue, can only ever be hypothetical. But there is a much stronger non-mysterious explanation, and that is related to the physiological conditions of the eyes as death approaches.

The Tunnel – Susan Blackmore and Gerald Woerlee

As we have already discussed, British psychologist Susan Blackmore has shown a great interest with regard to the NDE-facilitated tunnel perception. In 1998, an extremely influential and much-cited article was published in *The Journal of Near-Death Studies* in which she argued that the tunnel effect could be explained by anoxia, or a lack of oxygen. This is known to result in a narrowing of vision, fading first at the edges, that would create the illusion of a tunnel and light. Further, endorphins, internally-generated chemicals that block the perception of pain and increase feelings of well-being, released at the time of death and under stress, might serve as the source of euphoria associated with NDEs. (Blackmore, S., 1998) We shall return to this in greater detail later.

More recently, the NDE sceptic Dr Gerald Woerlee has expanded upon this explanatory theme. In an article he had published in the *Skeptical*

Enquirer in 2004, he argued that the tunnel is a somatic hallucination caused by oxygen starvation. (Woerlee, G. M., 2004) He states that this has to do with the structuring and functioning of the blood supply to the retina; as the oxygen supply drops off, peripheral vision starts to fail. This creates the tunnel experience. He further argued that the worsening levels of hypoxia, or oxygen deficiency, eventually lead to the failure of the retina and a total loss of vision. This, in Woerlee's opinion, is why some NDErs report a loss of peripheral vision and the perception of a tunnel.

Woerlee also discussed an incident that took place in January 1924 at the now long-defunct Hackney General Hospital in London. This was of interest to him because he had also worked at this hospital as an anaesthesiologist. Woerlee paraphrased a description of what took place written by Sir William Barrett in his book *Death-Bed Experiences*. (Barrett, 1986) He writes:

> *In Barrett's report, a dying woman first saw only darkness and subsequently saw a 'lovely brightness' as well as 'bright forms'. The obstetrician reported her observations. At one point she wrote: 'But then she turned to her husband, who had come in, and said, "You won't let the baby go to anyone who won't love him, will you?" Then she gently pushed him to one side, saying, "Let me see thy lovely brightness."' A matron was also present and reported: 'Her husband was leaning over her and speaking to her, when pushing him aside she said, "Oh, don't hide it; it's so beautiful."' (Woerlee, G. M.,* Darkness, Tunnels and Light, *2004, p. 29)*

Woerlee then argues that the 'lovely brightness' that the dying woman saw was because she was dying of oxygen starvation due to heart failure. He, quite rightly, points out that oxygen starvation causes the pupils of the eye to widen, in which case the person perceives an increase in the brightness of the light around them. After this, however, I became suspicious, especially when Woerlee went on to explain in greater detail how this process described what the dying woman perceived:

> *As an amateur photographer, I realized this was also an effect of pupil widening. Pupil widening reduces the depth of field. A person whose pupils are widely dilated not only sees a bright light but only clearly sees people upon whom the eyes are focused, while all other people are seen as bright and blurry forms. So this unfortunate woman interpreted the bright and blurry images of out-of-focus people elsewhere in the room as 'bright forms'. (Woerlee, G. M.,* Darkness, Tunnels and Light, *2004)*

What caught my attention was why Woerlee felt the need to stress that 'this unfortunate woman interpreted the bright and blurry images of out-of-focus people elsewhere in the room as "bright forms"', something that was of no real consequence regarding his debunking of the incident.

As I always do in these cases, I went back to the source material. Over the years, I have learned that biased reporting to prove a particular belief or point of view is used depressingly regularly by both believers and sceptics.

I discovered that Barrett was not present at the incident, but his wife, Florence, witnessed it and that the dying woman's name was Doris. In the book, Barrett quotes Florence in full:

> *When I entered the ward Mrs. B. (Doris) held out her hands to me and said, 'Thank you, thank you for what you have done for me – for bringing the baby. Is it a boy or girl?' Then holding my hand tightly, she said, 'Don't leave me, don't go away, will you?' And after a few minutes, while the House Surgeon carried out some restorative measures, she lay looking up towards the open part of the room, which was brightly lighted, and said, 'Oh, don't let it get dark – it's getting so dark . . . darker and darker.' Her husband and*

mother were sent for. Suddenly she looked eagerly towards one part of the room, a radiant smile illuminating her whole countenance. 'Oh, lovely, lovely,' she said. I asked, 'What is lovely?' 'What I see,' she replied in low, intense tones. 'What do you see?' 'Lovely brightness – wonderful beings.' It is difficult to describe the sense of reality conveyed by her intense absorption in the vision. Then – seeming to focus her attention more intently on one place for a moment – she exclaimed, almost with a kind of joyous cry, 'Why, it's Father! Oh, he's so glad I'm coming; he is so glad. It would be perfect if only W. (her husband) could come too.' . . . She lived for another hour and appeared to have retained to the last the double consciousness of the bright forms she saw, and also of those tending her at the bedside. (Barrett, 1986, p. 6)

So Woerlee deliberately did not mention in his precis that Doris saw her father in the brightness. She didn't state that she saw blurry figures. Not only that, but it is fair to say that she would have been aware of the locations of the others in the room from their voices and their outlines. But here she recognizes her father straight away. There is no hesitation. The reason for Woerlee's deliberate omissions became more apparent when I read further into Barrett's report to another quotation that was, for Barrett, 'the most important evidence'. This was the statement of the matron, Miriam Castle:

I was present shortly before the death of Mrs. B., together with her husband and her mother. Her husband was leaning over her and speaking to her, when pushing him aside she said, 'Oh, don't hide it; it's so beautiful.' Then turning away from him towards me, I being on the other side of the bed, Mrs. B. said, 'Oh, why there's Vida,' referring to a sister of whose death three weeks previously she had not been told. Afterwards the mother, who was present at the time, told me, as I have said, that Vida was the name of a dead sister of Mrs. B.'s, of whose illness and death she was quite ignorant, as they had carefully kept this news from Mrs. B. owing to her serious illness. (Barrett, 1986, p. 7)

It was later confirmed by Mrs B.'s mother that Vida had died on 25 December 1923, just two weeks and four days before Doris also died. She confirmed that nobody had told Doris of her sister's death. Furthermore, she added that Doris stated that Vida was not alone, but was standing next to their father, who was also dead.

So we now know why Dr Woerlee was so keen to precis the account and only use Florence's account of the incident. Doris 'saw' her dead sister with her father straight away. Again, there was no hesitation, which surely there would have been if the figures were blurred. However, the crucial element that Woerlee didn't want his *Skeptical Enquirer* readers to know was that Doris had no idea that Vida had died. She had knowledge supplied to her in her 'hallucination' that was correct. Her sister was with her father.

I find this deception profoundly disappointing, particularly as, up until this discovery, I had been very impressed with Dr Woerlee's seemingly balanced critiques of the NDE phenomenon. It seems that both sides in this important area of human experience are prone to being economical with the truth. This is so sad.

For me, a better argument, and a very intriguing one at that, is what has now become known as the Individually Tailored hypothesis. This was first proposed in 1995 by William Serdahely, whose work we encountered earlier. In a paper which appeared in the *Journal of Near-Death Studies* he took a refreshing new angle on the whole NDE industry. He argued that, for many years, researchers had created a typical 'prototype' NDE. But the outriders that did not fit into the mould were more interesting for him. In his article, he described how he created his non-random sample to investigate these unusual experiences. During a sabbatical he had taken, he had encountered 11 people who had a series of unusual out-of-body experiences following traumatic incidents. These involved a number of variations on the prototypical 'tunnel' experience:

> *One person experienced a 'clockwise spinning vortex' of blacks, whites, and grays; one reported an 'all gray whirlpool'; one said the tunnel was like a 'windsock', like a 'slinky covered with nylon'; another said the tunnel was not solid but 'net like', like a 'spider web'; and still another reported many side tunnels coming off the main tunnel, through which he and his two deceased grandfathers were traveling. Deceased people came out of the side tunnels to greet this NDEr. One person went through a mist or a fog (and not a dark void or tunnel) to get to the light, and another passed through the hospital wall into a fog or into a gray, cloudy mist before encountering the main tunnel with the multiple side tunnels (Serdahely, W., 1995, p. 189)*

In a subject we will return to in much greater detail later, some researchers have suggested that the tunnel experience can link the NDE to another great modern mystery, that of UFO encounters and, specifically, alien abductions. In a very important paper published in *Scientific American* in 1977, psychologist Ronald Siegel argued that most abduction scenarios contain reported imagery consisting of zig-zags, spirals, tunnels and webs. These are seen as rotating, exploding and pulsing. (Siegel, 1977)

For me, all these descriptions suggest a visual phenomenon known as Klüver Form Constants. These have been reported for many years and can be linked to hallucinogenics, hypnagogia and, most importantly, classic migraine auras.

But there may be another physiological answer to the light and the tunnel, something suggesting that consciousness may not be a creation of the neurons but of another, little known but incredibly chemical process that creates inner, biological light known as biophotism.

The Tunnel – Biophotons

If you press or rub your eye, you will 'see' light patterns. But what is the nature of these light patterns? Remember, your eyes are closed, so there is no natural light stimulating the retina. A similar effect takes place if you stare at a computer screen and then close your eyes. This is known as an after-image. Whatever the light is that you see, its source is not external to you. During 'hallucinations', people see geometric shapes (known as Klüver Form Constants), and in dreams, what we see is 'illuminated' by an inner light that even casts shadows.

These internally generated visual images are technically known as 'entropic images' (literally 'within vision' in Greek). They can only be seen by the observer and nobody else. These are usually after-images, of which there are two types: negative and positive. A positive after-image usually lasts for a fraction of a second, whereas a negative one can last for much longer (seconds or even minutes).

But this begs a huge question: how can our eyes sense light while there is no excitation happening simultaneously?

In 1923, an intriguing discovery was made by the Russian embryologist Alexander Gurwitsch. He found that the roots of one plant could stimulate the roots of another one nearby, but only if both plants were in quartz glass pots. It would not happen if the plants were in silicon glass pots. Intrigued, he decided to discover the difference between the two types of pots. He found that the crucial factor seemed to be that the silicon filtered ultraviolet light, whereas the quartz did not. He concluded that one plant was emitting light in the UV part of the spectrum, and the neighbouring plants were picking up the message. He became convinced that these rays had an effect on cell division and, for this reason, called them 'mitogenic rays'.

Over 50 years later, German biophysicist Fritz-Albert Popp read about Gurwitsch's work and decided to find out more about these mysterious photons. He was aware that the intensity of the photons was extremely weak, roughly 1018 of the intensity of visible light. To study this phenomenon, he developed an instrument called a photon multiplier. This is so sensitive that it can detect the light given off by a firefly 16 km (10 miles) away. Popp was successful in showing that this electromagnetic energy was actually stored and released not by living cells but, more precisely, by the DNA within the cells. He called this process 'biophotonic emission', and the photons themselves he called 'biophotons'.

Popp proposed that this internal light is profoundly coherent and, in many ways, similar to laser light. This creates a very effective tool for communication between cells right across the body. Within a healthy individual, biophotons show a great deal of coherence. However, when somebody is seriously ill, the natural rhythm breaks down. Literally, their 'internal lights' start going out. The converse is also true: sometimes, too much coherence or order can be damaging. For example, Popp found that individuals who have multiple sclerosis have a very high level of photonic rhythmic harmony. Unfortunately, this leads to a dangerous lack of flexibility when dealing with unusual biological challenges. It is as if the body is being blinded by the light and therefore unable to react in the correct way to new problems.

One of the most significant and frightening times in any living creature's existence is when it faces the end of its life. Indeed, this is another circumstance when the 'lights are going out'. However, from reports from individuals who have been close to death and have survived, it seems that the lights do not go out at all. Indeed, the 'light' is the major sensation reported by individuals who report near-death experiences.

As we have already discovered, books on the subject of the NDE can often be identified by the word 'light' in their titles. *Closer to the Light*, *Beyond the Light* and *Transformed by the Light* have all been very popular books on the subject, for example. In 2009, Hungarian pharmacologists István Bókkon and his associate, Vahid Salari, suggested that Popp's bioluminescence may be responsible for this intriguing altered state of consciousness. They wrote:

In near-death experiences (NDEs), seeing a brilliant light may arise in the recovery period following cardiac arrest, but the subjects can think that these experiences had happened during the actual period itself. Here we hypothesize a biophysical explanation about the encounter with a brilliant light in NDEs. Accordingly, meeting brilliant light in NDEs is due to the reperfusion that induces unregulated overproduction of free radicals and excited biomolecules among them in numerous parts in the visual system. Unregulated free radicals and excited species can produce a transient increase of bioluminescent photons in different areas of the visual system. If this excess of bioluminescent photon emission exceeds a threshold, they can appear as (phosphene) lights in our mind. In other words, seeing a brilliant light in NDEs may be due to bioluminescent photons simultaneously generated in the recovery phase of numerous areas of the visual system and the brain interprets these intrinsic bioluminescent photons as if they were originated from the external visual world. Although our biophysical explanation about brilliant light phenomena in NDEs can be promising, we do not reject further potential notions.

Indeed, in an earlier paper, Bókkon presented experimental proof that the human eye actually *gives off light*. The old idea that a person's eyes sometimes seem to shine has been proven to be more than a simple folk belief! Bókkon and his associates took the eye, lens, vitreous humor and retina from rats and they found that these tissue samples gave off bioluminescent photons. This suggests that phosphenes are generated internally from the cells of the eye. (Chao, Bókkon, Dai & Antal, 2011) In other words, when we see phosphenes, we are looking at light whose source is inside our cells and not from the external world. This is a fantastic discovery. We now have experimental evidence that the light that illuminates our dreams and our inner world comes from within.

And this inner light may create life itself.

In 2011, a burst of light was observed for the first time at the point of conception of a human embryo. In their initial experiment, Alison Kim and her team at the Feinberg School of Medicine at Northwestern University, Chicago, witnessed the flash of light in mice. (Kim et al., 2011) By 2014, an associated team at Feinberg School had found a way of filming the event for the first time as billions of zinc atoms were released at the exact moment when a mammal's egg was pierced by a sperm cell. They then managed to film the same event taking place in a human egg at the point of conception. Not only that, but it was also subsequently discovered that the size of the sparks is a direct measure of the quality of the egg. (Duncan, Que, Feinberg, O'Halloran & Woodroff, 2016)

I know there is no way to prove this, but imagine for a second that the light at the end of the tunnel reported by NDErs may be a glimpse of the light generated by their impending conception.

We will return, in much greater detail, to the role of oxygen starvation and increases in carbon dioxide when we discuss the so-called 'organic hypothesis' explanation of the near-death experience. But for now, we need to continue our review of the 'traits' and move our discussion to the element of the near-death experience that interests me the most, the so-called panoramic life review.

The Dying Brain Hypothesis – Explained?

Academics categorize three significant classes of explanation of the NDE: transcendental, physiological and psychological. All three are based on the assumption that the patients were near death when they had their experiences. However, little-reported research published in 1989 and 1990 suggested this is not always the case.

In response to the Gallup Poll discussed earlier, it was reported that 23 million Americans 'have, by prevailing medical definitions, died briefly or . . . come close to death' and that about 8 million of these persons 'have experienced some sort of mystical encounter along with the death event'. (Gallup & Proctor, 1982, p. 6) NDE researchers Dr Ian Stevenson of the University of Virginia, Emily Williams Cook of the University of Edinburgh and Dr Nicholas McClean-Rice of Twin County Community Hospital decided to review these claims in greater detail. They dug deeper into the medical records of patients who had reported NDEs and checked a handful of readily available records, including records from their own hospitals. They were surprised to discover that many of the patients were not near death. This concerned them, mainly because almost all of the writers making claims that NDE reports were literally 'near-death' experiences had not included any data on the medical conditions of the patients cited. Sabom and Morse were two notable exceptions.

Stevenson, Cook and McClean-Rice agreed that to follow up on these implications they needed to systematically examine the medical records of the 107 NDE cases they had previously investigated. They were able to obtain the medical records or testimony of the physician involved in 40 of the cases. With regards to the 'traits', 26 (65 per cent) reported an OBE; 15 (38 per cent) saw a bright light; 12 (30 per cent) described a tunnel; and 10 (25 per cent) saw or heard dead friends or relatives. A few life reviews were experienced; sadly, the paper did not report this.

Of the 40 patients, 33 (82.5 per cent) believed they were very near death or even clinically dead. On examining the actual medical records and by applying the agreed rules, the team designated 18 as being gravely ill and close to death, 8 who were sick or injured but with no danger to life, and 14 with no serious illness or injury. This conflicts strongly with the self-reported 82.5 per cent who believed they were dying or dead.

It was then discovered that in 22 of the cases, there was no indication from the medical records that these individuals had been near death. Eight of these cases had suffered severe illness or accidents, but not life-threatening ones:

> *One person suffered a concussion in an automobile*
> *accident, one person showed symptoms of shock following*

a blood transfusion, one had a ruptured ovarian cyst, one had taken an overdose of drugs, one had post-operative cardiac arrhythmias, two suffered a minor stroke, and one person escaped injury after an accident in which he was trapped under a truck for several minutes. (Stevenson, Cook & McClean-Rice, 'Are persons reporting "near-death experiences" really near death? A study of medical records', 1990, p. 48)

As regards the remaining 14 cases, 35 per cent of the total, there was no evidence of severe illness or loss of vital signs indicating clinical death. (Stevenson, Cook & McClean-Rice, 'Are persons reporting "near-death experiences" really near death? A study of medical records', 1990, pp. 48–49)

The researchers concluded that the belief that they were about to die brought about the experience rather than the fact that death was near. As such, it was the psychological explanation of the near-death experience rather than the transcendental one that had the support of the statistics. This information had the researchers suggest a new term: 'fear-death experiences'. (Stevenson, Cook & McClean-Rice, 'Are persons reporting "near-death experiences" really near death? A study of medical records', 1990, p. 53)

Intrigued by these results, Dr Justine Owens, also of the University of Virginia, joined Stevenson and Cook on a follow-up study of the data they used in the original research. In a paper published in *The Lancet* in 1990, they defined their objectives:

To find out whether the experiences of those subjects actually near death differed in any significant way from those subjects, not near death, and in the hope that the answers would shed further light on the strengths and weaknesses of the three major interpretations of NDEs, we have examined the features of the experiences according to

whether or not patients were near death. (Owens, Cook &
Stevenson, 1990)

They focused on the following features of the classic 'death experience': an enhanced perception of light, an experience of being in a tunnel and enhanced cognitive functions, with regards to patients who had perceived a 'near' death experience and those who perceived a 'fear' death experience.

The data was intriguing and of possible significance. Regarding enhanced light, 21 (75 per cent) of the NDErs reported this perception, whereas only 12 (40 per cent) of the FDErs reported this perception. Interestingly, the reports of the tunnel experience were lower than would have been expected from the general reports, with only 21 (46 per cent) of 46 patients reporting this experience; 12 had been near death, and 9 had not been. But for those who reported enhanced light during their experience, 19 (70 per cent) had the tunnel experience.

As regards the 'panoramic life review':

> *The two groups also did not differ in proportions reporting*
> *memories of earlier events in the subject's life (sometimes*
> *called 'life review' or 'panoramic memory'). 6 (27%) of*
> *22 patients near death and 4 (17%) of 23 patients not*
> *near death reported some such memories. Most patients*
> *reported only a few memories; only 2 (9%) patients near*
> *death and 2 (9%) patients not near death reported a*
> *review or replay of his or her whole life. (Owens, Cook &*
> *Stevenson, 1990)*

These results suggest that an NDE takes place if a person believes they are dying, rather than if they are. From this, it can be assumed that the experience is mind-generated rather than an autonomic physiological response to a death scenario. Of course, the mind-brain anticipation of death brings about physiological responses, as do many other sets of circumstances.

In this regard, a fascinating case was cited by psychiatrists Glen Gabbard and Stuart Twemlow in 1991. (Gabbard & Twemlow, 1991) Ten years earlier, they had written a paper suggesting that the elements of the near-death experience were not necessarily limited to situations in which survival was threatened. (Gabbard, Twemlow & Jones, 1981)

In 1982, in response to their 1981 paper, Gabbard, Twemlow and their associate and fellow psychiatrist Fowler Jones surveyed NDE accounts supplied by 339 subjects who had reported out-of-body experiences. Of these, only 10 per cent reported that they had been near death at the time of the experience. On further questioning, it was discovered that although there were no significant differences in the actual experiences in both groups, several features of the classic NDE were significantly more likely to occur if death looked likely:

> *These features included noises during the early stages, the experience of traveling through a tunnel, the sighting of one's physical body from a distance, awareness of other beings in nonphysical form, the perception of deceased loved ones, the experience of a brilliant light, and a sense of purpose connected to the experience. (Gabbard, Twemlow & Jones, 1982)*

However, in a paper published in December 2015 in *The Journal of Near-Death Studies*, Robert and Suzanne Mays presented evidence that there are no significant differences in intensity and content between life-threatening NDEs and NDE-like perceptions brought about by non-life-threatening circumstances. (Mays & Mays, 2015)

The Mays used the 2014 research project by Vanessa Charland-Verville and Steven Laureys of the University of Liège, Belgium, as their source. The results of this were published in the journal *Frontiers in Human Neuroscience*. They compared 140 'real' NDE scenarios with 50 NDE-like experiences facilitated by various situations, including fainting and meditation, in which the subject was aware that they were in no real danger of death. The 190 subjects completed Bruce Greyson's Near-Death Experience Scale (NDES), which we discussed earlier. Much to the researchers' surprise, there was no significant difference in either the intensity or the content of the NDE in either group. From this, it seems that there is no difference between a 'real' NDE and one brought about by other factors. In short, the NDE is not created by a psychological expectation on the part of the subject. The researchers concluded:

> *It seems that NDEs cannot be explained solely by the closeness to death or by the etiology of the precipitating factor. The question whether the NDEs' extraordinary features can be fully explained by cerebral activity is still a matter of debate. . . . (Charland-Verville et al., 2014, p. 6)*

What can we make of these seemingly contradictory discoveries? Indeed, these results also conflict with the 1990 analysis of Owens, Cook and Stevenson discussed above. (Owens, Cook & Stevenson, 1990) One possible explanation is the methodological differences between the 2014 Liège study and the earlier 1990 research. A broader classification of NDE features was applied in 1990, whereas the later research was restricted to the categories specific to Greyson's NDES. This is an area that needs to be explored in greater detail as it is crucial to understand whether the NDE is a series of perceptions that can happen at any time or whether it can only relate to an actual state of approaching death.

THE CATEGORIES – THE PANORAMIC LIFE REVIEW
Panoramic Life Review (PLR) – Introduction

In their influential 1995 book *The Truth in the Light*, Peter and Elizabeth Fenwick (Fenwick & Fenwick, 1995) have a chapter analysing the responses to their questionnaire regarding one of the most intriguing elements of the core NDE, the panoramic life review. Some of these are extraordinary, none more so than the experience of a 54-year-old ex-RAF pilot called Allan Pring. In 1979, he was having minor surgery when something went wrong. I think it is important to quote him in full:

On Monday, 6 August, the preparation for surgery was routine, and I lost consciousness within seconds of being injected with an anaesthetic. All perfectly normal. But the manner in which I regained consciousness was anything but normal. Instead of slowly coming round in a drowsy and somewhat befuddled state in a hospital ward I awoke as if from a deep and refreshing sleep and was instantly and acutely aware of my situation. Without any anxiety or distress I knew that I was dead, or rather that I had gone through the process of dying and was now in a different state of reality. The place that I was in cannot be described because it was a state of nothingness. There was nothing to see because there was no light; there was nothing to feel because there was no substance. Although I no longer considered that I had a physical body, nevertheless I felt as if I were floating in a vast empty space, very relaxed and waiting. Then I experienced the review of my life which extended from early childhood and included many occurrences that I had completely forgotten. My life passed before me in a momentary flash but it was entire, even my thoughts were included. Some of the contents caused me to be ashamed but there were one or two I had forgotten about of which I felt quite pleased. All in all, I knew that I could have lived a much better life but it could have been a lot worse. Be that as it may, I knew that it was all over now and there was no going back. There was one most peculiar feature of this life review, which is very difficult to describe, let alone explain. Although it took but a moment to complete, literally a flash, there was still time to stop and wonder over separate incidents. This was the first instance of distortion of time that I experienced but it was the beginning of my belief that the answers to many of the questions that are posed by NDEs lie in a better understanding of the nature of time and what we term reality. (Fenwick & Fenwick, 1995, p. 114)

Pring then experienced a form of trial done by four entities (he described them as 'persons' using the quote marks to show that he was not sure what they were). This sequence reminded me of the David Niven movie *A Matter of Life and Death*.

So, how common is the panoramic life review, and what may be its causes?

In their much-discussed review of past-life memories during near-death experiences from 1977, researchers Russell Noyes and Roy Kletti reported that 60 (29 per cent) of 205 subjects they investigated mentioned having had a life review. (Noyes & Kletti, 1977) Later, in 1980, in a similar review, Kenneth Ring found that 12 (24 per cent) of 49 subjects who had had an NDE reported a life review. (Ring, K., 1980) This agreed with findings published the same year by Ian Stevenson and Bruce Greyson of the University of Virginia, who found that 21 (27 per cent) of their 78 subjects mentioned a life review as part of their NDE. (Greyson & Stevenson, 1980)

In his late-1970s statistical analysis of the life review, Kenneth Ring noted that it occurred far more frequently in accident-related scenarios (55 per cent) than with those who were ill or had attempted suicide (16 per cent). I would argue that this suggests that the level of unexpectedness of the death encounter makes the panoramic life review more likely. Indeed, 24 per cent of Ring's group who had an NDE also underwent a life review. Several described how they felt they were shown millions of frames and pictures of their lives from childhood onwards. Another fascinating discovery of Ring's research was not just flashbacks but also what he termed 'flash-forwards', a subject we will return to in much greater detail later.

In 1995, Ian Stevenson and Emily Williams Cook of the University of Virginia published the results of an extensive review of cases of individuals who, after a near-death experience, reported that during the event they recalled memories from earlier in their lives. (Stevenson & Cook, 1995) They had two series as their source. The first consisted of 68 cases from published accounts in newspapers, magazines and autobiographies. They then presented an additional second series of 54 NDE cases that had been investigated by Stevenson and Cook's research group at the University of Virginia. These 54 were taken from an original total of 417 people who had reported unusual experiences during illness or accident. So, 13 per cent of the original total had experienced elements of the life review.

Of the 68 cases in series 1, four individuals reported that the life review was the only trait they experienced in their NDE; in a further six it was the initial, and significant, feature. (Stevenson & Cook, 'Involuntary memories during severe physical illness or injury', 1995)

Stevenson and Cook then embarked upon an in-depth analysis of the PLR experience. Ninety-two per cent described how the life review occurred at high speed. But this in no way impaired the perception of details. Indeed, 88 per cent reported how the images were unusually vivid or realistic. The words 're-lived' or 'seemed to relive' occurred in 24 per cent of the cases in the second group, with 45 of the 54 stating that there was an alteration in time perception, some reporting a slowing down of time and others that it speeded up. What I found of particular interest was that 26 per cent reported seeing or experiencing events that had long been forgotten.

Regarding the subject of early-life memories discussed earlier, five had memories of when they were under two years old, and, of possibly greater significance, six had birth memories, and two reported witnessing being conceived.

Of course, it could be argued that with the advent of photography and movies, the idea that your life can be recorded in some way is something that any 20th- and 21st-century person can relate to. A sceptic would argue that the NDErs are simply subconsciously creating a confabulation from things they have read and seen. Possibly, but historical analysis suggests otherwise.

PLR – History

Probably the earliest life review, which was accurately more of a variation on Kenneth Ring's 'flash-forward', was reported by the 1st century CE Greek philosopher Plutarch. He described a fascinating NDE-like series of perceptions reported by a man from Cilicia called Aridaeus, who was given the new name of Thespesius during his sojourn in the 'other world'. Like a small number of modern NDE reports, Thespesius experiences a 'flash forward' into his possible future:

> But he did hear, as he passed by, a woman's high voice foretelling in verse, among other things, the time (it appears) of his own death. The voice was the Sibyl's, the daemon said, who sang of the future as she was carried about on the face of the moon. He accordingly desired to hear more but was thrust back, as in an eddy, by the onrush of the moon and caught but little. Among this was a prophecy about Mt. Vesuvius and the surge of flame that would pass over Dicaearcheia, and a fragment of verse about the emperor of those days: /... good, he will through sickness leave the throne. (Plutarch, Moralia, p. 291)

Regarding the panoramic life review, we need to move forward many centuries to 10 June 1791, when Admiral Francis Beaufort, the creator of the Beaufort scale that measures wind speed, was a humble midshipman. While out in a rowboat that day, Beaufort fell into the sea when his vessel capsized. In a letter written around 30 years later, he recalled his feelings as he entered the water:

> *From the moment that all exertion had ceased, a calm feeling of the most perfect tranquillity superseded the previous tumultuous sensations – it might be called apathy, certainly resignation, for drowning no longer appeared to be an evil – I no longer thought of being rescued, nor was I in any bodily pain. On the contrary, my sensations were now of a rather pleasurable ease, partaking of that dull but contented sort of feeling which precedes the sleep produced by fatigue. Though the senses were thus deadened, not so the mind; its activity seemed to be invigorated in a ratio which defies all description.*

According to Beaufort's biographer, Nicholas Courtney, from whose book the above passage is taken:

> *Francis had total recall of those exact thoughts. It really was true that 'every past incident of my life seemed to glance across my recollection in retrograde succession; not, however in mere outline, as here stated, but the picture filled up with every minute and collateral feature; in short, the whole period of my existence seemed to be placed before me in a kind of panoramic view, and each act of it seemed to be accompanied by a consciousness of right or wrong, or by some reflection on its cause or its consequences; indeed many trifling events which had been long forgotten then crowded into my imagination.' (Friendly, 1977)*

All this took place in the two minutes or so he was in the water.

In his 1892 paper on climbing accidents in the Alps, 'Remarks on Fatal Falls', Swiss geologist Albert Heim quoted an experience he had read about in the 20 June 1891 edition of the *Swiss Protestant Journal*. It was a letter written by a theology student who had fallen with the collapse of a bridge a few days before:

> *Now there took place, in the shortest possible time, the ghastliest descent that one could imagine. I clung spasmodically to my seat. My arms and legs functioned in their usual way, as if instinctively taking care of themselves and, swift as lightning, they made reflex parries of the boards, poles, and benches that were breaking up around and upon me. During this time I had a whole flood of thoughts that went through my brain in the clearest way. The thoughts said, 'the next impact will kill me'. A series of pictures showed me in rapid succession everything beautiful and lovable that I had ever experienced, and between them sounded the powerful melody of a prelude I had heard in the morning: 'God is almighty, Heaven and Earth rest in His hand; we must bow to His will'. With this thought in the midst of all the fearful turmoil I was overwhelmed by a feeling of undying peace. (Noyes & Kletti, 1972, p. 48)*

Later, in his 1922 book *Death and its Mysteries*, French astronomer Camille Flammarion tells of an incident that his friend Alphonse Bue perceived while falling from a horse. In these few seconds Bue experienced his whole life from childhood onwards:

> *During this fall, which could hardly have lasted two or three seconds, his entire life, from his childhood up to his career in the army, unrolled clearly and slowly in his mind, his games as a boy, his classes, his first communion, his vacations, his different studies, his examinations, his entry into Saint-Cyr in 1848, his life with the dragoons, in the*

war in Italy [1857], with the lancers of the Imperial guards, with the Spahis, with the riflemen, at the Chateau of Fontainebleau, the balls of the Empress [Eugenie; wife of Napoleon III] at the Tuileries, etc. All this slow panorama was unrolled before his eyes in less than four seconds, for he recovered consciousness immediately. (Flammarion, 1922, footnote p. 142)

In 1960, German researcher Max Mikorey published an important paper investigating the panoramic life review. He concluded from the 24 cases he had reviewed that the life review occurred only after the subject had abandoned hope of survival and resigned themself to death. Mikorey argued that the brain creates 'harmless memory pictures of the past to avoid the trauma of such a circumstance'. How the brain does this was not explained. This explanation can be placed in the dissociation category. (Mikorey, 1960). It has many similarities with the interpretation detailed in a much later Noyes and Kletti paper from 1977, which places the panoramic life review as evidence of crisis-related depersonalization:

. . . in response to the threat of death, the endangered personality appeared to seek the safety of the timeless moment. There death ceased to exist as the person immersed himself in his experience. (Noyes & Kletti, 1977)

This observation must be read after considering the findings of Kenneth Ring, cited above. You will recall that Ring discovered that a much higher percentage of individuals perceive a life review in accident-related scenarios (55 per cent) against 16 per cent in semi-controlled and predictable circumstances, such as being critically ill in a hospital or when attempting suicide. (Ring K., 1980)

In 1979, Bruce Greyson and Ian Stevenson suggested that the panoramic life review may be related to the suddenness and unexpectedness of a life-threatening situation. This is precisely the same point I have made in my writings on the near-death experience. In 1985, Greyson surveyed 89 NDEs, which reinforced this suggestion. (Greyson, 1985) In several earlier books I have argued that this is why the panoramic life review is perceived as speeding past by near-death experience survivors – because the person survived to tell the tale. In a near-death experience, the operative word is the first one. I argue that in an RDE – a 'real-death experience', the person does not survive to tell the tale – the panoramic life review is experienced in real time, that is, as a second-by-second reliving of all events from the time of birth to the time of death.

An extraordinary example of the detail experienced in a full panoramic life review is described by renowned NDE researcher P. M. H. Atwater concerning her own encounter with this intriguing end-of-life perception:

> *The reliving included not only the deeds committed by [me] since birth . . . but also a reliving of every thought ever thought and every word ever spoken PLUS the effect of every thought, word, and deed upon everyone and anyone who had ever come within [my] sphere of influence whether I actually knew them or not. . . . I never before realized that we were responsible and accountable for EVERY SINGLE THING WE DID. That was overwhelming. (Atwater, P. M., 1980, p. 22) (Emphasis in original.)*

But could the panoramic life review be simply a cultural reaction to a highly stressful situation? As we have already acknowledged, it seems directly related to the unexpected and immediate prospect of personal annihilation. In the West, we have a very linear concept of time, where the future appears in the present and then disappears into the past. All that exists is the present moment. This linearity leads to a belief that time flows in one direction and can only be experienced in the ever-moving 'now'.

However, other cultures do not have this understanding of time. Is the panoramic life review experienced in the same way across all cultures?

It seems not. In a contributory chapter to the essential 2009 book *The Handbook of Near-Death Experiences* sociologist Dr Allan Kellehear of the University of Vermont focuses on the cultural aspects of the panoramic life review. (Holden, Greyson & James, 2009, pp. 152–154)

Kellehear points out that the PLR is one of the NDE features limited in non-Western cultures. For example, some aspects of the PLR can be found in Indian and Chinese NDEs but are unknown in indigenous Australian, North American, African and Pacific cultures. Following the work of the US sociologist Robert Bellah, Kellehear argues that the major religions of the cultures in which the PLR is prevalent are all what Bellah termed 'historic religions'. These are where there is a belief in two worlds: the physical world and the world of the divine. The divine world is perfect and eternal, whereas the physical world is debased and temporary. Within this flawed world, and trapped within it, is the human soul. This is an inwardly driven, individuated source of awareness that is flawed and in need of redemption. This redemption can only happen when the individuated essence, the ego, seeks it. Native Americans, Australian Aborigines and many Pacific cultures do not share this duality of existence. For these groups, animism is a central belief, that is, that everything is in some way alive and that individuated awareness is an illusion. Anxiety, guilt and all the psychoses found in 'historic religions' are part of the person. Still, their source, and therefore any responsibility for these feelings, is not from within but part of the external environment. This comes down to a belief in spirits rather than a belief in a personalized God. In this respect, Kellehear quotes the great sociologist of religion Max Weber, who stated that when this change takes place, 'transgression against the will of God is an ethical sin which burdens the conscience, quite apart from its direct results'. (Weber, 1965, p. 43). Once this change takes place, death is linked with consciousness and consciousness with identity after death. However, for animistic cultures, memories of a life are not contained in the mind but within the group and the environment.

In an earlier paper, published in 1993, and echoing his later position, Kellehear argued that in pre-literate cultures the life review is often replaced by a visit to the spirit world. In effect, a life review can be experienced there but as part of the spirit world, not as a personal experience. (Kellehear, A., 1993)

Kellehear's findings are supported by Todd Murphy's later research into South and East Asian NDEs. Murphy states that those younger than seven years old often avoid the life review and instead visit heaven or fairyland. (Murphy, T, 'Near-Death Experiences in Thailand', 2001)

Murphy's research also highlights that, so far, we have only discussed adult panoramic life reviews. It is reasonable to conclude that young children will have fewer 'life reviews' during NDEs simply because they have not experienced a great deal of life to populate the review. Indeed, Raymond Moody's research has noted that the review is absent in paediatric NDEs.

In the late 1980s, William Serdahely, a non-denominational hospice chaplain, NDE researcher and professor of health sciences in Montana, decided to do a review of childhood near-death experiences. He analysed four cases of individuals who had NDEs at an early age and published the results in the *Journal of Near-Death Studies*. His findings showed that of the four children whose cases he analysed only the oldest – a girl aged 15 – experienced a life review. Interestingly, as well as seeing images of her past, she also saw images from her future, including scenes showing how her relatives would react if she were to die. (Serdahely, W. J., 1990) Serdahely's conclusion, that the life review is absent in most childhood NDE cases, agreed with that of his fellow NDE researcher Melvin Morse and his associates, who in a study they conducted concluded that the 'childhood core NDE includes a number of the adult factors, but conspicuous in its absence is the life review'. (Morse, Venecia & Milstein, 1989) Additionally, Kenneth Ring echoed this absence. (Ring, K., 1980) Serdahely suggested that this may be because young NDErs are not equipped psychologically to deal with how their actions have impacted others, and a life review would be of no benefit.

From the findings of Morse et al., Ring, Serdahely and Murphy, it is reasonable to conclude that children report almost identical perceptions during an NDE to those reported by adults, with one or two possibly significant differences, which we shall discuss later. Again, this is evidence that the experience is real. The question is, what is its purpose with regard to human development?

In 1992, Melvin Morse and Paul Perry, taking the work of Wilder Penfield as their guide, suggested that the panoramic life review was related to the right-hemisphere Sylvian fissure in the brain. This deep fold separates the frontal and parietal lobes from the temporal lobe. They argued that, as death approaches, the body's electromagnetic field revives the memory-recall facilities of the right temporal lobe. (Morse & Perry, 1992) The major criticism of this model is that there is no measurable brain activity at death to create the self-awareness to perceive the memories and the processing power needed to evoke these memories. This is very much the position taken by transpersonal psychologist Jenny Wade, who argues that just because the Sylvian fissure can generate certain perceptions during life it does not mean it can reproduce these perceptions at the point of death. She states with a profound degree of assuredness that:

> Many NDE survivors have no measurable brain activity, often for an extended period. The gross alterations in consciousness represented by the merest variation in the frequency and amplitude of brain waves suggest that the cessation of all measurable EEG activity should have a dramatic effect. (Wade, 1996, pp. 232–233)

However, as we shall soon discover, a series of recent experiments have shown that the brain is highly active not only at the point of death but also immediately afterwards.

The fact that the panoramic life review is a real perception that takes place during a near-death experience is beyond question. As we have already discovered, it has been regularly reported for hundreds of years and seems to follow similar formats. But the question coming from this must be: how does it work, and where are the memories stored? In our search for answers, we need to return to Wilder Penfield.

PLR – The Source – Wilder Penfield

After he facilitated out-of-body experiences while stimulating the temporoparietal junction of patients in the early 1940s, Penfield made a series of other related discoveries that were even more extraordinary. He described these many years later, in June 1951, when he gave the presidential address at the seventy-sixth annual meeting of the American Neurological Association in Atlantic City. In this address, Penfield went into detail about the 'evoked recollections' that took place when he was using his electrode on conscious patients. These are of significance regarding the argument that human beings subliminally remember all their experiences and that these are available when circumstances are right.

It is important to stress precisely what Penfield observed with regard to the facilitation of these memories by the electrode:

> *Recollections which are clearly derived from a patient's past memory can sometimes be forced upon him by the stimulating electrode. The psychical experience, thus produced, stops when the electrode is withdrawn and may repeat itself when the electrode is reapplied. (Penfield, 'Memory mechanisms', 1951)*

There are two crucial points to be taken from this. The first is that all the recollections were elicited from the temporal lobes, and the second is that they started when the live electrode was placed on the temporal lobes and ceased when the electrode was removed. This suggests that the electrical stimulation was acting similarly to how the laser of a DVD player 'reads' the information encoded on a DVD to recreate the sound and vision in a form that can be both seen and heard. The 'data' exists whether or not the laser is reading it or not. And so it is, I would argue, regarding the 'memories' similarly 'encoded' within the brain.

Penfield then gives a series of extraordinary examples. The first is a patient identified as S.B.. When the electrode was placed on the first convolution of his right temporal lobe, he heard a piano playing. The electrode was removed, and it stopped. On re-application, he heard someone speaking. This again stopped when the electrode was removed. A new location was selected (point 16):

> When point 16 was stimulated, he said, while the electrode was being held in place, 'Something brings back a memory. I can see Seven-Up Bottling Company . . . Harrison Bakery.' He was then warned that he was being stimulated, but the electrode was not applied. He replied, 'Nothing.' (Penfield, 1951, p. 179)

Even though S.B. had been told that the electrode had been re-engaged on to his exposed temporal lobe, he did not react. This is robust evidence of my DVD analogy.

Penfield and his team had differing results in other brain areas away from what he termed the 'memory cortex' (effectively the temporal lobes). Stimulation of the auditory regions of the brain brought about buzzing or ringing sounds. This is significant as buzzing or ringing sounds are, as we shall discover, a regular perception as an out-of-body experience starts or during an NDE. DMT users also report buzzing or ringing sounds. Recall here the Hindu Vedanta concept of 'Aum' discussed earlier, which supposedly emanates from the brain's right hemisphere.

Similarly, Penfield discovered that stimulation of the visual cortex produced 'bright, lighted objects, such as stars or squares or streaks, or the opposite, i.e., black forms. It may produce a jumble of colors. The things seen may be stationary, but usually move or twinkle or dance. Thus, the images seen have light, darkness, or color.' (Penfield, 1951, p. 181)

Again, the patterns of light are similar to those reported in near-death experiences and during DMT 'trips'. But what is significant here is that this imagery, like the buzzing/ringing reported above, does not merge into a full sensory experience that can be likened to actual sensory perceptions. These only seem to take place in the temporal lobes.

Case R.W. is also very interesting. As the electrode was moved across the cortex towards the temporal lobes, the hallucinogenic quality moved from physical sensations of tingling of the skin to abstract visions of coloured lights and triangles floating in front of him. These became more real because they became comic-book characters, such as robbers with guns. These were images being drawn from his subconscious dreamscapes. It is important that the descriptor 'comic-book' characters were precisely the term Penfield used. As soon as the electrode arrived at the temporal lobe the quality and intensity of the imagery changed. It became an actual scene from everyday life that he was witnessing:

> . . . he heard a telephone conversation between his mother and aunt. When stimulation was carried out at 31 immediately afterward, he said, 'The same as before. My mother telling my aunt to come up and visit us tonight.' When he was asked how he knew this was a telephone conversation, he replied that he did not see them but he knew that his aunt was speaking on the phone by the way her voice sounded when she answered. In the original experience he must have stood very close to his mother as she telephoned. (Penfield, 1951, p. 182)

What I find extraordinary here is that Penfield, by his careful use of the words 'in the original experience', is sure that this is not a confabulation but an actual all-encompassing recall of an actual event in R.W.'s past. This is a literal re-living of an experience stimulated by the electrode. Indeed, if Penfield had stated earlier how the electrode stimulated these recalls, then if the electrode were placed back in precisely the same position, the event would have been experienced again and again.

My point is reinforced by what happened next. The team moved the electrode away from point 31 to point 32:

> *The recollection mentioned above was apparently no longer available to the electrode. This time, he said, 'My mother is telling my brother he has got his coat on backwards. I can just hear them.' He was asked whether he remembered this happening. 'Oh yes,' he replied, 'just before I came here.' He was then asked whether these things were like dreams, and he replied, 'No . . . It is just like I go into a daze.'*
> *(Penfield, 1951, p. 182)*

This is extraordinary. R.W. knew he was reliving a recent event that he had experienced in reality – the electrode had recreated an event in his past!

The panoramic life review needs one other of the NDE categories to be effective. If a whole life has to be reviewed in detail, something strange must happen regarding the subjective time perception of the NDEr witnessing this life review. It matters little whether it is speeded up or slowed down; it is perceived in another form of time. We need to now investigate in detail how this may occur.

THE CATEGORIES – TIME DISTORTION
Time Distortion – Introduction

Earlier, we discussed the implications of the difference in life review between adults and children. This suggests that the cognitive abilities of children, specifically how their brains are structured, open up different communication pathways from those available to adults. This is no more marked than in how children and young adults perceive non-human and non-living entities when in a near-death experience state.

I believe this is crucial if we are to understand the true meaning and significance of the NDE.

Significantly, changes in time perception occur in 78 per cent of cases of NDEs. (Noyes & Kletti, 1977) Finnish philosopher Valtteri Arstila (Arstila, 2012) has proposed that the experience of increased 'speed of thought' commonly reported during NDEs alters the perception of time and makes the world seem slower, permitting the individual to engage in purposeful rescue actions that can be life-saving. The correlation between changes in mental functioning and increased rescue efforts during NDEs may be consistent with an evolutionary scenario in which an NDE predisposition is directly selected because it increases survival probability.

Let us now review the evidence for this perception.

Time Distortion – Albert Heim

As I have discussed elsewhere, one of the most important pieces of writing on the time perception aspects of the near-death experience was by Swiss geologist Albert von St Gallen Heim, who, in the late 1870s and early 1890s, collected the subjective observations of survivors of falls in the Swiss Alps. These were subsequently published under the title of *'Notizen uber den Tod durch Absturz'* ('Remarks on Fatal Falls') in the 1892 *Yearbook of the Swiss Alpine Club*. (Heim, 1992) Heim discovered that nearly 97 per cent of climbers who survived their falls experienced time slowing down. In their 1972 paper, psychiatrists Russell Noyes and Roy Kletti discussed in detail Heim's paper, which was translated from the German by Roy Kletti. Here, Heim describes the subjective experiences of the climbers:

> *A dominant mental quickness and sense of surety. Mental activity became enormous, rising to a 100-fold velocity or intensity. The relationships of events and their probable*

outcomes were overviewed with objective clarity. No
confusion entered at all. Time became greatly expanded.
The individual acted with lightning-quickness in accord
with accurate judgment of his situation. (Noyes & Kletti,
1972, pp. 46–47)

Of great significance is how Heim also mentions a phenomenon that is
central to the modern reports of near-death experiences, the panoramic
life review. Remember, this piece of research took place decades before
the term near-death experience had been created, let alone the notoriety
of its 'traits':

In many cases there followed a sudden review of the
individual's entire past; and finally the person falling often
heard beautiful music and fell in a superbly blue heaven
containing roseate cloudlets. Then consciousness was
painlessly extinguished, usually at the moment of impact,
and the impact was, at the most, heard but never painfully
felt. Apparently hearing is the last of the senses to be
extinguished. (Noyes & Kletti, 1972, p. 47)

The above quote is taken from the early research into the phenomenon
by Noyes and Kletti. Four years later, they returned to the issue of time
dilation and depersonalization during times of life-threatening stress
with a survey. They found that the most frequently reported feature in the
survey was an apparent slowing down of external time (75 per cent of 85
participants reported this, with 68 per cent reporting an increase in speed
of thought). They commented:

Not only did elapsed time seem drawn out, but events
seemed to happen in slow motion. Yet, in contrast to the
outward slowing, individuals described their thoughts as
speeded up and expressed amazement at the number of

thoughts or mental images that passed through their minds
in a matter of seconds. These two aspects of the experience
of time were generally described together and were related
to one another. (Noyes & Kletti, 1976, p. 23)

It is important to emphasize that time dilation takes place in other, non-life-threatening circumstances that are just stressful. In their 1976 survey, Noyes and Kletti were aware of this distinction, and of the 59 respondees who believed that death was imminent, 80 per cent reported time slowing down. In contrast, such experience was reported only by 65 per cent of the subjects (26) who did not believe death was imminent. Of even greater possible significance was that hospital patients facing a threatening situation due to their illness did not report an increased speed of thoughts and altered attention. This suggests that for there to be a slowing down of time, the subject has to believe that death is imminent and additional subjective time is needed to take evasive action.

One of Noyes and Kletti's subjects narrowly missed being hit by a train and informed them that:

. . . as the train went by I saw the engineer's face. It was
like a movie run slowly so the frames progress with a jerky
motion. That was how I saw his face. (Noyes & Kletti, 1977,
p. 377)

Examples such as these intrigued a number of researchers, such as Stanford neuroscientist David Eagleman, famous for his work on time perception. With his associates Matthew Fiesta and Chess Stetson, he was involved in a paper that argued in its opening statement that this perception 'should entail consequences such as an ability to perceive things with higher temporal resolution. For example, watching a hummingbird in video slow motion allows finer temporal discrimination upon replay at normal speed because more snapshots are taken of the rapidly beating wings.'

In 2007, Eagleman and a handful of colleagues set up an elaborate experiment to see whether time really does slow down during life-threatening situations. (Stetson, Cui, Montigue & Eagleman, 2006) In this, volunteers fell backwards from a 50-m (164-ft) tower into a safety net, and, during the duration of the fall, they were asked whether it seemed that they were falling for longer than the three seconds of objective time that the descent involved. All reported that they subjectively felt that the fall took longer. According to neurologists, this sensation is caused by a linking together of time and memory. When the subjects recalled the fall, they felt that it took a longer time than three seconds. The team hypothesized that if time does slow down, then the subject should be able to perceive things that are usually denied, such as a mind functioning at normal temporal perception levels. For example, they should be able to see a hummingbird's wings when it is in flight or the individual frames of a cinefilm.

According to Eagleman, this is because traumatic memories are processed by the amygdala, the part of the brain that responds to fear-inducing situations. When processing perceptions, it is suggested that the amygdala lays down denser-than-normal memory formations. In simple terms, the memories are more detailed, which may contribute to the sensation of longer duration. This makes sense to me. However, I have specific observations to make in this regard.

Firstly, in the summer of 2007, quantum physicist Michio Kaku hosted a BBC television series that discussed time. In one episode, he featured the work of Dr Eagleman, specifically his time dilation experiment involving his subjects falling off the 50-m (164-ft) tower. Here, we see exactly how the experiment was set up. Each subject had what Eagleman calls a 'Perception Chronometer' on their wrist. This is like a huge LED wristwatch. On the screen are flashed a random sequence of numbers. The speed at which the numbers follow each other can be increased or decreased. The usual speed is so rapid that a normal brain cannot see what is being shown on the screen. The subject placed the perception chronometer on their wrist, and the experimenter increased the speed to ensure that no individual numbers could be read.

The programme showed a subject called Jesse, who confirmed that he could not see any numbers on the screen. Jesse was then sent to the top of the tower and leapt off backwards in such a position that he looked directly at the LED screen for the entire three-second descent. On his arrival back on solid ground, Jesse was asked to report what he saw on the screen. He immediately stated that he saw a number, and that number was 56. Dr Eagleman reported that the number that was presented was 50. As Eagleman stated:

> The zero looks a lot like a six, so this means that he was mostly able to see a presentation rate that he was not able to see under normal circumstances.[3]

The experiment is then repeated, and Jesse reported that he saw 96. The actual number was 98. According to Eagleman:

> These results are very encouraging because this is the first evidence that somebody's brain can speed up and they can see the world more slowly during a high adrenaline situation.[4]

Indeed, quantum physicist Kaku then adds his comment:

> This is the first demonstration that time really can slow down.[5]

What I find odd about this is that Dr Eagleman is now of the opinion that there is no evidence of any form of temporal resolution during stress

3 http://www.youtube.com/watch?v=RjlpamhrId8 – 3 mins 5 seconds in.
4 http://www.youtube.com/watch?v=RjlpamhrId8 – 4 mins 30 seconds in.
5 http://www.youtube.com/watch?v=RjlpamhrId8 – 4 mins 40 seconds in.

situations. On his website, he states:

> *By measuring their speed of information intake, we have concluded that participants do not obtain increased temporal resolution during the fall – instead, because memories are laid down more richly during a frightening situation, the event seems to have taken longer in retrospect.*[6]

Is this the same person who clearly stated the opposite in the TV programme? Jesse had a 1 in 100 chance of getting the number right on both occasions. I admit he did not identify the correct number, but as even Dr Eagleman acknowledged in the programme, 56 and 50 are similar shapes, as are 96 and 98. Remember, Jesse had a short glimpse of these numbers while in a highly unusual situation.

In my opinion, the circumstances that Jesse and his fellow subjects found themselves in were not in any way like a car crash or a near-death situation. They were well prepared for what was about to take place. They knew in advance that they were going to fall 50 m (164 ft). They also knew, and this is of utmost importance, that they were not in any danger of dying. In an actual NDE situation, car crash or climbing accident, the situation is totally unexpected, and the outcome is far from certain. Indeed, the two sets of circumstances cannot in any way be considered equivalent.

It is generally accepted that time dilation is a totally subjective experience. But encounters with other beings suggest a possible objective perception, particularly if those beings show independent motivations and give information not known by the perceiver. Of all the NDE traits, this is probably the most intriguing. Let's review this in more detail.

---

6 http://neuro.bcm.edu/eagleman/time.html

THE CATEGORIES – ENCOUNTERS WITH ENTITIES
Encounters With Entities – Introduction

Meeting with others is a very commonly reported element of the near-death experience. In a 2003 survey by Bruce Greyson and Jan Holden, 63 per cent of individuals who survived cardiac arrests reported that, during their NDE, they met dead relatives or beings of light. This intriguingly suggests that deceased loved ones exist in another part of the universe hidden from our everyday senses.

But is there more to this than initially appears? Who exactly are these entities, and do they have ontological independence from the person perceiving them? Are they simply wish fulfilment, or are they proof of post-mortem survival?

In my 2020 book *The Hidden Universe*, I reviewed in great detail what these entities may actually be, and I do not intend to repeat my conclusions here. With regards to this enquiry, I would like to focus on just one area, but one that brings into question the whole experience: evidence that the entities that are encountered are fulfilling the dying person's expectations of who they anticipate meeting when in an NDE state.

Entities – Cartoon Characters and Living People

In his introduction to his article 'Ketamine – near death and near birth experiences', psychiatrist Karl Jansen, whose intriguing theories we will return to later, opens up with the following comments regarding the Being of Light:

> *It is interesting to note that far more mundane accounts occur than those which have excited widespread interest. Children who have near-death experiences tend to 'see' their living schoolfellows and teachers, or Nintendo characters, rather than communicating with God, although there have been interesting exceptions (Morse, 1985).*

Young children may have no concept of death, but they
do have a sense of catastrophe linked to the birth trauma.
(Gabbard and Twemlow, 1984)

If young children see living individuals and Nintendo characters in their
NDEs, then surely this is powerful evidence that the brain creates the
whole experience from memories and expectations.

Paediatrician Melvin Morse was told of an intriguing case by Akiko
Murakoshi, a Japanese colleague. It involved the NDE of a four-year-old
Japanese boy who was seriously ill with pneumonia. The child described
floating out of his body and finding himself on a riverbank. Over on the
other side was a misty bright light, and in the light he could see several
of his playmates. They urged him to go back. It is unclear as to whether
these urges were by gesture or voice. But one clear thing was that all his
playmates were still alive. (Morse, M. L., 1994, p. 70)

In their book, *The Truth in the Light,* an excellent book I have cited
several times, Peter and Elizabeth Fenwick describe a case involving
Richard Hands, who, as a nine-year-old, suffered complications while
having his appendix removed. As his NDE began, he saw:

. . . a blackness with a pinpoint of light far off in the
distance. I feel drawn towards the light, but there is a terror
and a feeling that I do not wish it to pull me towards it. My
mother is with me in this scene, trying to pull me back from
the light. There is also a wind rushing past, towards the
light. (Fenwick & Fenwick, 1995, p. 173)

His mother was still alive, but here she was actively involved in his
NDE. Of course, the reasonable argument is that Richard was simply in
a dream sequence, in which case it is not at all surprising that his mother
would be trying to pull him back from entering the light. It is curious
that the Fenwicks fail to make any comment regarding the fact that a
living person was in a location usually only supposedly inhabited by the

deceased. One assumes that the reason for the lack of comment is that this case is contrary to the position held by the Fenwicks regarding the NDE being evidence of post-mortem survival. To their credit, they do acknowledge, later in the book, that Richard Hands derived absolutely no spiritual or religious feelings from his NDE and was, at the time of the writing of the book, a 'scientific journalist and an atheist'.

It could be argued that children may not have the cognitive reasoning to differentiate between life and death. Therefore, dream elements involving living friends may embroider and enhance the NDE environment. However, this cannot be used to explain cases where adults similarly encounter still-living associates, friends and loved ones. In another case cited by the Fenwicks, Mrs Jean Giacomozzi, who in 1977 suffered a heavy loss of blood during a hysterectomy, had what the Fenwicks considered an 'unusual' experience. She found herself floating outside her body and saw the doctors and nurses rushing her along the corridors to the operating theatre. She saw a doctor inserting a long cotton wool plug into her wound, and then she was pulled up into a very bright tunnel where she saw her father, who had died three years before. But then she heard somebody else calling her name from the end of the tunnel:

> It was Fabio [the man she was living with]. I remembered the doctor removing the cotton wool plug. When I later saw this doctor, I told him everything. Although he seemed rather shocked at my story, he had no explanation as to how I knew so much about the events of the previous night. Like most people, I had a tremendous fear of death. Now, believe me, it's the last thing I want, but I have lost that fear of the unknown because I truly believe I have had a preview. (Fenwick & Fenwick, 1995, pp. 32–33)

I find it extraordinary that, yet again, the Fenwicks, although commenting that 'her experience was unusual in that she met not only her dead father, but also her partner, who was alive, and very close to her', do not then focus on the implications of this NDE. Why not? Does such an encounter suggest that the NDE is a brain event created out of anticipations and memories? To meet with a living person is stark evidence that whatever these encounters are, they are more than just evidence of the survival of loved ones after death.

In his fascinating paper in which he introduces his 'Individually Tailored Hypothesis' of near-death experiences discussed earlier, William Serdahely cites an intriguing tunnel encounter involving a living individual:

> *One of the female NDErs saw a living female friend in her 'windsock' tunnel. The friend told her to go back to her body. It is rare to hear of a living friend or relative appearing during a near-death experience. However, the gender of the comforting spirit is consistent with previous reports of females appearing to women who are victims of sexual abuse and sexual assault, as this woman was. (Serdahely, W., 1995, p. 189)*

I would now like to return to Serdahely's 1990 paper on children's NDEs, which we discussed earlier, regarding the panoramic life review. You will recall that, in the late 1980s, he decided to do a review of childhood near-death experiences. He analysed four cases of individuals who had NDEs at an early age. Here is a particularly interesting case:

> *Pat was seven years old when he fell off a bridge into a lagoon.*

> *Pat found himself in a dark, black tunnel in which his two deceased pets, a cat and a dog, appeared to him. The former family cat brushed against his leg, and his dog licked his face, sending Pat back to his body. He did not encounter any other spirits or presence while in the tunnel.*

> *All of Pat's close relatives were alive at the time of his*
> *NDE. (Serdahely, W. J., 1990, p. 34)*

Pat saw his deceased pets but no adults. So, do children see deceased pets during NDEs, or is this a one-off case? It seems not. In another case, Serdahely describes the case of 'Amber', a ten-year-old whose heartbeat and respiration stopped when she was recovering from spinal surgery. During her NDE:

> *Two animals also appeared to Amber while she was in this*
> *'dark place'. She saw a shadow of what she believed was a*
> *dog and thought it might have been the family's pet, which*
> *had been put to sleep a few years earlier. She also saw a*
> *white lamb that came near her but did not touch her. The*
> *lamb was loving and gentle, and led Amber back to her*
> *body, after that she regained consciousness. (Serdahely,*
> *W. J., 1990, p. 34)*

Children also seem to have a different experience regarding the meeting of dead people. In a review of childhood near-death experiences, the much-respected NDE researcher Dr Melvin Morse and his associates noted that their sample of childhood NDEs differed further from adult experiences in that 'adults typically report meeting dead relatives and friends, while children report meeting teachers and living friends'. (Morse, Castillo, Venecia, Milstein & Tyler, 1986, p. 1112)

Another of Serdahely's cases was also somewhat unusual. A youngster called Mike felt the hand and heard the voice of a loving, friendly male whom he equivocally identified as Jesus. I am unclear as to how Mike, as a four-year-old at the time of his NDE, could determine the voice of Jesus rather than the voice of any adult. This suggests cultural programming. This is what Serdahely noted:

> *A warm hand touched his shoulder as he looked at his body*

below, preventing him from turning around. A comforting, loving male voice, coming from the presence whose hand was on his shoulder, told him: 'This is not your time. Do you want to go back or stay here?' (Serdahely, W. J., 1990, p. 35)

From these cases, it must be concluded that there is something far more complex going on than dying people encountering deceased relatives. Cartoon characters are fictional, and already living individuals perceived in NDE states are clearly not dead. More importantly, these living people encountered in the NDE world have yet to recollect the meetings. These facts suggest that some NDEs are more like dreams than actual incidents. But what of the beings encountered who show self-motivation and ones that impart information of which the NDEr had no previous knowledge? For example, Eben Alexander discovered after his NDE that the young woman with the startling blue eyes he met on the butterfly's wing was a long-dead sister that he did not know he had. And this is not an isolated case. This is an area that must be investigated in greater detail as it presents objective evidence that, although the NDE may be brain-generated, it still offers challenges to our present understanding of science.

In this regard, we need to dig deeper into the concept of life after death. But to do so, we need to define our terms. What do we mean when we use the terms life and death? What differentiates them? Indeed, what is consciousness and does consciousness end when the brain dies? It is to these timeless questions that we will now seek answers.

PART 4

The Science.
A Question of Life and Death

WHAT IS LIFE?

Our present scientific paradigm is based on a very simple but powerful philosophy known as material reductionism. It argues that we can understand how anything works by breaking it down to its constituent elements. For example, by breaking an automobile engine down into its bits and pieces, a person with a basic understanding of engineering, chemistry and physics will be able to understand how that automobile engine can create movement and speed. A biologist with knowledge of chemistry and chemical processes can take a plant apart and understand how the plant metabolizes energy from sunlight. This process of breaking things down to understand how they function is Western science's most influential contribution to our understanding of the physical universe. This has worked well over the last three or four hundred years. However, one thing that is immanent in the world defies such reductionism, because it is non-material and, therefore, cannot lend itself to a reductionist analysis. And that is the greatest mystery of all: life.

According to the *Oxford Dictionary of English*, life is defined as:

> *The condition that distinguishes animals and plants from inorganic matter, including the capacity for growth, reproduction, functional activity, and continual change preceding death.*

In other words, life is a property that distinguishes matter with biological processes from matter without. But living things are composed of complex biological molecular compounds, which are, in turn, made up of less complete individual molecular systems known as proteans and nucleic acids, such as DNA and RNA. That is it. But here lies a huge problem. In themselves, these components are not alive. It is only when they get together in particular structures that life spontaneously appears, seemingly out of nowhere, with all its self-replication abilities. It is as if life is a process created by the interface of substances that share none of its nature.

From ancient times onwards, the general understanding was that living things have an inner force that motivates them and facilitates movement. This force is not part of the external world but is generated from within the organism. The ancient Greeks called this force *enérgeia*, a word that has no direct translation in English. The closest translation is 'being at work'. From the 5th century BCE, it was also known that, in some way, the brain was responsible for creating this motive force. For example, the school of Hippocrates noted that if there was injury to one side of the head, sometimes muscular spasms were observed in the opposite side of the body. Then, in the 2nd century BCE, Galen presented a series of dramatic public vivisections in which he proved that the nerves along the spinal cord were responsible for a pig squealing. Carefully opening a live swine, he traced the nerves from the brain and followed them along the spinal cord. By tying off the nerves that controlled the pig's vocal cords, he could halt the sound of the animal's squealing while its breathing and movement continued. He then released the ligature on the nerves, and the pig began squealing again. In this way, he showed that signals from the brain caused the vocal cords to emit sounds. He concluded that the movement and actions of all living creatures were created by something he called the *pneuma zootikon* ('animal spirit'), which was formed in the brain. This was an example of *enérgeia*.

This model of understanding continued for centuries, and even in the mid-17th century, the French philosopher René Descartes argued that the animal spirits were filtered from the blood as it left the heart and that the most subtle and active particles ascended to the brain where they were focused in the pineal gland. From there, the spirits flowed into the pores of the brain and the nerves themselves. So, the motive force was a form of *enérgeia* that had the *pneuma zootikon* as its source.

By the 19th century, the word 'energy' was used to describe the quantitative property that must be transferred to an object to heat it. Nowadays, the generally accepted definition is 'a condition that describes the capacity to do work', similar to Galen's concept.

But 'life' comes in many forms. From single-celled organisms to the complexity of mammals. What seems to be a dividing line is the evolution of a brain capable of creating a mind that is aware of its environment and uses that awareness to maximize the survival potential of the body it is part of. It does this by focusing the *enérgeia* under its control to negotiate the hazards, challenges and dangers lurking in the world surrounding it. In lower animals such as insects, fish, reptiles and amphibians, the mind is simply a series of autonomic responses to threats. It is reasonable to conclude that no actual awareness motivates such actions. However, in higher animals such as mammals, there seems to be an awareness that can sometimes override the instinctive responses. This is an aware mind, otherwise known as consciousness. Life itself is a mystery, but consciousness is a total enigma. It is to this intriguing puzzle that we will now turn our collective attention by asking the question, what is this 'mind', and from what does it emerge?

WHAT IS MIND?

The mystery of the mind has preoccupied philosophers and scientists for hundreds, if not thousands, of years. How can we account for the reality of mental sensations? Our senses show us a physical universe with our body placed firmly within it. We can see the visible parts and can see our reflection in a mirror. We perceive other bodies similar to our own within the space that surrounds us. But what we can never sense is their minds. We can assume them and compare them to our own inner consciousness, but we can never prove them. This is because, unlike our bodies, mind, and its partners consciousness and thought, are totally non-physical. We cannot apply the materialist-reductionist model to mind. We cannot break it down into its component parts, nor can we even locate it. That it is in our head is simply because this is the location of the majority of our sensory organs, specifically our eyes and ears. But this is an illusion. If our eyes and ears were on our kneecap, then we would feel that our mind was located in the knee. As Descartes argued, the mind does not have any *res extensa*, Latin for 'extended thing', in that it has no extension in space in the way that physical objects do. He described mind as being *res cogitans*, a 'thinking thing'. But herein lies a huge problem: how can something with no physical attributes act on solid objects in space? How does the mind make the body move? How does my mind make my fingers move to type these words on my computer keyboard? .

In 1792, the Professor of Anatomy at Bologna University, Luigi Galvani, was surprised to discover that attaching a wire with an electric charge running through it would make a dead frog's leg twitch. Although it was also found that strong electric currents could stimulate nerves and the spinal cord of humans, it was not until the 1860s that German neurologist Eduard Hitzig made an astonishing discovery. He was working with wounded soldiers at a military hospital, some of whom had pieces of their skulls blown away in battle, exposing their brains. Hitzig, being aware of the discoveries of Volta and Galvani, decided to apply weak electric shocks to the surface (cerebral cortex) of the exposed brain of one patient. When he did so this caused the patient's eyes to move. Later, in 1870, when working with another doctor, anatomist Gustav Fritsch, he set up a makeshift laboratory and stimulated the brains of live dogs. He had been intrigued that a specific area at the back of the brain caused his earlier patient's eyes to move, whereas identical stimulation of the other regions did not. This led him to conclude that specific brain areas controlled specific movements. Fritsch decided to see if an experiment could be set up using live dogs. He discovered that when an electrical source was applied to the exposed brain of a sedated dog, the dog could be made to move its paw as though it was making a voluntary movement. Even more intriguing was that it was a paw on the opposite side of the body to the side of the brain stimulated. It was then discovered that the opposite paw could be moved by stimulating the other side of the brain.

From this, it was concluded that electricity was related to the motive force in the body and that this form of energy could be applied to the brain to stimulate this motive force. But it was also known that it was conscious intention that moved the body, so were mind and consciousness just another form of energy, or *enérgeia*? If this was the case, there must be a way of measuring it.

In the late 19th century, physicists and physicians such as Gustav Fechner, Theodor Meynert and Albert Lehmann applied the conservation laws to the mind-brain problem. In 1892, Meynert argued in a lecture that if the total sum of cerebral energy was not constantly partitioned and conserved, the human soul would violate the first law of thermodynamics. (Meynert, 1892) He argued that when energy is produced to bring about a thought or movement in one part of the brain, an equal amount of energy must disappear in another part of the brain to ensure that the total amount of energy is conserved. This issue was solved when, in the early 20th century, Albert Einstein, in his famous $E=MC^2$ equation, merged the first law of thermodynamics with another conservation law, Antione Lavoisier's Conservation of Mass from 1785, which stated that matter is neither created nor destroyed. This means that the total amount of mass and energy in the universe is constant. Mass can be converted into energy and energy into mass without changing the total amount of both. So if life, and its outcome consciousness, is a form of energy, then it can also be converted into physical mass.

This may seem of no real importance regarding what happens to consciousness at the point of death, but it is: consciousness is a form of energy, and the application of these laws brought about a series of discoveries about the brain.

In August 1875, physician Dr Richard Caton gave a lecture to the British Medical Association in Edinburgh. Caton had applied a galvanometer (an electromechanical measuring instrument for electric current) to the exposed brains of live rabbits and monkeys, and reported that he had discovered distinct variations in current, which increased when the animals were asleep. In a later paper, Caton explained how he measured what happened to the electrical current when the animals were killed. He discovered that immediately before the death of the animal, the electrical current increased, and immediately afterwards decreased, but did not cease as soon as the death occurred. (Caton, 1875)

These results intrigued a young German physician, Hans Berger, and motivated him to use the discoveries as the basis for his own research into objectively measuring *enérgeia* within the brain.

Berger's story is very interesting, evidencing that the borderline between science and the magical is larger than modern materialist reductionism is willing to accept. In his book *Entangled Minds*, author Dean Radin describes how, in 1893, while taking some time out from his studies as a mathematics student at the University of Jena, Berger was training with a cavalry unit of the German military. His horse became startled, throwing Berger into the path of a fast-approaching horse-drawn cannon. (Radin, 2006, pp. 21–22) Fortunately, the driver of the cannon managed to stop it in time, but Berger was left very shaken by this close encounter with severe injury or even death. That very same day, many miles away, his sister was overcome by an incredible feeling of dread regarding her brother and pleaded with her father to send a telegram asking if Hans was okay. He later described how this incident affected his appreciation of the brain's power. He wrote:

> *This is a case of spontaneous telepathy in which, at a time of mortal danger and as I contemplated certain death, I transmitted my thoughts while my sister, who was*

particularly close to me, acted as the receiver. (Radin, 2006, p. 22)

This encounter with the power of the mind changed the course of Berger's academic and subsequent professional career. On his return to university, he switched to medicine and psychology to understand more about how thoughts can be transferred across time and space. He never doubted that telepathy was genuine, and his objective was to discover the mechanism by which it was facilitated. His discovery of Caton's findings reinforced his belief that a hidden force was transmitted from and received by the brain.

His interest in the source of telepathic powers within the brain was further reinforced by a book published the year before by experimental psychologist Albert Lehmann, an advocate of the law of conservation with regards to the brain (Lehmann, 1892). Lehmann believed that the chemical energy created by metabolic processes within the brain could be converted into three major forms of energy in the brain: heat, electricity and what he called 'P-energy', the psychic energy associated with different mental states. To test this, he measured the peripheral blood flow when his subjects concentrated on certain mental states.

Lehmann's theory of cerebral energetics, in which theoretical changes in energy levels could be measured as particular mental states were experienced, inspired and motivated Berger to embark upon a 35-year search to measure brain activity. In public, he was a brooding, introverted character pursuing science in a totally structured way. One of his students, Raphael Ginzberg, described him as being 'the personification of static'. (Ginzberg, 1949) But, in private, Berger wrote expansive poetry, and his diaries contained fascinating musings on spirituality and the deeper meaning of life. Indeed, a little-discussed fact is that Berger never ceased to be interested in the implications of his discoveries with regard to psychic phenomena and, more importantly, what takes place in the brain at the point of death. In his world-famous 1929 academic paper in which he announced to the world his discovery of electrical activity in the brain, he referred back to Caton's discoveries over 50 years earlier:

There were found distinct variations in current . . . and with
the onset of death, strengthened, and after death, became
weaker and then completely disappeared. (Berger, 1929)

After a number of less-than-successful attempts, Berger devised a machine that could measure the electrical activity of the brain. By 1928, he had perfected a machine he called an electroencephalogram (EEG). This was able to measure small changes in the electrical activity of the brain's surface while the subjects were following certain mental activities. He noted that these electrical fluctuations had wave-like qualities, and they, not surprisingly, subsequently became known as brain waves.

To appreciate what Berger discovered, we need to digress from our narrative and discuss what scientists mean when they use the term 'wave'.

All forms of waves are defined by three measurements: frequency, wavelength and amplitude. Waves move in 'cycles,' which, as the name implies, are circular motions.

Imagine making a mark on the rim of a wheel and then starting the wheel, rolling forward. We will note that after one complete revolution, the mark returns to its starting position. This is one cycle. If we measure the time the wheel takes to do one cycle, we have discovered its 'period'. This is usually measured as the number of cycles completed in one second, known as its 'frequency'. Hertz is the unit of frequency, so if a wheel completes 20 revolutions in a second, its frequency is 20 Hertz (Hz).

Wavelength is the distance it takes for the spot on the wheel to return to the same position in the cycle. Usually, this is taken from the highest point to the highest point (the crest) or, less usually, from the lowest point back to the lowest point (the trough), but it doesn't really matter. It is measured in metres.

Finally, we have amplitude, which measures the size of the wave. It is the height of the highest point of a crest or the lowest point of a trough measured from the equilibrium point (also measured in metres).

Berger was surprised to discover that when a subject closed their eyes, the surface of the brain had brain waves at a frequency of 8 to 13 Hz, but when the subject opened their eyes, the frequency changed to between 13 and 30 Hz. He called the first alpha waves and the second beta waves.

In the 1930s, British-American neurophysiologist William Grey Walter improved on Berger's EEG, in which he detected a new form of very slow brain waves, known as delta waves, with a frequency of 0.5 to 4 Hz. These were of particular interest because they are usually associated with a form of deep sleep now known as SWS (slow-wave sleep) or NREM (non-rapid eye movement sleep). What was also of significance for our enquiry into the near-death experience is that delta waves are also associated with epilepsy, specifically temporal lobe epilepsy (TLE). We shall return to this later.

In 1938, German researchers Richard Jung and Alois Kornmüller announced the discovery of theta waves with a frequency of 4 to 8 Hz. These waves seemed to be focused on a small structure in the brain called the hippocampus. They have been found to relate to dreaming, meditation, hypnotic states and, of possible significance, memory retrieval.

Much later, in 1964, a new form of electrical oscillations in the brain was discovered in the visual cortex of awake monkeys. These were termed gamma waves. They are the fastest waves discovered to date, registering at above 35 Hz and going up to 100 Hz. In humans, and presumably in all other higher mammals, gamma waves have been associated with higher brain functions such as cognition and memory. As we shall discover later, the role of gamma waves may prove crucial to our understanding of the near-death experience.

However, with all of these measurements of brain activity, we have found a way of linking our inner experience to brain activity. But this gets us far from answering the question of what life is. We are discovering how inner intentions and perceptions manifest on the surface of the brain. From this must be asked: has this got us any closer to the mysterious 'Ghost in the Machine', as British philosopher Gilbert Ryle so dismissively termed it in his hugely influential 1949 book *The Concept of Mind*?

How does 'mind' come about, this amorphous nothingness that can generate alpha, beta, gamma, delta and theta waves?

Indeed, in 1989, British philosopher Colin McGinn asked this question in a wonderfully poetic way in a paper published in the academic journal *Mind*. He asked:

> *How can technicolour phenomenology arise from soggy grey matter? . . . How could the aggregation of millions of individually insentient neurons generate subjective awareness? . . . Neural transmissions seem like the wrong kind of materials with which to bring consciousness into the world, but it appears that they perform this mysterious feat in some way. (McGinn, 1989, p. 349)*

What we know is that as life evolves through the instructions contained within its DNA, it becomes more and more complex and, in some way, learns from its environment. But this learning is, using a term we will return to later, 'in the dark'. There is no awareness or sentience cognizant of the information being received. But then, just as life came about through complexity, another 'magical' event happened: consciousness. This was followed by self-aware consciousness and referential-self-aware consciousness, the 'something' that is processing these words from shapes on a page on a computer screen into images and ideas. It is that something that is central to each and every one of us. Self-referential consciousness is an awareness that knows it is aware and can ponder on the fact of this awareness. Furthermore, this awareness is the focus of all the incoming sensory data provided by the sense organs, and it is this awareness that uses this data to ensure the continuation of the meat machine it finds itself seemingly located within. But what is this awareness? Does the brain create it? And by what process can inanimate quarks and electrons come together within energy fields to create such awareness? This is a question that we will try now to address.

What Is Mind? – The Hard Problem

McGinn's question is of profound importance, and it is my intention, over the following few pages, to explain in layperson's terms what modern science knows (and does not know) about the functioning of the mass of cells located a couple of inches behind the eyes you are using to read these words, or the ears you are using to listen to this audiobook, something that is, as far as we know, the most complex mechanism in the universe. Furthermore, suppose we are to understand the true meaning of the near-death experience. In that case, we must define clearly what we mean when we use the terms 'life', 'consciousness' and 'death', all of which are states totally dependent on the functioning (or lack of it) of this 1,400 g (50 oz) of goo we call the brain.

Our technology is now sufficiently advanced for us to monitor those 1,400 g and isolate what parts of the goo do what. Modern techniques such as PET scans, CAT scans and other machines can show exactly what parts of the brain light up when certain actions are considered or certain perceptions are perceived. Radical surgery and brain injuries have shown us where memory is processed (but not stored) and how personality can be changed by damage to certain areas of the brain.

However, this is still an overview. It does not tell us how self-referential consciousness is created. There is something in my head that looks out on the world. It has memories, hopes, fears, loves, hates, ambitions and many other traits. It is self-aware and is keen to understand itself and where it has come from. How can I 'be'?

Now, let us try to apply the materialist-reductionist model to the brain in an attempt to find consciousness. We need to break down the brain into its basic building blocks.

If you look at a section of brain matter, you will discover that it comprises neurons or nerve cells. At birth, the brain contains around 100 billion of these cells. Each neuron has a cell body and tens of thousands of tiny branches called dendrites. These dendrites receive information from other neurons. Each neuron also has what is called a primary axon. This is a projection that can travel great distances across the brain. Each neuron makes contact with each other neuron at a point known as a synapse. The neurons do not actually come into contact with each other. At each synapse is a tiny gap between it and its neighbour. These 'synaptic gaps' are extremely short, about 200 to 300 angstroms across. (One angstrom equals one hundred millionth of a centimetre.) Messages are transferred across the brain via the synapses. Depending upon what you are thinking, specific synapses transfer electric currents between them in the form of calcium ions. This is called 'firing'. Some synapses will fire, and others will not. So, similar to traffic lights on red or green, the flow of messages across your brain can be channelled in various directions. The width of these synaptic gaps is so tiny that they are approaching the atomic scale of dimensions.

A receptor site is at the end of each synapse. These are of many different types, each designed to work with one of several internally-generated chemicals known as neurotransmitters. There are two types of neurotransmitter: excitatory and inhibitory. Simply put, the excitatory variety stimulates the brain to do something, and the inhibitory variety calms it down. Over 100 of these have now been identified. The major excitatory neurotransmitters are glutamate, norepinephrine and epinephrine. Regarding the inhibitory variety, GABA (gamma-aminobutyric acid) and serotonin are the major players. Those that bring about a response to the adjoining receptor site are technically known as agonists, and those that block a response are known as antagonists. With regards to this book, there is another major neurotransmitter that facilitates both excitatory and inhibitory responses in neighbouring receptor sites. This substance is known as dopamine.

So, what have we found? An amalgamation of inanimate molecules reacting to a sea of similarly inanimate electrons. In other words, chemistry reacts with electricity. It seems that the best answer we can find is that consciousness is an 'epiphenomenon' of brain processes. It just kind of happens at some point when a crucial level of complexity is reached. By the addition of one more process, one more molecule, and one more electron, consciousness pops out of nowhere. This reminds me of the cartoon by Sidney Harris in which two scientists stand in front of a blackboard. On one side of the blackboard is a mass of mathematical notation, and on the other side is another mass of mathematical notation. Linking them is the words 'then a miracle occurs'. The older scientist points at the comment and says to the creator of the formulae, 'I think you should be more specific here in step two.'

A growing band of scientists believe that the only viable explanation for how inanimate molecules and electrical impulses can create a self-referential consciousness is that the brain does not 'create' consciousness; it 'receives' it. This is analogous to a radio or TV receiver. The source of the TV programme viewed on the screen is not inside the back of the TV in the same way that the radio announcer is not in the radio. An even better analogy is the location of the internet. It is not located on your computer's hard drive but is supplied on a needs/demand basis. It exists in an informational 'field' that surrounds us. This radical model is known as 'orchestrated objective reduction' and was proposed as a specific response to a famous question raised by Australian philosopher David Chalmers. Chalmers argued that with regard to consciousness, there are two problems: the first is understanding how the brain works, its neurochemistry and its physiology. To gain an understanding of how the brain does what it does is what Chalmers calls the 'easy problem'. By this, he means that our present scientific paradigm has the tools to crack this mystery eventually. However, solving the easy problem will only supply us with an overview. The solution cannot tell us how self-referential consciousness is created.

A considered and balanced attempt to dismiss the complex problem as simply a misunderstanding of brain processes can be found in the 2004 book *Consciousness: Creeping up on the Hard Problem* by neurophysiologist Jeffrey Gray. (Gray, 2004) In this robust defence of materialist reductionism, Gray agrees with computer scientist Marvin Minsky's famous statement that 'the mind is what the brain does'. (Minsky, 1988)

Gray comes to these conclusions because he addresses the hugely complex question of how the brain creates subjective, conscious experiences, such as the colour red or the sensation of pain. (Gray, 2004, p. 301) From this, he argues that the relationship between brain activity and consciousness is a causal one. In other words, his position is one of *emergentism*. Although Grey argues otherwise, this is simply a new form of the much-maligned and generally dismissed proposition of Cartesian dualism: that 'mind' and 'matter' are totally different things. Indeed, it has been long argued that the phenomenon of consciousness cannot be explained in physical, that is 'scientific', terms, nor can a causal relationship be found between consciousness and brain activity. In many ways, this is identical to the problem of how perception (particularly vision) works in an out-of-body state, which was discussed earlier. There is no known scientific process that can begin to explain how a disembodied 'soul' can see or hear anything, just as there is no known scientific process whereby inanimate matter can spontaneously bring into existence consciousness. They are both 'impossible'.

But materialist reductionists are happy to announce that these impossibilities show that life after death, out-of-body states and all parapsychological perceptual states can be dismissed as scientifically impossible. However, there is not the same sweeping admission regarding how the brain creates consciousness. One position is shouted from the rooftops, whereas the other is swept under the carpet.

But there is an escape mechanism for the materialist reductionists. It was originally called 'promissory materialism' by the philosopher of science Karl Popper. He argued that modern science avoids addressing the problem of consciousness by stating that we may not know how inanimate matter creates self-aware consciousness now. Still, scientific advances in the future will explain them. Clearly, Popper was somewhat dismissive of this position, so the defenders of promissory materialism have coined a new term, 'inclusive physicalism'. This argues that the phenomenon of consciousness will eventually be shown to be entirely caused by brain activity and that this will work using processes consistent with the already established laws of physics and neurophysiology. In this way, consciousness becomes a physical property in the same way that electricity is.

However, the major problem is that self-referential awareness is qualitatively different to the brain matter from which it spontaneously seems to appear. Matter is physical; it has an extension in space and mass. It can, therefore, be quantified and measured. Consciousness has none of these qualities. It has no extension in space and no mass. If it did, then surely there would be a difference in mass between a living brain and a dead brain? Indeed, this would be a definitive measure of death. But as we shall discover, there is no such objective test. In this regard, I am aware of the much-quoted 1907 Duncan MacDougall experiment, in which he weighed six patients at the moment of death and afterwards discovered that one patient lost 21.3 g (0.74 oz). (McDougall, 1907) Unfortunately, it was pointed out that this could be accounted for by a loss of liquid from the body due to excess sweating at death.

One well-respected academic who does not share Gray's optimism is psychologist Max Velmans, who, in his review of Gray's book, makes several crucial observations regarding the areas of the 'Hard Problem' that are generally ignored by neuroscience. He cites the discovery that much of what we think of as conscious, voluntary mental activity is carried out unconsciously or preconsciously. Experiments have shown that a conscious wish to take a particular physical action, such as flexing a muscle, can be detected by measuring something called a 'readiness potential' on the surface of the cortex. The only problem is that the readiness potential is detected at around 350 milliseconds *before* the subject decides to act. From this, Velmans asks the perfectly reasonable question, 'Who or what is responsible?' (Velmans, 2005, p. 529) Indeed, such discoveries have profound implications for our ideas not only on free will, but also on the true nature of the self.

However, it is with regard to the mysteries of perception that Velmans takes issue with the materialist-reductionist model of consciousness. He points out that central to Gray's argument is that the individual qualities of experience are processed in different parts of the brain, creating an inwardly generated facsimile world that is presented to consciousness. From this, he makes the following profoundly important observation:

> *Given his acceptance that the experienced 3D world is a construct of the brain and his adoption of biological naturalism, Gray is committed to the view that the entire perceived world is really inside the brain, with the consequence that the real skull (as opposed to the phenomenal skull) is outside the experienced world, that is, beyond the dome of the perceived sky. (Velmans, 2005, p. 530)*

In other words, by dismissing one mystery, that of how the brain creates consciousness, Gray dismisses the existence of a world external to that of the perceiver. This world contains the very brain that supposedly creates that world.

It is fairly clear that Chalmers's 'Hard Problem' remains an issue to science, and it seems that until a satisfactory answer is found our understanding of the workings of the universe will continue to be incomplete. And, more importantly, how can we ever come to a conclusion about the meaning of the near-death experience when we have no idea what life and consciousness really are?

But there is one thing we can measure and quantify, a state we all have waiting for us at an undetermined date in the future: death. It is to this netherworld that we now turn our attention.

WHAT IS DEATH?

On 19 October 1967, Harvard Medical School (HMS) anaesthesiologist Dr Henry Knowles Beecher presented a paper to his university's Standing Committee on Human Studies. It was entitled 'Ethical Problems Created by the Hopelessly Unconscious Man'. In this, he asked a profoundly important question: 'Under what circumstances, if ever, shall extraordinary means of support be terminated, with death to follow?' He then went on to add that, 'When it becomes evident that the brain is dead, there is an obligation to discontinue extraordinary supports.' (Nair-Collins, 2022, p. 44) This caused quite a stir, and soon afterwards, the Dean of HMS, Robert Ebert, proposed that a special committee should be set up to look into these issues. Under the chairmanship of Beecher, the Ad Hoc Committee of the Harvard Medical School to Examine the Definition of Brain Death (alternatively, 'the Brain Death Committee') was set up. The Brain Death Committee aimed to define the criteria regarding irreversible coma and death to serve two purposes: to specify the circumstances of the withdrawal of life-sustaining treatment from those determined to be brain dead and the procurement of organs for transplantation from such patients.

On 3 December 1967, the issue became crucial when South African surgeon Christiaan Barnard performed the first heart transplant in a hospital in Cape Town. The question arose as to whether, during such procedures, the donors were dead at the time that the heart was removed or whether it was the removal of the heart that killed the donors.

The subsequent report was published in August 1968. It laid out specific medical criteria that defined the new category of 'irreversible coma' or 'brain death'. These criteria included no movements or breathing, lack of responsiveness or specific brainstem reflexes. (Beecher, 1968)

As the years progressed, people became uncomfortable with the decision-making process regarding who lives and who dies. It was felt that a much more precise definition of death was needed, specifically the differentiation between 'brain death' and 'biological death'. Indeed, James Bernat, a neurologist at the Dartmouth School of Medicine in New Hampshire, argued that the two states were identical.

A moment's reflection discloses that it is primarily the brain that is responsible for the functioning of the organism as a whole: the integration of organ and tissue subsystems by

neural and neuroendocrine control of temperature, fluids and
electrolytes, nutrition, breathing, circulation, appropriate
responses to danger, among others. The cardiac arrest
patient with whole brain destruction is simply a preparation
of unintegrated individual subsystems since the organisms a
whole has ceased functioning. (Bernat, 1984, p. 48)

This argument was accepted, so, in the US in 1981, the Uniform Determination of Death Act (UDDA) defined death as 'the irreversible cessation of circulatory and respiratory functions, or the irreversible cessation of all functions of the entire brain, including the brainstem'. (President's Commission for the Study of Ethical Problems in Medicine and Biomedical and Biobehavioral Research, 1981).

Since 1981, there has been further refining of these definitions of death. In 1995, the American Academy of Neurology stated that 'brain death' necessitates coma, absence of brainstem reflexes and apnoea (lack of breathing).

Subsequently, most US states adopted the UDDA and AAN guidelines. Still, several maintain different standards, which means, in practice, that a person could be legally dead in one state and alive in another.

It is of profound importance with regard to the near-death experience that there has never yet been a case of anyone who has been correctly diagnosed as brain dead who has ever had neurological recovery. But medical science is constantly advancing, and new developments like deep-brain stimulation may be able to reverse brain death.

And this brings about another huge problem: if death is the separation of the soul from the body, then there must be a moment in time when this happens. A scenario of 'before' and 'after'. One moment, a person is alive; the next, they are dead. So, we have a concept of 'the moment of death'. Developments in modern science and our abilities to assist the body in continuing to live after fairly traumatic damage suggest that there is no 'moment' of death. It is more a process of death. This is reflected in the central argument that death is a loss of integrity.

So, it must be asked, what is responsible for the integration of the brain if the brain does not function? Integration is impossible, and the soul and the body part company. This 'integrator theory' of the brain has another, even more pressing issue: how can we know if the entire brain has ceased functioning?

In my previous writings I have asked is it the addition of one molecule, one atom or even one quark and then suddenly consciousness pops out of nowhere in a magical cloud of epiphenomena?

In 2020, The World Brain Death Project published a report seeking international consensus on the minimum criteria for brain death. (Greer, Shemie, Torrance, Varelas & Goldenberg, 2020) This report proposed eight criteria: (1) no evidence of arousal or awareness to maximal external stimulation; (2) pupils fixed in a midsize position and unreactive to light; (3) absent corneal, oculocephalic and oculovestibular reflexes; (4) absent facial movement to noxious stimuli; (5) absent gag reflex to bilateral posterior pharyngeal stimulation; (6) absent cough reflex during deep tracheal suctioning; (7) no brain-mediated motor response to noxious stimulation of the limbs; and (8) lacking spontaneous respirations during apnoea test targets of pH < 7.30 and $Paco2 \geq 60$ mm Hg. (Greer, Shemie, Torrance, Varelas & Goldenberg, 2020)

Effectively, death is caused by cardiac arrest. The heart stops beating, and the blood ceases circulating, which means that all body areas cease receiving the oxygen needed. Technically known as ischaemia, this is particularly devastating for the brain and its 86 billion or so neurons. Because they cannot store energy, they die quickly.

Currently, the modern-day versions of Berger's EEG prototype are the most widely utilized tool to record neurophysiological activity in the dying brain. EEG recordings can be applied in two ways in the clinical setting. The first method involves the placement of 16 electrodes spaced equally on the surface of the skull, which can measure surface electrical activity across all brain regions. This is known as the 10–20 System, with an internationally recognized notation of each electrode location on the scalp. The '10' and '20' refer to the actual distances between adjacent electrodes as either 10 per cent or 20 per cent of the total front–back or left–right distance of the skull. Each electrode placement site has a letter to identify the lobe or brain area being monitored, with a number isolating the placement more precisely.

The second method is the so-called Bispectral Index (BIS) monitor and was introduced in 1994 as a way to measure the degree of sedation of the patient. This is of particular importance in the operating theatre, where the surgeon and the anaesthetist need to know that the patient is unconscious and incapable of feeling pain. BIS monitoring consists of two to four channels placed on the patient's forehead. The sensors receive EEG signals from their respective area and send them to a monitor.

This is crucial during surgery, where consciousness during an operation would be intensely distressing to a patient. Known as 'awareness', this is a critical factor in Gerald Woerlee's critique of the Pam Reynolds case discussed earlier. BIS analyses a frontal cortical EEG signal, which converts into digital data. This data is processed so that an easily comparable score between 0 and 100 is produced; the lower the score, the more sedated the patient is. For example, 0 is total EEG silence with a BIS value of 40 to 60 when a patient is effectively anaesthetized.

This is now known as the Patient State Index (PSI). Over the years, and having been applied to patients in various types of sedation, the PSI has become an essential tool in measuring levels of awareness. But BIS has its drawbacks. For example, because BIS consists of only two to four electrodes placed on the forehead, it can only measure neuronal activity in that area of the brain. In contrast, the 10–20 System can capture all brain areas.

So, during a death scenario in an operating theatre, BIS could not measure activity in the temporal lobes. Now, if, as I suspect, the temporal lobes are crucial to the near-death experience, then such activity will never be picked up in an operating theatre where BIS is the standard EEG measurement tool.

Another problem with BIS is that, until recently, it could monitor brain activity in real time but could not record the activity for later analysis.

This has changed with the development of a BIS monitor known as the SEDLine Root device by a Californian company called Masimo. This does not overcome the monitor location difficulties of BIS, but it has allowed records of brain activity to be kept when the patient dies.

It was a SEDLine Root monitor that recorded an extraordinary case of brain activity after death. In 2009, Washington-based anaesthesiologist Dr Lakhmir Chawla and his associates published a paper in which they described how they were able to capture a raw EEG signal in a patient who had just died. (Chawla, Junker, Jacobs, Seneff & Akst, 2009) This was part of a study on end-of-life neurological activity. They reported on seven critically ill patients who, for various reasons, had had life support removed. The case involved a patient whose brain activity was recorded by a SEDLine.

As we have already discovered, one of the most valuable aspects of the SEDLine is that it can measure and record EEG signals. What Chawla and his team found when they checked the recordings was intriguing. They noted that after the patient had died the SEDLine recorded a sudden surge of gamma-wave activity.

You will recall earlier that gamma-ray activity is consistent with cerebral arousal. And this is precisely what Chawla et al. observed in the recordings:

> . . . a multitude of these BIS spikes (>20) in other patients who were immediately ante-mortal, and the timing of these spikes is consistent, although not all patients will demonstrate a surge of activity. (Chawla, Junker, Jacobs, Seneff & Akst, 2009, p. 1097)

The term ante-mortal is crucial here. It is another way of saying 'after death'. So, brain activity involving awareness was measured (and recorded) after the patients had died.

What is intriguing is that this was not the first time a BIS spike had been observed but not recorded in a similar clinical setting. In 2005, a

BIS monitor detected a massive spike in brain activity as a 79-year-old woman began the dying process. Although this was not post-mortem, it is again evidence that the activity starts before brain death and continues afterwards. (Gambrell, 2005) This is supported by several clinical and experimental settings involving human and animal subjects dating back to the mid-1980s. (Clute & Levy, 1990; Hansen, 1985)

Chawla et al. stated that the BIS spikes observed with their seven patients lasted between 30 and 180 seconds.

The team was concerned that external electromagnetic interference may have caused the spikes. However, they argued that the constant similarities of timings observed in each patient and different environments suggest that this was not the case. They added that electrical activity that was not strong enough to cause physical movement in the patients and yet sufficient to generate electrical activity in the brain was also doubtful.

Interestingly, the team argued that this brain activity prior to death may be the source of many of the reported near-death experience traits that we shall discuss later. These include the out-of-body experience (OBE) and the panoramic life review.

Although not referenced directly, it is likely that, among others, the Chawla et al. 2009 paper inspired, at least in part, the research of neuroscientist Jimo Borjigin and her team at the University of Michigan in 2013. (Borjigin, J., 2013) In their abstract, the team explained that they were keen to understand how, during a near-death experience, a malfunctioning and oxygen-starved brain can create images of such lucidity and vividness. To do this, they monitored EEG signals from rats in three states of awareness: wakefulness, anaesthetization and cardiac arrest. The electrodes were implanted in the brain rather than the usual surface electrodes used in standard 10–20 EEGs. This gave a far more accurate reading of brain activity with much less chance of external electromagnetic interference. After the first wakeful measure was taken, the rats were anaesthetized, and the second measure was taken. When fully unconscious, the rats were placed in a state of cardiac arrest. To their surprise, the team observed a massive increase in gamma-wave activity in the dying rats, together with a phenomenon known as coherence. This is when all the different wave frequencies in the brain become synchronized. As we have already discovered, gamma-wave activity suggests heightened, not declining, consciousness. But even more astonishing was that the global coherence of low gamma oscillations in the 35–55 Hz range continued for more than 15 seconds after the rats were clinically dead. Further tests in which the rats were killed using carbon dioxide inhalation induced a similar surge of global coherence. The paper states, 'Our results clearly show that mammalian brain activities become transiently and highly synchronized at near-death'. (Borjigin, J., 2013)

As I discuss in greater detail in my previous book, *Cheating the Ferryman: The Revolutionary Science of Life After Death* (Peake, 2022, pp. 145–149), of possible significance here are the similarities between the surge of brain activity recorded in the dead rats' brains and a temporal lobe seizure. As previously discussed, gamma waves are the fastest brain waves possible, oscillating from 35 Hertz up to 100 Hertz. This would mean that everything perceived by the rats during such brain activity would be hyper-real. Their sense of time would slow down profoundly, especially regarding the temporal flow perceived by an observer experiencing standard brain-wave frequencies. In effect, this means that if the rats could perceive anything in this seemingly 'dead' state, a second of 'normal' time would be perceived as a much more extended period, possibly hours, weeks or years. As we have already discovered, this is precisely what is reported during near-death experiences and by individuals with other neurological conditions. These are also the perceptions reported by individuals experiencing temporal lobe epilepsy aura states. It has been discovered that gamma-wave activity in the brain is directly related to TLE seizures. (Hughes, 2008) This presents a direct link between Borjigin's findings, TLE and NDE.

It is essential to add that, in October 2013, Jimo Borjigin, Michael Wang and George Mashour, in a letter published in the journal *Biological Sciences*, replied to Chawla and Seniff's paper. (Borjigin, Wang & Mashour, 2013). In this, they agreed with the importance of gaining a scientific understanding of the dying process. They took issue with Chawla and Seneff's claim that Borjigin's earlier paper had largely confirmed their conclusions that 'end-of-life electrical surges could be responsible for near-death experiences'. Borjigin et al. argued that the two groups used different EEG devices and that BIS monitors and the SEDLine had been 'designed to monitor depths of anaesthesia during surgery and had not been validated for monitoring features of conscious information in waking humans', adding that the parameters used in their study had been. They finished the letter by stating:

> *To compare our studies with those using the BIS or other monitors, one must perform the two kinds of analyses simultaneously in the same individuals (rats or humans). This type of study may bridge human and animal studies and facilitate the understanding of the neurophysiology of the dying brain. (Borjigin, Wang & Mashour, 2013)*

There was a degree of disagreement on the implications of these results.

Not deterred, in 2017, Dr Chawla, with another group of associates based in Washington DC, expanded upon his 2009 paper by describing some new research he had been involved in regarding end-of-life electroencephalographic surges in critically ill patients. (Chawla et al., 2017) In the introduction, Chawla and his team discuss how the end-of-life surges that Chawla et al. had discussed in the 2009 paper have now gained their own acronym, ELES (End-of-Life Electroencephalographic Surges). Additionally, the discoveries of van Rijn et al. (van Rijn, Krijnen, Menting-Hermeling & Coenen, 2011) and Jimo Bojijin et al. (Borjigin, J., 2013) had effectively proven that the surges could not be attributed to external influences but were EEG signals emanating directly from the brain being monitored. Indeed, a second independent report of ELES from 2010 showed that an ELES tends to occur 30 to 180 seconds after the loss of blood pressure in the body and lasts between 15 and 240 seconds. (Auyong et al., 2010)

Chawla et al. examined the medical records and raw EEG data of 35 terminally ill patients undergoing palliative care at the ICU at George Washington University Hospital. Of the 35 patients, 13 had ELES recorded. The team concluded that they had demonstrated that ELES are 'common in patients who die in the ICU'. (Chawla & Seneff, 2013, p. 5)

One of the team was able to observe an ELES taking place as the patient died. They reported that the patient appeared unconscious with no signs of any movement, and yet the neuromonitoring showed that the patient was in a state of full consciousness. From this, it can be assumed that had such levels of 'awareness' been recorded in the brain of a person undergoing surgery, extreme actions would have had to have been taken to avoid powerful trauma, both physical and psychological. Indeed, what implications does this have for cases such as Pam Reynolds's?

In their conclusion, they cited supporting evidence from the findings of Jimo Borjigin et al., stating that this demonstrated 'cohesive gamma-wave electrical activity after death'. (Chawla & Seneff, 2013, p. 8) They also asked why it is that while approaching 50 per cent of terminally ill patients experience ELES, a small but significant number do not. If it was, as they describe, an evolutionary 'last-gasp survival mechanism', why are ELES not found in all cases? And, of possibly even more significance, why is ELES never observed in patients who are diagnosed as being clinically brain dead?

However, I can confirm that Pierpaolo Pani and his associates presented further evidence for post-mortem brain activity at Sapienza University in Rome in 2018. In a letter published in the journal *Resuscitation*, they reported that they had observed the presence of cortical electrical activity persisting for about two hours after death by cardiac arrest of an adult male macaque monkey. As with the human patients of Chawla et al., the spike in activity started before death and continued afterwards. What is fascinating about this discovery is that Pani et al. stated in their abstract that:

Importantly, this activity appears after a period of relative silence, and it is characterized by a peculiar temporal relationship between LFP and MUA in several electrodes, suggesting a non-local origin. (Pani, Giarroccoa, Brunamonti & Stefano, 2018)

Interestingly, in the letter, Pani et al. argue that their discovery of the 120-minute post-mortem cortical electrical activity contradicts the tens of seconds reported by Jimo Borjigin and her team at the University of Michigan in 2013. (Borjigin, J., 2013)

In this respect, we need to discuss a series of related but morally questionable decapitation experiments that were undertaken by Clementina van Rijn and her associates in 2010 and reported in January 2011. (van Rijn, Krijnen, Menting-Hermeling & Coenen, 2011)

In justification, it seems that the series of experiments involving the beheading of live rats was to decide whether such a process is a humane method of euthanasia for awake animals. The experimenters decapitated 22 male Wister rats aged between 6 and 8 months. Nine rats were guillotined while fully conscious, and eight were anaesthetised. During the procedure, all the animals' brains were monitored with an EEG before, during and for at least 5 minutes after execution.

The results were startling. It took on average 17 seconds for the electrical activity in the decapitated brain of the previously awake rats to flatline (technically known as being 'iso-electric'). Furthermore, the post-decapitation brain activity was similar in awake and anaesthetised animals. One conclusion was that 'the animal's consciousness is briefly enhanced immediately after the neck cut'. In other words, an anaesthetised rat's previously unconscious brain becomes aware AFTER it is decapitated from its body.

But what was totally unexpected was that it was discovered that around 50 seconds after the decapitation, when the brain is in a state of iso-electricity, a large-amplitude wave suddenly appeared. This differed slightly between the previously 'awake' rats and those who had been anaesthetized. For the latter group, the wave appeared after 80 seconds.

Interestingly, the authors noted similarities with the findings of Chawla's 2009 experiment.

In the summing up of their findings, the team coined the terrifying phrase 'the wave of death':

> *The wave thus might reflect a massive opening of ion channels: a depolarization wave. The still functioning of these ion channels in the period before the wave might be responsible for the observed difference in the pre-wave and post-wave power of the EEG. Hence, it is thought that the wave represents the synchronous death of brain neurons, expressed in a 'wave of death'. (van Rijn, Krijnen, Menting-Hermeling & Coenen, 2011)*

In 2014, a group of New Zealand-based researchers at Massey University followed up on the findings with a similar experiment to van Rijn et al. This time, all ten rats were anaesthetised and then beheaded. Again, at around 15 seconds after decapitation, significant increases in brain activity were noted, specifically in two areas of the EEG power spectrum, at the median frequency (F50) and F95. (Kongara, McIlhone, Kells & Johnson, 2014)

In 2015, Borjigin continued her research in this critical area and, together with a large international team, she published an article in the academic journal *Neuroscience*. In this, the team found consistent heart rate changes in rats undergoing experimental asphyxia, including four distinct stages, starting with the onset of asphyxia and ending in ventricular tachycardia and asystole. (Li et al., 2015)

The team made a series of continuous electrocorticographic recordings using electrodes implanted in the rats' left and right frontal, parietal and occipital lobes. These revealed increased coherence in the gamma band (65 to 115 Hz) and the theta band (5 to 10 Hz) between all cortical sites, with increased functional connectivity between the frontal, parietal and occipital cortices in multiple frequency bands. The degree of connectivity between neural networks, feedback and feed-forward directions in which network connectivity between brain regions increased, and the frequency band in which connectivity was principally observed varied consistently in relationship to the stage of asphyxia.

Dramatic surges in the levels of multiple neurotransmitters were reported, including norepinephrine, serotonin, dopamine, GABA and acetylcholine in both the frontal and occipital cortex, and levels remained elevated for as long as 20 minutes following the onset of experimental asphyxia.

They conjectured that surges in neurotransmitters in the first minute of asphyxia may help explain widely reported features of NDE phenomenology. They postulated that the observed 30-fold increase in central norepinephrine might be consistent with transiently increased alertness, attention and arousal; a 12-fold increase in central dopamine may be consistent with increases in arousal, attention cognition and affective emotions; and a 20-fold increase in central serotonin may help explain visual hallucinations and mystical experiences. The authors inferred that the observed surge in synchronized cortical gamma activity stimulated by asphyxia signifies an internally aroused brain and supports the hypothesis that the mammalian brain is capable of high levels of complex information processing at near death.

In relation to these findings, further support was supplied in February 2022 when a paper appeared in the peer-reviewed academic journal *Frontiers in Ageing Neuroscience*. (Vicente et al., 2022) Under the reasonably innocuous title of 'Enhanced Interplay of Neuronal Coherence and Coupling in the Dying Human Brain', the article described what may be one of the most astonishing discoveries about what happens in the dying human brain in the history of science.

What was also of interest was the geographic scope of the authors, who were located in China, Estonia, Canada and the USA, and were describing an event that took place in Germany involving an 87-year-old Canadian male who was being treated in a hospital emergency unit after a fall in which he sustained a head injury. After a series of tests, it was concluded that his 'Glasgow Coma Scale' (GCS) was 15.

The GCS is the most common scoring system used to describe the level of consciousness in a person following a traumatic brain injury. It is used to help gauge the severity of an acute brain injury. Fifteen is considered to be very minor. However, he rapidly deteriorated to a score of 10, which concerned the attending physicians. Although his gag reflexes and corneal reaction were preserved, one of his pupils was much larger than the other (an effect known as aniscoria). Under a CT scan, it was discovered that he had several bilateral acute subdural haematomas, areas of bleeding in the outermost layer of the brain, between the inner surface of the skull and the surface of the brain. He was operated on to clear the blood and was stable for two days before he declined again. An electroencephalography (EEG) scan was obtained, which showed that his left hemisphere had gone into a state known as status epilepticus, in which a series of epileptic seizures take place one after the other. In this case, at least 12 were recorded. His breathing then became very laboured. It was agreed with the family that a DNR (Do Not Resuscitate) status be applied, and soon afterwards, the patient died. During this time, his brain continued to be monitored using the EEG. And what they discovered was astonishing, as was reflected in the introduction to the paper:

> *Here, we report what is to our knowledge the first continuous EEG recording from the human brain in the transition phase to death. We find decreased theta activity and an increase of absolute gamma power after bilateral suppression of neuronal activity. Post cardiac arrest, relative gamma-band power is increased while delta, beta and alpha bands show reduced activity. Finally, we observe strong modulation of narrow- and broad-band gamma activity by the alpha band.*

This is of significance. There was decreased theta activity and an increase in 'absolute gamma power' as cardiac arrest started. This is, in layperson's terms, the point of death. 'Post cardiac arrest' means after the person has died.

In the discussion section, the authors refer to the paper by Borjigin et al. (2013) and observe the similarities. Borjigin and her associates made a point about how, in the dying rodents, an increase of low-gamma-band frequencies was observed 10 to 30 seconds after cardiac arrest. But there were intriguing and possibly significant differences. One of these can be observed when comparing phase-amplitude coupling (cross-frequency coupling): post cardiac arrest, delta, theta and alpha modulate low-gamma activity in the rodents (Borjigin et al., 2013), whereas, in the human brain, such modulation occurs in all gamma bands and is mainly mediated by alpha waves, and to a lesser degree by theta rhythms. The alpha band is thought to critically interfere with cognitive processes by inhibiting irrelevant or disruptive networks.

This is so because it is known that the 'cross-coupling between alpha and gamma activity is involved in cognitive processes and memory recall in healthy subjects'. And then, the authors throw in this incredible observation:

> *it is intriguing to speculate that such activity could support*
> *a last 'recall of life' that may take place in the near-death*
> *state. (Vicente et al., 2022, p. 9)*

This is precisely what I suggested may have been happening with Borjigin's rats in my last book. (Peake, 2022, pp. 145–149)

But it is important to note that a degree of caution in over-reacting to this discovery was argued by NDE luminaries Bruce Greyson, Pim van Lommel and Peter Fenwick in a 'commentary' on the paper published in the same journal on 18 May 2022. (Greyson, van Lommel & Fenwick, 2022). They argued that the EEG recordings, as described, did not show an absolute gamma activity increase after cardiac arrest. Indeed, it showed a decrease, pointing out that only the relative amount of gamma increased compared to alpha, beta and delta. Also, increased gamma and gamma synchronization are not exclusively related to consciousness perception but have been observed in several brain activities. (Muthukumaraswamy, 2013) They also suggested that the gamma-wave activity could have been caused by muscle contractions, pointing out that this type of contamination is well known.

Indeed, a few years earlier, in 2013, and in response to Borjigin's original paper, Bruce Greyson was again determined to question the idea that the discovery of brain activity during the cardiac arrest of rats could be associated with the near-death experience. He questioned the use of the term 'hyper-aroused' with regard to the rats' brains and argued that what happens in a rat's brain may not apply to a human brain.

Although these points seem reasonable, I cannot help but feel that the enthusiastic way in which Greyson et al. are willing to dismiss the findings of Vicente et al. may be related to the fact that all three are very much advocates of the 'survivalist' position with regards to NDEs, and any form of neurological explanation based on brain activity suggests that the NDE is a brain-generated phenomenon. Indeed, I find it curious that Dr Fenwick, whose own book, as we have seen earlier, is full of experiences of the 'panoramic life review' – for example, the much-cited case of Allan Pring, who was given glimpses of what can only be described as a speeded-up video of his future life (Fenwick & Fenwick, 1995, pp. 120–121) – takes this stance. Is it not more likely that the source of such information is brain-programmed memories than something outside of the experiencer's brain?

The latest research exploring this crucial area was described in a paper published on 1 May 2023, in the journal *Neuroscience*. Gang Xu and a group of neuroscientists, again including Jimo Borjigin, describe how the team investigated further evidence for the brain's gamma oscillations and functional connectivity at the point of death. They analysed the electroencephalogram and electrocardiogram signals in four comatose dying patients before and after the withdrawal of ventilatory support.

The objective of this study was to discover if there is any evidence of high-level awareness in the brains of dying patients, awareness that could justify the perceptions reported by near-death experiencers. For example, there is evidence that the visual and hearing systems in the brain are fully functional or at least functional enough to create dream states. It has been discovered that the stimulation of two brain areas, the occipital and parietal cortices, can create visual images that have no relationship with any external visual stimulus. (Mazzi, Mancini & Savazzi, 2014) This can be linked with how it is known that the temporal and parietal cortices are crucial to perceptual awareness. From this, it can be concluded that the area where these three cortices come together, the temporo-parietal-occipital (TPO) junction, is where visuospatial processing occurs. Indeed, it has been shown that this area is involved in dreaming. (Siclari, et al., 2017) We discussed this area extensively earlier in our enquiry, and it is now evident that some crucial correlations have been drawn.

However, the most exciting thing is how these discoveries can be linked to the earlier referenced Borjigin et al. paper from 2017. In their summing-up, the team made the following comment regarding their findings:

> *Our results clearly indicate that mammalian brain activities*
> *become transiently and highly synchronized at near-death.*
> *(Borjigin, J., 2013)*

So, whatever the near-death experience is, it is part of the dying process or, more specifically, what happens in the brain as it prepares for death. This does not mean it is not a 'real' event, as modern quantum mechanics tells us that 'reality' is a slippery concept. However, from our present understanding of neurology and neuro-chemistry, a model of dying can be formulated, which is most neurologists' position. They believe that their 'Dying Brain Hypothesis' successfully explains the NDE. It is my task to present you with the facts supporting this model and allow you to decide whether the case is made.

THE DYING BRAIN HYPOTHESIS
The Dying Brain Hypothesis – Introduction

As we have already discovered, sceptics have long argued that NDEs are purely brain-generated hallucinations created by the brain during times of extreme stress. This is, not surprisingly, known as the 'dying brain hypothesis'. Central to this is the idea that the NDE is caused by the brain entering a state known as 'neural disinhibition' induced by the brain being starved of oxygen, termed anoxia. But this can also be triggered by several neurological factors such as illness, trauma, confusion, pathology, epilepsy, migraine, drug use, sensory deprivation and brain stimulation. These can all be associated with the generation of hallucinations.

This model raises a huge question: if the NDE is organically induced, then why don't all patients close to death report NDE-like experiences? One explanation is that only some individuals are predisposed to potent neurochemical activity in the temporal lobes. In 2004, a study by University of Arizona psychologists Willoughby Britton and Richard Bootzin showed that individuals who had reported NDEs had more temporal lobe epileptiform EEG activity than control subjects, and the activity was primarily found in the left hemisphere. The researchers also noted that the NDErs reported altered sleep patterns with shorter nightly sleep duration and delayed REM sleep compared to the control group. (Britton & Bootzin, 2004) Other research has postulated that rapid eye movement (REM) sleep induces hallucinatory experiences that have many similarities with those described in NDE states.

The Dying Brain Hypothesis – TLE and NDEs

One of the great mysteries of the human brain is the causes and effects of epilepsy. What is of particular significance with regard to our enquiry is the relationship between epilepsy-facilitated seizures and the status of the dying brain. As we shall discover later, in his influential *Skeptic* article, Jason Braithwaite, when describing the dying brain hypothesis, points out that the brain does not react well to any changes in its chemical structure. As we have discussed, the most critical brain cells seem to be the neurons, which send messages across the brain by releasing and receiving chemicals that contain the messages. These, not unsurprisingly, are known as neurotransmitters. Some are excitatory, and others are inhibitory. As the words suggest, excitatory neurotransmitters stimulate actions in the receptor sites of the neurons and inhibitory inhibit reactions. The primary inhibitory neurotransmitter in the human nervous system is gamma-aminobutyric acid, or GABA for short. This is synthesized from another neurotransmitter, glutamate, which is considered responsible for the brain synchronization observed at death. (Lee et al., 2014). So, a release of GABA will lessen individual neurons' ability to receive, create or send neurochemical messages to other nerve cells. And this is where it gets interesting. It has been discovered that just a 10–15 per cent reduction in the inhibition facilitated by GABA is sufficient to hugely increase seizure propagation in the brain.

In this regard, it has long been known that seizures can be generated in a non-epileptic brain. Indeed, seizure generation recognizes that the neuronal mechanisms that participate in seizure generation are precisely those that are used in and essential to normal brain function. (Schwartzkrion, 1997, pp. 853–854) So the question has to be asked: what possible function can seizure generation have and, more importantly, what possible evolutionary advantage can a seizure-prone brain give to any species, particularly high-functioning primates like *homo sapiens*?

Could it be that we have evolved such a neurological state to facilitate death and that we all die in a seizure? After all, it may be that we are all born into this world in a brain state similar to epilepsy. When electrodes have been attached to a woman's stomach in late pregnancy, the brainwaves of the foetus are usually recorded as slow delta waves at a frequency of less than three cycles per second. However, this regular pattern is sometimes interrupted by more significant discharges similar to the spike recordings obtained from adults in an epileptic attack. As the baby approaches full term, these convulsive spikes become more frequent until, at birth, they are almost continuous as the child thrashes its way into the world. The implication seems to be that we are all born with something like epilepsy. And, if we consider that the surge of brain activity discovered by Jimo Borjigin and her team at Michigan University in 2013 can be applied to all mammals, then it is reasonable to conclude that we also die in an epileptic seizure.

This is precisely what would be observed if my 'Cheating the Ferryman' (CTF) hypothesis is correct. (Peake, 2022) To consider this as a viable model, we have to differentiate between near-death experiences and real-death experiences. When somebody is in an RDE state, they will experience a greater level of disinhibition than during an NDE. For example, in an RDE, the panoramic life review would be far more intense and meaningful than in an NDE. So, the reports we have received from NDE survivors are just a snapshot of the true, all-encompassing RDE-facilitated panoramic life review.

Indeed, Brathwaite adds to his support of the CTF model by discussing the role of epilepsy and epileptic-like seizures observed in the brain during RDE-like circumstances. The brain cannot tolerate any form of abnormal states and usually reacts to them. This tends to be seizure or disinhibition states. He writes:

> Very small changes in the neural environment have been shown to be more than sufficient to impact on the fine balance maintained in the brain. For example, a 10–15% reduction in GABA inhibition is sufficient to significantly increase seizure propagation in cortical tissue, and changes of a few millimoles in extracellular potassium levels can turn a stable neural population into an epileptogenic one. (Chagnac-Amitai & Connors, 1 989; Haglund & Schwartzkroin, 1 990; Korn, Giacchino, Chamberlin & Dingledine, 1 987) The ranges of these values are well within those encountered under normal brain functioning. The real question then becomes not one

of whether disinhibition or seizure could be involved in contexts conducive to NDE but, as Schwartzkroin (1997) states, why seizures are not indeed far more common and why are we not all having seizures constantly! (Braithwaite, 2008, p. 12)

The important points here are where he states that 'reduction in GABA inhibition is sufficient to significantly increase seizure propagation in cortical tissue, and changes of a few millimoles in extracellular potassium levels can turn a stable neural population into an epileptogenic one'. He then focuses on the question asked by Schwartzkroin as to 'why seizures are not indeed far more common and why are we are not all having seizures constantly'.

Braithwaite next makes a critical point. He asks the simple question of how any form of memory creation and retrieval can occur in a brain with no neuronal activity:

Applied to the NDE, this means that there must have been sufficient neural activity to encode the experience, to represent the experience, and to store the experience (even a glimpse of an afterlife would require this). As far as current science is concerned, it is not at all clear how a memory of an experience can occur without the use of memory itself. The very fact that these experiences were 'remembered' in the first place suggests that memory itself was functioning and encoding at the time of the experience (meaning there was neural activity in those brain regions during the experience, which may indeed have been responsible for the experience). (Braithwaite, 2008, p. 12)

Of course, if my 'Cheating the Ferryman' model has any form of validity (Peake, 2005), then the answer to the mystery of the near-death experience will be found not in parapsychology but in neurology and neurochemistry.

Indeed, for many materialist reductionists, the only answer will be found in physiology and the mechanics of the human brain. And this 'organic hypothesis' is where we will now turn our attention.

THE ORGANIC HYPOTHESIS
The Organic Hypothesis – Introduction

Central to our anthropological survey of the near-death experience in various cultures was how these traditions linked life after death with altered states of consciousness. Meditation is linked to all the cultures reviewed, from shamanic beliefs to the various forms of Hinduism, Buddhism and many modern esoteric traditions.

In both Buddhism and Hinduism is found a tradition that has its roots in shamanic practices, using meditation to access higher levels of consciousness. This is known as samadhi. This is a state of undifferentiated 'beingness' in which time and space cease to be, and an inner perception of the real, timeless universe is perceived. Over the centuries, various techniques and processes have been perfected to facilitate immediate access to the state of samadhi. These include Hatha Yoga postures, rigorous breathing practices called Pranayama, focused levels of meditation or the working with subtle vibrations by the repetition of certain resonant words (mantra). One of the most intriguing is known as Khecarī Mudrā. This involves placing the tongue above the palate and rolling it back as far as possible. It is believed that this awakens the spiritual energies in the body by facilitating the rising of the kundalini (a form of energy) from its sleep. We will return to the significance of this enigmatic concept in greater detail later. The word mudra is actually an amalgamation of two Sanskrit words, *mut*, which means 'bliss', and *ra*, which means 'to draw'. So here, we have an exact meaning. It is a process by which the practitioner draws bliss.

This state is discussed in Hinduism, Buddhism, Sikhism and esoteric Islam (Sufism), as well as many schools of Yoga. One factor that links all these different approaches to the same state of consciousness is that it is regularly accompanied by a sweet taste at the back of the throat that goes by many names: amrita, ambrosia, the Living Water, the Nectar of Sublime Awareness and many others. The process by which the amrita drips down the back of the throat is known as *shaktipat*. This Sanskrit word is made up of *shakti* (psychic energy) and *pāta* (to fall).

A phenomenon associated with *shaktipat* is the perception of an intense white light that emanates from within and engulfs everything. This white light sometimes takes the shape of a tunnel or vortex. It is usually accompanied by intense buzzing and whirring sounds. So here we have some of the classic NDE traits being experienced during an altered state of consciousness brought about by a curious liquid that falls down the back of the throat. What is of even greater significance is that both the words ambrosia and amrita have the same Sanskrit root, *amrta*, which means 'elixir of immortality'. Indeed, it is of possible significance that the Greek word 'nectar' has as its root the much earlier Proto-European words *nek* ('death') and *tar* ('to overcome'). This substance is believed to overcome death and place the recipient of the liquid in a location outside space and time. Is it this nek-tar that brings about the near-death experience? And what exactly is it?

The Organic Hypothesis – Endorphins

Our first port of call is to explore the substances known as endorphins. Endorphins are one of a number of brain chemicals collectively known as neuropeptides. These act as natural stress-relievers that also serve as painkillers. The word is a contraction of 'endogenous morphine'. The hypothalamus and pituitary glands usually release them, but they may also come from other parts of the body. They were first discovered in 1973 and, eight years later, in 1981, Daniel B. Carr of the Endocrine Unit at Harvard Medical School wrote a letter to *The Lancet* suggesting that endorphins may be involved in the near-death experience. (Carr, 14

February 1981) He argued that 'peptide neuromodulators released into the brain shortly before death may trigger complex psychological responses apart from passivity and analgesia'. Citing the discoveries of Karlis Osis and Erlendur Haraldsson on close encounters with death, which had been published in 1975, he observed that the subjects reported euphoria, involuntary recall of memories, a sense of disassociation from the body and auditory, olfactory and visual hallucinations. From this, he suggested that the cause might be what he termed a 'limbic lobe syndrome'. Such was the interest engendered by this letter that he subsequently expanded his ideas into a paper that was published the following year in *Anabiosis*, the then journal of the International Association of Near-Death Studies (IANDS).

If it is correct that endorphins facilitate the NDE, then it should be the case that all NDEs are pleasant and enjoyable. But this does not seem to be the case. Although rarely reported in the literature, negative and 'hellish' experiences do occur, as do similar experiences facilitated by DMT, 5-MeO-DMT and other entheogens. Indeed, some researchers have argued that horrific NDEs are far more common than previously suspected. (Atwater, 1992)

In 1996, Dr Karl Jansen, then of the Maudsley Hospital in south London, argued in a contributory chapter to an anthology on near-death experiences that another agent rather than endorphins may facilitate them. He argued that the artificially created hallucinogenic anaesthetic ketamine can reproduce all the features of the near-death experience. (Jansen, K. L., 1996) Ketamine was first used as an anaesthetic on wounded US soldiers during the Vietnam War. As Jansen observed, although very effective, it was never used on civilians because it had some peculiar side effects. Since then, ketamine has become a very popular (but illegal) recreational drug. This means that here are many available accounts of its effects, one of which Jansen cited in a no-longer-available paper. In this, the person gave an interesting description of what they perceived:

Almost from the beginning of my ketamine adventures, the trip would start with a ringing in my ears. The room would disappear, and I would suddenly find myself going down tunnels at high speed. And I mean fast. Sometimes it was a tube, sometimes like going through the plumbing behind the fabric of everything, and sometimes I would be on an underground railway, but I wasn't in a carriage. I seemed to be actually mounted on the rail itself. Then I would suddenly arrive. On one memorable trip, I came out into a golden Light. I rose into the Light and to my astonishment, having been raised an atheist by atheists, found myself having an unspoken 'interchange' with the Light, which I believed to be God. (Jansen, K., 1998)

In this experience, you will recognize a number of the NDE 'traits'that are used to identify a near-death experience. With this in mind, I am sure that if this person had completed the Greyson questionnaire, there would be no doubt that they had experienced an NDE.

So why does this artificially created chemical so effectively reproduce many, if not all, the NDE traits that the brain produces naturally during times of extreme stress?

Once in the brain, ketamine attaches itself to a glutamate receptor called the N-methyl-D-aspartate or the NMDA receptor. You will recall that glutamate is one of a group of chemical substances known as neurotransmitters and is known to be the critical neurotransmitter within the temporal lobes, the hippocampus and the frontal lobes. So, when ketamine is introduced into the brain, it disrupts the flow of this crucial chemical messenger.

As a reminder, it is helpful to imagine these receptors as tiny harbours with several docks. What ketamine does, in effect, is to blockade the harbour, therefore stopping any glutamate from getting through to its receptors. Generally, glutamate is not harmful, but vast amounts are generated under certain circumstances, causing what is termed a glutamate flood. Excessive amounts of glutamate can lead to the death of brain cells by a process called excitotoxicity. What happens is that glutamate opens the harbour even wider and, in doing so, allows water to rush in, causing the neuron cell to literally burst apart. This process of cell death can also be brought about by a lack of oxygen (hypoxia), low blood sugar (hypoglycaemia) and, significantly, epilepsy.

The circumstances that lead to a glutamate flood exist at times of extreme threat or crisis, particularly during life-threatening situations. However, it is counter-productive when a potentially damaging flood of chemicals enters the brain, particularly if the life-threatening situation proves to be a false alarm.

Jansen argued that during a real near-death experience, the glutamate flood is prevented by the internal generation of a substance that protects the NMDA receptors by binding to one of the 'docks' in the NMDA 'harbour'. This 'dock' is called the PCP receptor. The substance must, by its very nature, have a very similar effect to ketamine on the psychological state of the person involved. This endogamous (internally created) drug is the trigger for natural near-death experiences.

So, what could this endogenously generated substance, known to the ancients as nek-tar, soma or ambrosia, be? Well, it seems that it may have been found, and there is growing evidence that we may not only be close to understanding what facilitates the near-death experience but also why it happens.

The Organic Hypothesis – DMT and 5-Meo-DMT

As you will recall from our earlier discussion, neurotransmitters are chemicals released by a neuron (brain) cell to stimulate other neurons in its vicinity and transmit impulses from one cell to another. This facilitates the transfer of messages throughout the whole nervous system.

Since their first discovery in the 1930s, 50 or so neurotransmitters have been found, the most critical being serotonin, noradrenaline, glutamate and a group of pain-killing opiates called endorphins. However, one internally-generated substance was to remain a mystery. In 1972, Nobel Prize-winning chemist Julius Axelrod made a shocking discovery.

In a routine test of some brain material, Axelrod found traces of a substance we have already discussed in passing, the powerful hallucinogen dimethyltryptamine. Known as DMT, this chemical is a member of the amine family. Seven years earlier, another amine had been found in human blood. This was a surprise as, until then, amines had only been found in the cells of invertebrates. The discovery of an amine in the brain was a total puzzle. It was believed that these chemicals had no function within the human body. Why was DMT in the brain?

The mysterious function of amines within the body was further questioned in 2001 when a new receptor cell family was discovered. Called Trace Amine-Associated Receptors (TAARs), these cells were like locks in which only one key could be used: an amine. What this suggested was that amines are a form of neurotransmitter. (Liberles, 2009) As DMT is a form of amine, its reason for being in the brain was apparent: DMT exists in the brain because it is designed to work with it.

DMT is known to be one of the most potent hallucinogenic substance yet discovered. Shamans have used it for centuries to communicate with the 'upper' and 'lower' worlds. But now, neurologists have found that the brain may generate it naturally and that DMT is a natural element of how the brain functions.

Some scientists believe there is one specific place in the brain where DMT is produced – the pineal gland. Indeed, researcher Dr Rick Strassman of the University of New Mexico has further suggested that DMT may be responsible for the near-death experience itself. (Strassman, R., 2001)

We have, on several occasions, referenced the astonishing discovery of Dr Jimo Borjigin and her team regarding the discovery of post-mortem brain activity in the brains of euthanized rats. However, in another experiment, she made another equally stunning discovery – and one that is directly relevant to our enquiry here.

Dr Borjigin worked with Dr Steven Barker's Analytical Systems Laboratory at Louisiana State University. Barker was interested in testing the brains of live rats to see if he could isolate what neurotransmitters were active at the time of the rats' spike in neurological activity. If this could be shown to be a particular neurochemical, we may be closer to understanding the near-death experience. With funding from an organization known as the Cottonwood Research Foundation, Barker did a series of tests on the brain material and found an enzyme's presence. He was looking for evidence of our already discussed friend, dimethyltryptamine (DMT).

As we have already discussed, DMT and its associate substance 5-MeO-DMT are powerful hallucinogens that bring about profound experiences. Of significance is that the reported sensations and perceptions are, again, somewhat similar to those perceived during a near-death experience. The founder of Cottonwood Research, Dr Rick Strassman, has long been associated with research into the true nature of DMT. In the early 1990s, Strassman was involved in an extensive US government-funded research project into the effects of the substance. In his book *DMT: The Spirit Molecule*, Strassman suggested that DMT was highly likely to be active in the human brain. This is unsurprising, as DMT has been found in virtually all living things. This is best described by chemist Alexander Shulgin:

> *DMT is . . . in this flower here, in that tree over there, and in yonder animal. [It] is, most simply, almost everywhere you choose to look. Indeed, it is getting to the point where one should report where DMT is not found rather than where it is. (Shulgin & Shulgin, 1997, p. 247)*

Strassman was sure that DMT would be discovered in one particular location within the brain: the mysterious pineal gland. Furthermore, he believed that the pineal gland may indeed create DMT as an endogenous (internal) neurotransmitter. He thought this may be the case because:

It possesses the highest level of the necessary enzymes and
precursors; the pineal gland is the most reasonable place
for DMT formation to occur. (Strassman, R., 2001, p. 67)

In February 2009, Strassman's suspicion that DMT was a possible human neurotransmitter was confirmed in a paper written by University of Wisconsin-Madison pharmacologist Arnold Ruoho and published in the academic periodical *Science*. In the article, he described how his team had discovered that DMT activated a receptor known as sigma-1. (Ruoho, 2009)

Around this time, Dr Jimo Borjigin, whose ground-breaking discoveries of brain activity in dead rats we encountered earlier, became interested in the role of DMT in the mammalian brain. She had been researching the pineal gland for many years but had not heard of Strassman's work. When she discovered his theories on internally-generated DMT she contacted him and they agreed to work together and pool their knowledge and resources. This led to a collaboration that resulted in an influential paper published in 2013, explicitly finding direct traces of DMT in the pineal gland of a rat for the first time. (Barker, Borjigin, Lomnicka & Strassman, 2013)

The suspicion that the subjective perceptions perceived during an NDE were facilitated by endogenous (internally-generated) DMT was reinforced a few years later by the findings of Christopher Timmermann and his team based at Imperial College in London. These were published in 2018 in the academic journal *Frontiers of Psychology*. (Timmermann et al., 2018) A group of volunteers were administered either a dose of DMT or a placebo and were then asked to complete Bruce Greyson's NDE Scale questionnaire which we discussed earlier. These results were compared with the responses of individuals who had experienced actual NDEs. There were significant similarities. In their conclusion, the team made the following observation:

This study's findings warrant further investigation
to address the putatively strong overlap between the

phenomenology and neurobiology of DMT (and other psychedelic) experiences and 'actual' near-death experiences, particularly given some of the scientifically problematic yet influential claims that have been made about NDEs. (Timmermann et al., 2018)

Inspired by the Imperial College results, Borjigin worked again with Strassman and other researchers to explore in greater detail the evidence for DMT in the mammalian brain. What the team found was that the enzyme indolethylamine N-methyltransferase (IMMT), a crucial catalyst needed for DMT to be synthesized from tryptamine, is in the brain, together with another enzyme critical for this transformation process, aromatic-L-amino acid decarboxylase (AADC).

This discovery offers the first clear and plausible mechanistic explanation of how a mammalian brain may create DMT. Even more exciting was the discovery that these enzymes are to be found not only in the pineal gland but also in many other parts of the brain, including the neocortex and the hippocampus.

But there was more. In the paper, the team made the following comment:

A significant increase of DMT levels in the rat visual cortex was observed following induction of experimental cardiac arrest, a finding independent of an intact pineal gland. These results show for the first time that the rat brain is capable of synthesizing and releasing DMT at concentrations comparable to known monoamine neurotransmitters and raise the possibility that this phenomenon may occur similarly in human brains. (Dean et al., 2019)

This has extraordinary implications for our discussion here and my own model of the near-death experience. Borjigin and her associates replicated the experiment in rats who had had their pineal gland surgically removed.

This brought about no difference in cortical DMT levels – suggesting that the pineal gland is not a major DMT-producing part of the brain, something contrary to Strassman's longstanding hypothesis, but that the hallucinogenic molecule is generated quite widely across different parts of the animal's brain, particularly the visual cortex, the place that creates internal images and the perception of light. Furthermore, this was discovered to be most active when the rats were placed in cardiac arrest. It seems that DMT is programmed to be released across the brain with a focus on the visual processing system at the point of death.

From this, it is reasonable to conclude that the link between endogenous DMT and the near-death experience has been made. This in no way invalidates the reality of the experience but does suggest a facilitator.

Individuals who have taken DMT consistently report that as soon as the DMT takes effect, there is a sensation of being shot down a tunnel at great speed and finding, at the end of the tunnel, an alternative reality inhabited by entities that offer guidance and advice. Even more curious is that these entities seem to recognize the DMTer and welcome them back as if the DMT world is the real one and our perceptual universe is an illusion or a hallucination. A personal friend of mine, who was one of the volunteers involved in Timmerman's Imperial College research, told me that on arriving in the DMT world the first time, he was approached by an entity who told him in no uncertain terms that he should not be using DMT to enter its realm. Two weeks later, he was back in the laboratory and had the DMT injected into his veins to find himself in exactly the same environment as two weeks before. Then, to his utter astonishment, the same entity approached him and stated, 'I told you last time, this is not the way to do it.'

This suggests that whatever this being was (or is), it has an independent existence from the mind of my associate and, indeed, seemed to be waiting for his return. So, who are these beings?

In September 2020, studies at the Center for Psychedelic and Consciousness Research, Johns Hopkins School of Medicine, under the leadership of psychiatrist Dr Alan Davis, sought to examine what kinds of entities people encounter during the DMT experience. (Davis et al., 2020) They had 2,561 individuals complete an online survey in which they were asked to describe the single most memorable entity encounter after taking DMT. The most common descriptive labels used were spirit guide, alien and helper. Interestingly, 41 per cent said they felt fearful during the encounter, but the majority did not have this sensation. In their summation, Davis et al wrote:

> *Most respondents endorsed that the entity had the attributes of being conscious, intelligent, and benevolent, existed in some actual but different dimension of reality, and continued to exist after the encounter. Respondents endorsed receiving a message (69%) or a prediction about the future (19%) from the experience. (Davis et al., 2020, p. 220)*

Indeed, more than half of the respondents considered the encounters to be among the most meaningful, spiritual and psychological events of their lives. With this in mind, the team came to the following intriguing conclusion:

> *N, N-dimethyltryptamine-occasioned entity encounter experiences have many similarities to non-drug entity encounter experiences such as those described in religious, alien abduction, and near-death contexts. Aspects of the experience and its interpretation produced profound and enduring ontological changes in worldview. (Davis et al., 2020, p. 1020)*

But the entities sometimes also manifested as elves and, rather disturbingly, as insectoid or reptilian humanoids, exactly the entities encountered during many reported UFO 'abduction' cases, specifically those involving surgical procedures and dismemberment.

I am surprised to discover that academic researchers, such as Alan Davis and his team, seem to be unaware of the earlier research in this field by Lorraine Davis, which was published in the *Journal of Near-Death Studies* in 1988. I believe that the results of these various avenues of research need to be taken into account. Sadly, academic 'siloism' is still all too prevalent.

Lorraine Davis used the questionnaires from Kenneth Ring's book *Heading Towards Omega* (1984) as her information source. She sent these to 206 individuals who had experienced UFO encounters. Of interest here is that she was particularly interested in whether the respondees reported apocalyptic visions similar to those reported by some of Ring's NDErs.

A UFO experience, which can last from just a few seconds to hours, may consist of (1) sighting an unusual light in the night sky, often moving but sometimes stationary, and/or (2) sighting an unusual object, often circular but sometimes cigar- or other-shaped, out-of-doors that often moves soundlessly through the sky, frequently in mountainous areas; and/or (3) what might be termed an 'inner experience', sometimes fearful, sometimes occurring in or near a bedroom, which can involve dreams, out-of-body experiences, hypnosis and/or time loss. Some individuals experience being on board a UFO and seeing beings who can communicate with, physically examine, advise and/or hypnotize the abductee. The experience may include witnesses who are often, but not always, aware of what the abductee is experiencing.

I found the account of one of Davis's respondees of significance in that it had many themes that suggested a case of REM intrusion and/or sleep paralysis, themes we have discussed extensively earlier. Davis paraphrases this person's description (at the time of the response, she was a 56-year-old homemaker, but she was actually recalling an incident that happened 30 years before):

At approximately 2 a.m. a small white light entered through the top of her bedroom window, grew in size and color (yellow-orange-red) as it traveled down the window to the floor, along the baseboard and toward the bed. It changed from a ball to the shape of a fire to a golden glow with nondescript lines and shadows. It left the room following exactly the same pattern but in reverse order. The experience left the respondent 'frozen' on the spot and trembling. She subsequently checked the entire house for signs of fire but found none. She concluded her description by saying: 'It was not unusual for me to awaken and study from 2 a.m. to 5 a.m.. . . . My mind was sharp and functioning best at this time of morning. This was not a dream.' (Davis, 1988, p. 245)

I cannot help but link this to a section of my own 2019 book *The Hidden Universe: An Investigation into Non-Human Intelligences.* (Peake, *The Hidden Universe: An Investigation into Non-Human Intelligences*, 2019) Below is a precis of an incident I discussed in detail there.

In 1992, a 13-year-old boy, James Basil, had an uncanny experience while lying in bed. He stretched out his hand to come in contact with another hand, but this was not human. It was smooth and lizard-like, with curled fingers. He then opened his eyes and saw two aliens standing at the end of his bed. This was the start of a series of encounters with these creatures over a period of years.

In 1997, he discussed his experiences with somebody whose work we have encountered many times in our enquiries, Susan Blackmore. He contacted Blackmore as part of his student project. Blackmore was sure that he was suffering from a form of sleep paralysis. However, he was able to present Blackmore with physical evidence: he argued that the aliens had implanted a small object in his mouth, and a few weeks later, in another operation, they removed it. For some reason, the aliens left the implant with him, and he promised he would bring it in for Blackmore to examine. She subsequently saw the object and described it as being 2 x 3 mm and a dullish grey colour. Analysis showed the 'implant' to actually be a tooth filling.

Of significance here is that James Basil's alien encounter took place in a seeming state of sleep paralysis, something also associated with out-of-body experiences and a number of other NDE traits. But, here, he encounters an entity that seems to wish him harm and also has a distinct reptilian aspect with shamanic overtones. We need now to explore what this may tell us about all these altered states of consciousness.

THE PSYCHOLOGICAL HYPOTHESIS

Is there a psychological predisposition that makes certain individuals more likely to experience NDE-like perceptions during any life-threatening scenarios? This was the opinion of Noyes and Kletti in their influential 1976 paper. (Noyes & Kletti, 'Depersonalization in the face of life-threatening danger: a description', 1976)

This has long been suspected as individuals have often reported NDE-like perceptions when, although the person believed they were about to die, this was not the case. In 1981, well-known NDE researchers Glen Gabbard and Stuart Twemlow, whose work we have encountered several times in our discussion, argued that, in some individuals, just the expectation of possible death was sufficient to trigger an NDE. (Gabbard, Twemlow & Jones, 1981) This suggests that the NDE results from a dissociative defence mechanism in response to extreme danger. Added to this was the suggestion by Sheryl Wilson and Theodore Barber that several NDE experiencers may be susceptible to what has become known as 'fantasy-proneness', a facility some people have for entering a state of rapt immersion in a world of self-created fantasy. (Wilson & Barber, 1983) A preliminary study by James Council and Bruce Greyson, presented at a conference in 1985, confirmed this suspicion. (Council & Greyson, 1985)

It was these discussions, among others, that inspired the co-founder of The International Association of Near-Death Studies (IANDS), psychologist Dr Kenneth Ring, to take a sabbatical to write a book entitled *Heading Toward Omega: In Search of the Meaning of the Near-Death Experience*. This was published in December 1984 and proved groundbreaking. (Ring, K., 1984) In this work, it was clear that Dr Ring wished to move away from the standard interpretation of the NDE and broaden it. In doing so, he became more and more intrigued with regard to the seeming similarities between near-death experiences and UFO encounters, specifically UFO 'abductions'.

Ring was particularly interested in the two psychological traits that had intrigued Noyes, Kletti, Gabbard and Twemlow: 'dissociation' and 'fantasy-proneness'.

Mainstream psychologists generally argue that all altered states of consciousness (ASCs) involve turning one's attention inward and, in doing so, using the contents of one's mind to replace the external world presented by the senses with an internally-generated facsimile created by the mind. The classic examples of this are dream environments and encounters, but in the opinion of most psychologists and perception scientists, out-of-body experiences, near-death experiences and all 'mystical' experiences are included. In simple terms, what they mean is that an ASC is simply a brain-generated 'hallucination'.

So, the argument goes, individuals with a high propensity for dissociation and fantasy-proneness regularly retreat to this inner world when the real world becomes too challenging or dangerous. It has been discovered that another psychological state known as absorption usually works in association with dissociation to create a typical fantasy-prone personality.

To expand on the earlier work, in September 1988, Ring and his associate researcher, Christopher J. Rosing, sent out hundreds of letters inviting potential participants into something he called 'The Omega Project'. The details of these individuals were sourced from the archives of the International Association of Near-Death Studies (IANDS) and from the list of UFO experiencers supplied through the cooperation of various UFO groups across North America. They received responses from 264 individuals who were broken down into four categories: NDE:

persons who reported an NDE (74); NDC: persons who were interested in NDEs but had never had one themselves (54); UFOE: persons who had reported some kind of UFO encounter. (97); and UFOC: persons who were interested in UFOs but had no significant UFO-related experience themselves (39). After doing a preliminary statistical analysis, they were surprised to discover that all the experiential groups had no distinctive psychological differences between them. This suggested that those who report abduction experiences are not in any way distinct from others who just had a non-abduction UFO encounter.

Ring and Rosing were keen to analyse in greater detail something they suspected was significant: the incidence of childhood-related entity encounters. For this, they created the CEI: the Childhood Experience Inventory. This provided measures of three psychological factors that may facilitate sensitivity to anomalous phenomena such as near-death experiences, out-of-body experiences and UFO encounters.

The first factor Ring and Rosing called fantasy proneness. Yes-no answer options isolated this to statements such as, 'As a child, I had a vivid imagination' and 'When I was a child, I daydreamed a lot'. They believed that if their respondents had a propensity for higher levels of fantasy proneness than non-NDE/UFO experiencers, this would be statistically evidenced in their responses.

This resulted in the publication of Ring's *The Omega Project: Near-Death Experiences, UFO Encounters and Mind at Large* (Ring, K., 1992), which can be considered a sequel to his 1984 book, *Heading Towards Omega* (Ring, K., 1984).

Ring observed that there is usually an eerie quality to such encounters involving a sense of being watched or that something strange is about to occur. This can be followed by a feeling of being swept up in the air into a place where the rules of time and space do not apply. He noted the similarities with the NDE experience, specifically the out-of-body elements.

Further, Ring made the observation that the appearance of the creatures encountered is remarkably uniform. They are usually small in size, with large, prominent black eyes set in a head that is disproportionately large compared with the body. This is virtually identical to the UFO entities known as the 'greys'. (Ring, K., 1992, p. loc 751)

He then notes the 'drop-in' nature of the encounters. This is suggestive of a classic lucid dream in that the standard differential between a lucid dream and an out-of-body experience is that there is no sensation of transition, such as rising out of bed or seeing one's body asleep in the bed. Here, the person finds themselves in a location. This could be linked to hypnapompia or REM intrusion, but there is no associated sleep paralysis.

In 1990, Ring and Rosing returned to this theme in a paper published in the *Journal of Near-Death Studies* (Ring & Rosing, 1990). They sent nine separate questionnaires by mail to 74 NDErs and 54 individuals who stated they were interested in the phenomenon. The questionnaires included the Childhood Experience Inventory, the Home Environment Inventory, The Experience and Interests Inventory, and the Psychological Inventory. From this, they discovered that NDErs have significantly greater dissociative tendencies than non-NDErs and suggested that childhood trauma makes victims more prone to dissociation and, thus, NDEs. (Ring & Rosing, 1990, p. 211)

From these observations, Ring created the term 'encounter-prone personality'. (Ring, K., 1992, p. loc 401) These are individuals who are psychologically sensitive to low-stress thresholds caused by traumatic childhood experiences. He does not see this as a negative issue. On the contrary, he argues that such a psychological makeup develops 'an extended range of human perception beyond normally recognized limits'. (Ring, K., 1992, p. loc 2123)

In 1993, and further support of Ring's 'encounter-prone personality' hypothesis, Australian psychologist Harvey J. Irwin discovered that NDErs were more likely to have suffered childhood trauma than non-NDErs. He suggested that NDErs are predisposed to dissociate during unexpected, highly stressful situations in order to 'escape' from the pain or anxiety of their environments. (Irwin, H. J., 1993, p. 99)

Furthermore, in 2018, a team of neurologists from two Belgian universities conducted a survey concerning fantasy-proneness in NDE survivors. (Martial, Cassol, Charland-Verville, Merckelbach & Laureys, 2018) They interviewed 108 experiencers; 51 had their NDEs in the context of a life-threatening situation, and 57 had their NDEs not related to a life-threatening situation. Of those who did not meet the criteria to be considered 'experiencers', 20 had their NDE in the absence of a life-threatening situation; 50 had faced death but did not recall an NDE and finally, 50 were healthy people without a history of life threat and/or NDE. All completed the Greyson NDE questionnaire and a measure of fantasy-proneness called the Creative Experience Questionnaire. The results were interesting:

> *People reporting NDE-like scored higher on fantasy proneness than those reporting classical NDEs, individuals whose experiences did not meet the NDE criteria and matched controls. By contrast, individuals reporting classical NDEs did not show different engagement in fantasy as matched controls. The reported intensity of the experiences was positively correlated with engagement in fantasy. (Martial, Cassol, Charland-Verville, Merckelbach & Laureys, 2018)*

A year later, Charlotte Martial, the lead author of the paper cited above, returned to this theme by testing out how hypnotism may be used to reproduce the near-death experience. In the abstract, the team explains the process they used. (Martial et al., 2019) The results again supported Ring's 'encounter-prone personality' model.

Martial and her associates had five volunteers who had previously experienced a positive NDE to actively try to recall as best they could their original NDE and then follow a similar recollection of a pleasant autobiographical memory encountered at roughly the same time. This was then followed by a session whereby the memories were evoked using hypnotism to place the subjects in an altered state of consciousness.

The volunteers monitored their brain activity using a high-density EEG during both procedures.

The team noted increased alpha activity in the cerebral cortex's frontal and posterior areas during the NDE recall sessions. What was also of interest was that three out of the five volunteers proved to be highly susceptible to hypnotism according to the Stanford Hypnotic Susceptibility Scale, even though this had not been part of the initial selection criteria. In the paper, Martial and her associates made the following observation:

> *We may assume that NDE experiencers have a propensity to enter dissociated states when faced with acute stress or other suitable physiological and/or psychological conditions. Hypnotic state can be regarded as a spectrum, covering distinct but related concepts such as dissociation or fantasy proneness. (Martial et al., 2019)*

The team also concluded that the association between the active recollection of NDE memories and increased alpha activity in the brain was significant and warranted further research.

Although this research involved a very small sample (5), it does suggest that a preference for dissociation may contribute to an NDE-proneness, as suggested earlier.

These results support the view that the strong engagement with fantasy concerning those who reported NDEs in the absence of a life-threatening situation might make these individuals more likely to report such experiences when exposed to social conditioning. In this regard, I am particularly interested in the implications of out-of-body experiences in non-life-threatening scenarios. Such experiences cannot really be explained by psychological dissociation, suggesting that the OBE is a far more complex altered state of consciousness. And if this is true for non-NDE-associated OBEs, then it is reasonable to conclude that the NDE-associated OBEs and related perceptions are similarly complex.

As a caveat to the above discoveries, I would like to add my own observations. Mainstream psychologists generally argue that all altered states of consciousness (ASCs) involve a process of turning one's attention inward and, in doing so, using the contents of one's mind to replace the external world presented by the senses with an internally-generated facsimile created by the mind. The classic examples of this are dream environments and encounters, but in the opinion of most psychologists and perception scientists, out-of-body experiences, near-death experiences and all 'mystical' experiences are included. In simple terms, what they mean is that an ASC is simply a brain-generated 'hallucination'. By definition, a hallucination is a perception not shared by anybody else and, thus, by implication, not real. Of course, the major problem with this is that modern perception studies and neurology tell us that everything we perceive is a brain-generated 'hallucination' in that the brain creates a facsimile reality through its various sensory inputs. It is this which is presented to consciousness. This suggests a need for much greater research in the area and that prejudices should be overcome. I believe the answers to these questions include the discoveries of modern quantum mechanics, neurochemistry and perception studies. We should look where the finger points rather than at the finger.

PART 5

Discussion. NDEs and Kundalini Experiences

NDEs and UFO Abductions – Introduction

I have long been intrigued by this curious NDE explained in a letter
written to Peter and Elizabeth Fenwick by Mrs Nita McCallum, after
their appearance on the British TV programme *QED* in the late 1980s. It
was included in their important 1995 book *The Truth in the Light*:

> At the time of my NDE I was a practising Roman Catholic.
> Had I died I would most certainly have expected that any
> visions I had would have related to my faith, and that if I
> was to see a being of light I would have related it to Jesus
> or Mary or an angel. As it was, when I suddenly found
> myself in this gentle glowing light and standing a little
> below the three beings above me, they appeared as young
> Indian men, and, though they were dressed alike in high-
> necked silver-coloured tunics with silver turbans on their
> heads, I felt they were young Indian princes, or rajas. Two
> were facing each other and the third facing me. And from a
> jewel in the centre of each forehead or turban three 'laser'
> beams emitted, meeting in the centre. My whole lifestyle
> was changed as a result – much reading about various
> religions and philosophies. (Fenwick & Fenwick, 1995,
> p. 81)

This, to me, is more like an encounter with alien beings as described by numerous 'contactees' and 'abductees' in UFO literature.

So, what is going on here? This seems to involve far more than simply transitioning into a heavenly realm full of benign spiritual beings. For example, in his 2000 book *My Descent into Death*, American art historian Professor Howard Storm described a disturbing near-death experience he suffered in Paris. He was hospitalized with a perforated duodenum. As he was lying in bed in extreme pain, he realized he was dying. He said goodbye to his wife, sitting beside the bed, and drifted into darkness. He then found the darkness clear to realize he was standing up and looking at his wife, still beside his bed. He spoke to her, but she did not respond. He then looked at the bed to see a person lying in it. He was astonished to notice that the person was himself. He heard, off in the distance, several disembodied voices, both male and female, calling to him in English. In his disembodied state, he walked towards the source of the voices. As he did so, he became surrounded by an ever-darkening fog. The voices then manifested as dark shadows surrounding him and mocking him. This mocking turned violent, and entities began tearing at his flesh with sharp nails and long teeth. He found the pain they inflicted upon him, both physical and mental, almost unbearable. What followed was an intervention by a voice telling him to 'pray to God'.

This seemed to make the entities back away and fade into the gloom. In the distance, he saw a light that became brighter and brighter as it approached him. Inside the light was a being that he later described as about 2.4 m (8 ft) tall. He felt himself rising up as the light healed the wounds inflicted by the entities and subsequently experienced a panoramic life review and a meeting with a being he identified as 'God' before returning to life. (Storm, 2005)

But there are many parallels here with shamanic initiation. As we have already discussed, anthropologists generally believe that shamanism is the core religion of all humanity and that all subsequent belief systems are simply adaptions of this central credo. Using hallucinations, facilitated by various techniques or induced by personal neurological conditions, shamans were able to access other realms of reality and bring back information for the tribe or family unit. These techniques include rhythmic dancing to a regular and powerful drumbeat, spinning, jumping and chanting. Some shamans can enter altered states of consciousness spontaneously, possibly through the channel of epileptic seizures or other neurological conditions. These methods allow the shaman to travel outside their body and perceive non-ordinary realities. This is known as the 'shamanic journey'.

On entering the shamanic world, things can become extremely macabre. The trainee shaman encounters an entity known as the 'totem'. This usually appears in the guise of an animal. It can be a small creature, such as a rabbit or an owl, or a larger predator, such as a wolf or a lion. At the same time, or soon afterwards, the 'teacher' will appear. This will be a human-like entity, usually wearing a hooded cloak that obscures the face, who will facilitate the brutal and horrific dismemberment of the initiate shaman's body. There are cultural variations, but in general, the shaman's body is torn open, their entrails drawn out, and their limbs chopped off. This may be done by the claws and teeth of an animal totem, such as a wolf or a tiger, or by the humanoid 'guide' using weapons or surgical tools. It is all part of the initiation. Soon afterwards, the body will be reassembled, and the initiate becomes a practising shaman.

The shamanic world involves many themes found in near-death experiences. For example, the 'teacher' can be compared with the 'being of light', but these themes can also be found in two other variations on travelling to alternative realities: UFO abductions and encounters with DMT entities.

In this regard, I would like to return to the extraordinary NDE of 'Andrew', cited by Canadian anthropologist Dorothy Ayers Counts in 1983, which we discussed earlier. You will recall that, in 1981, Counts was undertaking research into near-death experiences in the Kaliai people, an isolated community on the north coast of West New Britain Province in Papua New Guinea. She asked her contacts if they knew of anyone in the community who had died and returned to life. She was told of three men who had died and returned to life with memories of the time they were dead. Andrew (not his real name) was one of them. As we have already discovered, his account contained a number of the standard Moody 'traits' but with unique, possibly culturally-influenced tropes. But for me, what was of great significance with regards to the themes of this book was the peculiar element in which he encountered a flying 'house':

> *But I saw the dead woman that I had met on the road. I saw her leave me. I wanted to call out, 'Hey, come back!' but I couldn't, for this house turned in a circle. I couldn't see the man who talked to me, but I did see children lying [on platforms] over the doors and windows. As I was walking around, trying to see everything, they took hold of me and took me back down the steps. I wanted to go back to the house, but I couldn't because it turned and I realized that it was not on posts. It was just hanging there in the air, turning around as if it were on an axle. If I wanted to go to the door, the house would turn and there would be another part of the house where I was standing. (Counts, D. A., 1983, p. 120)*

This section is quite extraordinary. 'Andrew', guided by two entities, climbed a long ladder into what he identified as a house. But this house was not what it seemed. He realised it was not on stilts, as would be the case with a typical New Guinea building, but hovering high above the ground. So what we have here is some form of flying machine accessed from a long ladder that runs down to the ground. The machine was moving in circles on its own axis. Around it, or inside it (this is unclear), were small child-like entities 'on platforms'.

You will recall from earlier what Andrew encountered next. I will repeat this quotation:

I was to come back, but there was no road for me to follow, so the voice said, 'Let him go down'. Then there was a beam of light and I walked along it. I walked down the steps, and when I turned to look there was nothing but forest. (Counts, D. A., 1983, p. 120)

He came down from the hovering 'house' (UFO?) and was guided by a 'beam of light'. This is a widespread process described by UFO abductees where they are drawn up into and down from a UFO. For example, here is a description of his 1975 UFO encounter by abductee Travis Walton:

I rose to go and was half out of my crouch when a tremendously bright, bluegreen ray shot from the bottom of the craft. I saw and heard nothing. All I felt was the numbing force of a blow that felt like a high-voltage electrocution. The intense bolt made a sharp cracking, or popping, sound. The stunning concussion of the foot-wide beam struck me full in the head and chest. My mind sank quickly into unfeeling blackness. I didn't even see what hit me; but from the instant I felt that paralysing blow, I did not see, hear, or feel anything more. (Walton, 1996, p. 42)

This is just one of a number of UFO-like themes found in Andrew's NDE. For example, we have the much-reported 'you must go back' instruction from the 'being of light':

The man took my hand, and we entered a village. There we found a long ladder that led up into a house. We climbed the ladder but when we got to the top I heard a voice saying, 'It isn't time for you to come. Stay there. I'll send a group of people to take you back.' I heard his voice, but I couldn't see his face or his body. (Counts, D. A., 1983, p. 120)

If this had been the only incident involving a seeming encounter with aliens in a flying machine reported in New Guinea then Andrew's encounter can be reasonably described as a hallucination. But 22 years before, on the evening of 27 June 1959, Father William Gill, an Australian Anglican missionary, came out of the dining hall at the Boainai Missionary School in Eastern New Guinea to see a large sparkling object in the sky close to Venus. He was joined by 39 other members of the school, including five teachers, two medical assistants and a large number of local people. The object was soon joined by two others. As the main object came closer to the school, the witnesses stated that they could see human-shaped forms on what the later witness statements described as the 'top deck' of the flying machine. The entities were dressed in silver suits and seemed to be working on repairing sections of the deck. Occasionally, the object projected a thin beam of bright blue light into the sky above it. Then something extraordinary happened. When one of the figures seemed to look in the direction of the crowd, Father Gill waved at them. The being waved back. What then took place was a form of semaphore communication as Gill and some of the locals raised both their arms. Two of the entities responded by doing the same. The encounter lasted for another 20 minutes or so before the blue beam was switched off, and the UFO moved behind a cloud. (Salisbury, 1967, p. 23)

Note here that, yet again, we have the 'beam of light' associated with the UFO. Travis Walton described a 'bluegreen' beam, and Andrew described a 'beam of light'. I find the linkage here of interest.

In his book *Dreamtimes and Inner Space*, Holger Kalweit describes a curiously similar experience recounted by a Korean female shaman called Oh Un-sook. She had dreams of thunder and lightning:

> *Soon after, she encountered a pillar of light three times, and three men appeared to her from heaven. Inner luminosity is often preceded by a visible physical phenomenon of light, such as a ball of fire, lightning, pillars of fire, a figure of light, or simply a light beam. In most cases, however,*

the inner light can only be perceived when a higher level
of consciousness has been reached, if the subject is in a
trance, or if mind and body are sufficiently exhausted and
unbalanced to become open to new insights. (Kalweit,
1988, pp. 205–206)

Again, we have extraordinary echoes of the Walton case.

So, what are we to make of this? Clearly, there are links between shamanic practices, near-death experiences and UFO encounters. It seems that such scenarios take place under unusual circumstances. In 1988, British UFO researcher Jenny Randles coined the term 'The Oz Factor' to describe such situations. She defined this as:

. . . a set of symptoms very commonly reported by a witness
to an abduction . . . time standing still . . . all sound
vanishing . . . the impression of temporarily having left
our material world and entered another dream-like place
with magical rules, just as it did to Dorothy in the famous
fantasy story The Wizard of Oz. *(Randles, 1988, p. 22)*

In one of her cases, Randles described how a man was having dental treatment when he suffered a reaction to the drug being administered. This nearly killed him. While in an unconscious state, he felt himself float out of the dentist's chair and up through the ceiling. He then found himself entering a UFO, where he met a group of aliens who discussed their involvement with the Earth with him. She also described a similar case regarding a Leeds-based ambulance driver, lying on his bed after an exhausting shift, who fell into what seems like a sleep-paralysis state; he then saw a group of classic 'greys' with large faces and huge black eyes standing around his bed. Curiously, they asked him for his help in fixing their damaged UFO. He then found himself floating up to the ceiling and into a strange room with a long table in the centre. He lay down on the table, and the entities gave him a medical examination. Then, after the standard confusing message from the aliens, he found himself back on the bed, still paralysed. He woke up fully convinced that he had experienced an abduction. (Randles, *Alien Contact: The First Fifty Years*, 1997, p. 108)

Kundalini Experience – Introduction

Earlier, in our discussions of Hinduism and Buddhism, we looked at the state of samadhi, an undifferentiated 'beingness' in which time and space cease to exist and an inner perception of the real, timeless universe is perceived. Some consider this an awareness of the 'God within' and that we are all part of a greater being, the 'Godhead'.

In the Hindu Vedanta philosophy there is a force that animates and sustains life within all living creatures. This force is known as *prana*. This literally 'fills' a body with vital energy. Within the body are three main channels, known as *nadis* ('rivers'), in which *prana* flows. *Ida* flows in the right-hand side of the brain and the left-hand side of the body, with *pingala* flowing along the left-hand side of the brain and the right-hand side of the body. This is quite intriguing. Modern neurology informs us that each hemisphere of the brain controls the opposite side of the body. For example, the left, usually dominant, hemisphere moves the right-hand side. How did the writers of the Vedanta know this? This must lead to the conclusion that the original source of information used by Vedanta to create its philosophy had a sound basis, and therefore, any information it offers regarding the true nature of reality must be taken seriously.

The third *nadi* in which the *prana* flows is named the *sushumna*. This runs along the spinal cord and through seven centres of force known as chakras (Sanskrit for 'wheels'). Sometimes called the 'silver cord', the *sushumna* is the most important of all the *nadi*. There are believed to be over 72,000 minor *nadi*, which connect all the major areas of what is known as the 'subtle body' or *sukshma sarira*. This is not the same as the physical body; it is the body that carries consciousness from one life to another. The physical body is simply a manifestation of the subtle body that is visible within the illusion that is Maya.

The chakra found at the base of the *sushumna* – in other words, at the base of the spine – is called the *muladhara*. This is also known as the 'root chakra'. It is significant to us because Vedanta tradition has it that sleeping quietly within the *muladhara* is the Kundalini. The name Kundalini comes from the Sanskrit for 'coiled'; the Kundalini is depicted as coiled around itself three and a half times, like a tiny serpent. This is the one part of the subtle body that has a direct link with Brahman and, when awoken, gives the atman direct awareness of the true nature of reality. In other words, according to the Vedanta, a Kundalini experience – an awakening of enhanced awareness – gives us direct access to the Absolute.

Within Chinese and other East Asian cultures, there is a concept known as qi. This concept is very similar to the Hindu *prana* and has its roots in the ancient Chinese philosophy known as Taoism. It has been embroidered into Chinese life for at least 2,500 years and was originally codified in a book called *Tao Te Ching* (*The Way and Its Power*), traditionally believed to have been written by the philosopher Lao Tzu.

Qi has many different meanings, but in most cases it is interpreted as a special substance in a constant state of flux which acts as the guiding force for the universe. This energy force runs throughout all living bodies and follows hundreds of separate pathways crossing 12 primary meridian points, spread across the body. These can be accessed from over 400 specific locations. The flow of the qi can be moderated and controlled by acupuncture, which involves the insertion of hair-thin needles into the flesh above the locations.

The lines and meridian points depicted on a diagram of the human body found in acupuncture manuals are based on the anatomical knowledge used in ancient Chinese surgical practices. Ancient texts indicate that the meridians are three-dimensional in nature, run deep inside the human body and connect all the internal organs.

I can understand how the more scientifically-based reader will, quite rightly, consider that this theological and experiential description is all well and good, but where is the supporting science?

Reissner's Fiber and Kundalini

In my opinion one of the most important researchers attempting a scientifically-based understanding of altered states of consciousness is Connecticut-based physician Dr Lawrence Wile. Wile has written a series of papers discussing a fascinating structure discovered in the brain and spinal column in 1860, a structure that he believes facilitates such perceptions as the near-death experience, the out-of-body experience and, most importantly, the Kundalini experience.

In 1994, Wile wrote an article for the *IANDS Review* in which he explained the inspiration that led him to his extraordinary hypothesis:

> *A personal mystical experience led me to the belief that a little known structure in the center of the spinal cord, Reissner's fiber, is identical with the anatomical entity described by Kundalini yoga. My struggles to understand the meaning of that experience have led me to believe that an understanding of the deeper realities underlying quantum phenomena can be integrated with an understanding of the mysterious realities of near-death and other mystical experiences, and that Reissner's fiber can serve as an empirical basis for a scientific investigation of these phenomena. (Wile, 1994)*

In the article, Wile describes how, when he was a medical student, a series of synchronicities and his unconventional fascination with Kundalini took him to the work of Charles Loeser, the Chairman of Neuroscience at the University of Connecticut. It was these synchronicities that led

Loeser and Wile to begin a collaboration to study the possible functional connection between the terminal ventricle at the base of the central canal of the spinal cord and the pineal gland as the analogues of the Muladhara chakra and the Ajna chakra.

Wile is now convinced that Reissner's fiber (a.k.a. primo-vascular system or PVS, see below) interacts with the brain's internally-generated opioids. He points out that the PVS's fibrils make surface contact in the ventricular section of the central grey area. He also argues that the receptors surrounding the fibres contain photosensitive proteins (Blackshaw and Snyder, 1999), which may be linked to a phenomenon we discussed extensively earlier in this book: biophotons.

Finally, Wile also makes a direct reference to Reissner's fiber and entheogenic substances like dimethyltryptamine and 5-MEO-DMT:

> *Mystical experiences generated by RF's facilitation of the actions of endogenous psychoactive substances, though, would not justify faith in revelations, theophanies and prophecies from divine sources. Viewing RF's 5-nanometer diameter filaments, embedded nanostructures, and hollow core through the lens of modern physics, however, provides new perspectives on the borderland between the natural and supernatural. The mysteriousness, ineffability, immateriality and holism of the subatomic realm, and its intimate relationship with the forces of creation have inspired comparisons with the esoteric traditions. (Wile, L., 2022, p. 3)*

So, how was this structure discovered, and what supporting evidence is there for Wile's claims?

As we have already discovered, it all started in 1860 when a German anatomist, Ernst Reissner, found in the body of a lamprey eel an enigmatic, thread-like structure that began at the bottom of the spine, travelled up the central canal of the spinal column and entered the brain, where it terminated at a location just below the pineal gland called the subcommissural organ (SCO). In 1863, Reissner's discovery was confirmed by Karl Kutschin, who recognized this by calling it 'Reissner's fiber'. Unfortunately, in 1868, German anatomist Ludwig Stieda, on re-examining the samples, concluded that the spinal fluid and the chemicals used to preserve the specimens had coagulated to create the thread. Many anatomists accepted this argument but, in 1899, a Harvard doctoral candidate, Porter Sargent, rediscovered the fibre in a lamprey and in 1904 published his research, arguing that the fibre was a highly specialized conduction path. Sadly, although Sargant's conclusions were generally accepted, he left research and became a poet, leaving the enigmatic Reissner's fiber to return to obscurity.

But in East Asian cultures, interest in parallels between the discoveries of Reissner and the teachings of ancient Chinese medicine was such that, in 1960, a North Korean scientist called Kim Bong-Han made an astonishing discovery when investigating possible scientific support for acupuncture. He injected some radioactive phosphorus into the abdomen of a rabbit. The spot was chosen precisely because, according to traditional Chinese medicine, this was where several crucial meridian points crossed. Bong-Han and his team were able to trace the flow of the phosphorus along the meridians of the rabbit's body. Of significance was that the phosphorus was only detected where the qi lines were believed to be. (Bong-Han, 1962) The primary structure that Bong Han's phosphorous trail highlighted was Reissner's fiber. As Bong-Han was unaware of Reissner's discovery, he named the fibre after himself, the Bong-Han duct. Indeed, in an unusual cross-border association of interests, in 2009 a team of researchers at South Korea's Seoul Nation University began testing Bong-Han's claims using fluorescent magnetic nanoparticles and confocal laser-scanning microscopy, and rediscovered his 'ducts'. (Soh, 2004) Then, in 2008, Byung-Cheon Lee and his team at the Biomedical Physics Laboratory, also at Seoul National University, published their discovery of threadlike structures running afloat in the cerebrospinal fluid of the brain ventricles and the spinal central canal of a rabbit. In the article, they also confirmed that:

> *Although the Bong-Han theory has not been reproduced for a long time, recently, some portions of the Bong-Han duct network were confirmed in various mammals' organs, including blood vessels, lymphatic vessels, and enteric organs. The novel threadlike structure in the central nervous system, more specifically in brain ventricles, is one in a series of findings in an attempt to rediscover the Bong-Han duct network. (Lee, Kim & Soh, 2008, p. 29)*

Reissner's fiber and the Bong-Han duct network are now known collectively as the primo-vascular system (PVS), which has been discovered within human beings. According to Wile, whose writings I acknowledge as the major source of the material cited in this section, the first discovery was recorded in 1922 when it was observed in a 14-year-old in Germany. (Wile, L., 2018, p. 57) Wile also cites a paper from 1935 when evidence for the PVS was found in a 15-week-old human foetus. (Keene & Hewer, 1935)

With regard to the PVS, we need to return to the teachings of Vedanta. You will recall the three *nadis* (rivers) in which the *prana* life force flows: the *ida*, the *pingala*, and the *sushumna*. According to ancient texts, the *sushumna* runs along the spinal cord in a channel. This is precisely what modern anatomy tells us the PVS does.

The implications of Reissner's discovery and the teachings of Tantric Yoga were not lost on American initiate Theos Barnard, living in Tibet in the late 1930s. He believed that there was something of extreme significance regarding the role of this puzzling fibre with regards to human spiritual evolution. In a book published in 1940 entitled *Heaven Lies Within Us*, he argued that Reissner's fiber was none other than the Sanskrit concept known as Chittra, the 'Heavenly Passage' that runs down the centre of the *sushumna*. Sadly, in 1947, Barnard disappeared under mysterious circumstances in northern India, and his ideas languished in obscurity.

Could it be that what Reissner discovered in 1860 was the physiological basis for the Kundalini experience? This is what Lawrence Wile believes. In an article he wrote in 2019, he observed:

> Yoga describes three concentrically arranged tubes (Brahman, Chittra and Vajra *nadis*) inside a hollow passageway in the center of the spine (Sushumna *nadi*) which opens to a cavity in the center of the brain (Cave of Brahman). Coiled in a triangular region (Mooladara chakra) the base of the Sushumna *nadi* is a dormant energy called Kundalini. Yogic practices can awaken Kundalini and promote its ascent through the central *nadis* along a series of energy vortexes (chakras) resulting in increased well-being and wisdom. When the Kundalini reaches the penultimate chakra (Ajna chakra), the yogi attains paranormal powers (*siddhis*). When the Kundalini reaches the ultimate chakra (Sahasrara chakra), individual consciousness (atman) unites with ultimate reality (Brahman). (Wile, L., 2019, pp. 3–4)

It is important here to realize that where Reissner's fiber ends (or starts) its journey is a location in the brain between the pineal gland and next to a structure known as the preoptic area of the hypothalamus (POA) which coordinates sleep and body temperature. So, this area of the brain is responsible for increasing body temperature and facilitating sleep and dreaming. A Kundalini experience is regularly described as a feeling of a powerful, unbearable form of energy starting at the base of the spine, searing its way up the spinal column to explode in the centre of the brain. This is accompanied by sensations of intense heat followed by an intense wave of bliss, visions and insight.

You will recall that I argued that biophotons are the source of the internal light that 'illuminates' the environment encountered in a near-death experience. This is an inner world created from our mind that is more real than this one. This internally-generated source of electromagnetic energy is also responsible for the alternative world of out-of-body experiences, dreaming and the universe encountered when experiencing entheogens like dimethyltryptamine and LSD. All these experiences are related, and although they are technically 'hallucinations', they are still subjectively real. In this regard, it is also important to realize that electromagnetic energy exists in many forms, depending on its wavelength. For example, it can be perceived as visible light in one form and heat in another. Is this the source of the extreme heat (and sometimes cold) perceived during a Kundalini experience? Is this not clear evidence that all these perceptions are just variations of the same phenomenon?

But what evidence do we have for such speculation? Indeed, what physiological and neurochemical processes can be implicated in creating the NDE and associated altered states of consciousness? I want to discuss just two areas of possible investigation, firstly something known as the Default Mode Network and, secondly, to return to Lawrence Wile's investigations into the role of the mysterious Reissner's fiber.

The Default Mode Network and Kundalini

Several astonishing discoveries have been made in recent years regarding how entheogens modify the brain's functioning. Until 2012, neurologists assumed that psychedelics increased brain functioning, and this was why the inner perceptions created by these substances were so much more elaborate and intense than everyday perceptions.

This belief was, to a certain extent, based upon empirical research. For example, a team in Zurich administered psilocybin (the active ingredient of 'magic' mushrooms) to a group of volunteers whilst monitoring their brain activity using positron emission tomography (PET) scans. It is known that psilocybin activates specific receptor sites in the brain (called the 5-HT2A receptors), which are normally activated by the neurotransmitter serotonin. This showed a considerable increase in brain activity in the frontal areas of the cerebral cortex, including the anterior cingulate cortex and the anterior insula. Interestingly, this was facilitated by the release of large amounts of glutamate, which, in turn, activates the NMDA receptors. (Vollenweider et al., 1997)

Interestingly, these findings contradicted similar research undertaken by Robert Carhart-Harris at Imperial College in London. Using fMRI scanning, Carhart-Harris and his team were able to show that a medium-sized dose of psilocybin, administered intravenously, led to an immediate reduction in activity across many areas of the brain. (Carhart-Harris et al., 2012)

Inspired by this discovery, a whole series of laboratory-based experiments have confirmed Carhart-Harris et al.'s findings, and others have had results suggesting that this is how other psychoactive substances bring about powerful altered states of consciousness, including dimethyltryptamine (the psychoactive component of ayahuasca). (Palhano-Fontes et al., 2015)

To be clear, these substances decrease brain activity. In effect, they start to shut it down. This is precisely what happens in the brain at the point of death. These substances mimic the circumstances of a near-death experience.

This disintegration of activity across the brain thus coincides with the frequently experienced disintegration of the self. In particular, reduced activity in the cingulate cortex and diminished functional connectivity between these regions (the default mode network of the cortical midline, an area discussed earlier in this chapter) and the other regions of the brain were related to subjective alterations in the experience of the self. The default mode network is linked to mental 'time travel' into the past and the future and is responsible for situating the self within time. Accordingly, the disintegration of the self and time and the disintegration of the connections with the default mode network go hand in hand.

In what I consider a crucially important paper, Megan McGill and her associates made a series of interesting observations regarding what is known as 'idiopathic generalized epilepsy' (IGE) and abnormalities in the default mode network (DMN). (McGill et al., 2012, p. 353)

To clarfy: the word 'idiopathic' means of unknown cause. This is of great importance in that modern neurology has no idea why certain people, with no abnormal brain anatomy or an identified focus area of seizure activity, experience seizures and aura states. So it is that modern science cannot explain how consciousness is created by the brain (the 'Hard Problem') and has no idea what is facilitating the powerful altered states of consciousness that create out-of-body experiences and near-death experiences. And yet, as an escape clause, materialist-reductionist scientists are happy to use these unknown processes to 'explain' near-death experiences and out-of-body experiences. A classic magic trick is going on here, using something you don't understand to 'explain' something else you don't understand. Watch this hand, folks, as the other scrambles in the dust and clutches at straws. Hubris does not even begin to describe this. This is what I call 'Idiopathic Science'.

It is because it decreases brain activity during specific cognitive demands that the DMN is also known as the 'task-negative network'. Note also that it is a 'network' because its activity is synchronized across a number of separate locations spread across the brain. These communicate via low-frequency oscillations identified by what are known as BOLDs, spontaneous increases in the blood oxygen level dependent signals. These create functional integrity across the network. In healthy individuals, there are negative correlations between the activity of the DMN and other brain areas.

However, it has been discovered that abnormal DMN functional connectivity occurs in several brain disorders, including Alzheimer's disease (Greicius, Srivastava, Reiss & Menon, 2004), schizophrenia (Garrity et al., 2007), ADHD (Tian et al., 2006), Parkinson's (Van Eimeren, Monchi, Ballanger & Strafella, 2009) and depression (Greicius et al., 2007). However, what is of more note for our enquiry is that functional connectivity has been shown to decrease with regard to temporal lobe epilepsy. Of significance is also the discovery that this has also been observed in individuals who experience IGE.

So, it seems reasonable to suggest that altered states of consciousness and a perception of an alternative reality that can be facilitated by a decrease in brain activity may bring about the various 'traits' associated with the near-death experience. We have also discussed earlier evidence that endogenously-generated psycho-active substances like N, N-Dimethyltryptamine (DMT) may directly influence the creation of such ASCs and that these substances are active in the mammalian brain. (Barker, Borjigin, Lomnicka & Strassman, 2013) If the source of this DMT is not in the brain, it must be transported from elsewhere in the body. But where?

Kundalini Experiences and the NDE

As we have already discovered, there seems to be a direct link between mystical experiences, altered states of consciousness and temporal lobe epilepsy. Indeed, I have written extensively about this in the past, suggesting that there is a continuum from classic migraine, through TLE, to schizophrenia, Alzheimer's and autism. In this regard, I coined the term 'The Huxleyian Spectrum'. (Peake, 2016, pp. 42–44) So, can this be linked in some way to the Kundalini experience? To attempt an answer, I would like to return to the work of psychiatrist Lawrence C. Wile.

You will recall that Wile presents robust evidence that a structure known as Reissner's fiber (RF) may facilitate altered states of consciousness such as the Kundalini experience. He has noted that this structure, which runs along the inside of the spinal column from the bottom of the spine to the centre of the brain, interacts directly with the brain's endogenous opioids, such as leu-5-enkephalin and met-5-enkephalin. It is known that fibrils (tiny fibres) that branch out from the main body of the RF project into the areas of the brain that contain the highest density of these endogenous opioids. (Kohno, 1969)

The problem is that, after death, RF is too thin to be detected by current neuroimaging devices, so it is impossible to show any relationship between it and consciousness. Furthermore, it undergoes rapid post-mortem degeneration, so the activity of this mysterious structure at the point of death cannot be detected. However, it is known that, due to its location in the spinal column, it is continually bathed in cerebrospinal fluid (CSF), and it is also known that within the CSF can be found amounts of N, N-Dimethyltryptamine (DMT). So, in effect, RF interfaces directly with endogenous DMT. Could it be that what stimulates a Kundalini experience is its absorption of DMT and its transfer from the CSF to the brain's centre and the pineal gland?

Is this where we will finally find the answer as to what happens to consciousness at the point of death?

Epilogue

We have almost reached the end of our journey across space and time in our quest to understand more about the enigmatic near-death experience. What have we discovered? Well, it seems that it is far more intriguing than the materialist reductions would have us believe. Yes, it is, in a very real sense, a hallucination. But then again, so is all our sensory experience. It is 'brain-generated' in that what is perceived during an NDE involves the firing of neurons and chemical reactions.

For me, one of the most fascinating cases whereby the near-death experience metamorphoses into an encounter with non-human intelligences that may be related to the UFO abduction experience involves an associate of mine, a Swiss-based Croatian-Canadian musician-inventor whom I will identify as 'Subject A'.

Subject A's first NDE took place when he was six years old. He was visiting a beach in Croatia with his aunt. While playing in an inflatable plastic boat, imagining he was a pirate on the high seas, he saw a seahorse swimming in the water below him. He became fascinated by the play of light on the water and seemed to go into a form of trance state. This brings about the much-reported oceanic feeling; he then falls into the water and starts to drown. He finds himself in the clouds floating in the sky. He looks down to see the mountains and the coastline, with a small boat floating in the water. He sees a beach with a car coming off the beach road on to the beach itself and driving towards a group of people surrounding a small figure of a child. As he falls closer, he realizes that the child is him. He enters the body in a flash of light. He then opens his eyes, and he is looking up at a group of people surrounding him.

The second NDE happened when Subject A was seventeen. By this time, he had moved with his family to Canada and was a member of a rock band. One Saturday night, they were playing a concert at a local venue. A friend had loaned him a large amplifier specifically for the concert, and he was keen to check that it was in full working order. He plugged a lead into the amplifier and switched it on. As he did so, there was a pop, and all the lights went out. He had blown a fuse. As there was no time to drive into town to purchase a replacement fuse, he decided to improvise. He asked a friend for the tin foil from their cigarette packaging, rolled it into a cylinder, and placed it in the location where the fuse would have been. He turned on the amplifier, and it gave off a satisfactory humming sound. His improvised piece of electrical engineering had worked, but not in the way he had anticipated. He picked up the lead with the intention of plugging the other end into his synthesizer, but there was a huge flash and he found himself hovering in the air and moving away from the stage. He recently explained to me that this moving away was not linear but in discrete steps. He perceived what was happening around him like a series of film stills, moving from one to the other. There is then a transition and he finds himself floating in space as a point of consciousness and surrounded by stars. As he travels towards the stars, more and more of them pop into his field of view, first hundreds, then thousands, then millions. The star field then takesa the shape of a human body, thousands of light years across. There is another flash, and he finds himself looking up at the rigging above the stage and the sound of people's voices in a state of panic. He is helped up, with pulsations running through his body. The exposed jack plug had given him a powerful electric shock that, his fellow band members told him, had thrown him through the air. Much to his, and everybody else's, surprise, he recovered quickly and was soon well enough to continue with the concert.

But something had changed in him. He felt different. This came to a head a few weeks after his electrocution when he was drifting off to sleep one evening at his parents' house. As he fell into a doze, he heard what he later described as a loud hissing sound accompanied by a noise similar to a distant thunderstorm. He opened his eyes, and the sound stopped. He got up and looked out of his bedroom window. Everything outside was calm. He returned to his bed and the noise started again, now with the added complexity of strong vibrations. He felt that his room, the house and the whole street were enveloped in this maelstrom of sound and movement. He tried to get up again but found he could not move. It seems that he was in a state we have already discussed in detail: sleep paralysis.

And then things became even stranger. Looking up at the ceiling above him, he saw a distinct glow appear. This became brighter, and in the centre, he could discern the silhouette of a human-like figure. The entity 'spoke' to him, using one single word, 'peace'. The being then stated that it was there to help him and would be with him for the rest of his life. Subject A originally identified this entity with the name 'HeSheIt' because he could not identify a gender. But he has informed me that it subsequently identified itself by the name of Kalaman. Kalaman informed Subject A that it was in his life to impart information, information that Subject A would only fully understand and use in the future. For this reason, Kalaman insisted that that he must write down everything he was told in a series of notebooks. Subject A agreed he would do as instructed. With this, the entity vanished, and his bedroom returned to normal.

This was the start of a series of communications from Kalaman. Although Subject A was grateful and dutifully kept notes of all he was told, he was concerned that others would think him crazy if he told them what he was experiencing. Kalaman promised that soon it would provide him with something tangible to prove that what the young man was experiencing was far from a hallucination.

One November day, by the sea, Kalaman kept its promise. At that time Subject A was visiting family for the wedding of one of his cousins. The location was a beautiful seaside resort, and one day, to kill time, he decided to take a bracing stroll next to the beach. Suddenly, a woman appeared out of nowhere and handed him an object, saying, 'This is yours.' Taken aback, he looked down at his palm to see a greenish coin-like object. He looked up again, and the woman had vanished. He recently told me he did not see the woman's face because she was wearing a hood.

Subject A's third brush with death happened in Canada when he was 24. It was in deep winter with freezing conditions. He was driving to an appointment in his VW Beetle and came over the brow of a hill along

Lansdowne Avenue in Toronto; as he started to drive down the other side, he saw parked trucks in the centre of the road. He slammed on the brakes, but the car had no ABS and began to slide. He realized he was going to hit them at speed. As with his last NDE, time slowed down and became a series of images merging into a slow sense of movement. He hit one of the trucks, and bits of metal smashed through the window of his car and hit him on the head. Then he is somewhere else entirely, a place full of bright light with a portal in front of him. Standing next to him is a being of light that he immediately recognizes as Kalaman, but this time, it is a distinctly female being. She says to him, 'You really were doing something stupid there.' She then adds, 'You can pass over if you wish.' He replies that he feels this is not his time and has more to do in his life. She says, 'Okay, you can go back in time and take a different path. With that, Subject A sees time run in reverse; the impact runs backwards, with the smashed windscreen's shattered shards of glass coalescing back into a sheet of glass. The car then reassembles itself and reverses back along the road. There is another flash of light and he finds himself sitting in a totally undamaged car jammed between a grass verge and a telephone pole. He explained to me later that it was so close to this pole that he could not open the door. He stated that this was only about 5 cm (2 in). He has visited the site a number of times over the years and has never been able to understand how the car could have ended up in this position.

So who, or what, are the beings that Subject A has encountered over the years? Kalaman seems to manifest in his life during near-death experiences, out-of-body experiences and general altered states of consciousness. But Kalaman also has aspects more in keeping with alien encounters and shamanic travelling. With one extraordinary difference: the object promised by Kalaman in an NDE that was subsequently given to Subject A by the mysterious woman that windswept November day.

Subsequently, Subject A was to call this object 'the octastone' as it has eight sides. I have seen this object, and it is very intriguing. Indeed, over the years, Subject A has worked with a number of scientific laboratories to identify what the object is made of. To date, it has proven a total mystery, refusing to give up its secrets to either spectrometry or tunnel scanning microscopy. It seems to be made of no known substance. Was this the proof that Kalaman said it would supply? It seems that an object not made by human hands is available to uncover its secrets.

And what about the information promised to Subject A during his sleep paralysis and out-of-body experience? Well, over the years, he has received hundreds of 'downloads', details of which are found in several notebooks. As promised by Kalaman, Subject A finds that suddenly he is drawn to a particular page and understands fully what the words and diagrams mean. He now has a number of patents for inventions whose details were contained in the notebooks. These have been extraordinary and involve totally unique technologies. If evidence was needed that these communications are from somewhere beyond everyday human experience then these patents present that evidence.

I am of the opinion that the near-death experience and its associated states of consciousness offer modern science a huge opportunity to develop a whole new paradigm of understanding. Throughout history, each civilization has considered its science to be the correct model by which the true nature of reality can be understood. These models of understanding were called 'paradigms' by Harvard University-educated physicist Dr Thomas Kuhn in his 1962 book *The Structure of Scientific Revolutions*. In simple terms, Kuhn argued that these paradigms change not gradually but in sudden leaps of understanding, 'revolutions'. He cited the example of how medieval schoolmen used the writings of Aristotle to show that the Earth was the centre of the universe, with all the known planets revolving around the Earth. The problem was that there were a number of observed astronomical phenomena that seemed to suggest otherwise; for example, the perceived motion across the sky seemed to go in reverse at certain times of the year. As you may know, the word planet means wanderer. It comes from the fact that the planets appear to wander across the sky, with some of them doing so in a strange 'back and forth' pattern, which became known as retrograde motion. This was only observed in three of the known planets: Mars, Jupiter and Saturn.

Venus and Mercury orbited exactly as predicted by the earth-centred model. To explain this, the astronomers and mathematicians of the time came up with an elaborate set of calculations to create what they called 'epicycles'. These were ever-smaller mini-revolutions that were believed to exist in the larger revolutions. They became ever more complicated. This was all to change in 1543 when Nicolaus Copernicus, a Polish priest, had a book published that proposed that all the planets revolved around the sun. Seventy years later, the German astonomer Johannes Kepler made a few changes to Copernicus's model, and suddenly, epicycles were no longer needed and a new paradigm was born. Since then, two more paradigm shifts have occurred, the one initiated by Isaac Newton in 1687 with the publication of his book *Principia* and then the one that totally revolutionized our understanding of the universe, the discovery of quantum mechanics in the first 25 years of the 20th century.

In each case, the objective evidence for the principles of the new scientific paradigm was already known; it was just that the scientists interpreted the evidence wrongly, effectively refusing to accept anything that didn't complement the paradigm they were so not wanting to abandon.

I believe that we are at the start of a new paradigm, a paradigm that will explain a great deal more about the true nature of reality and the role of consciousness within the universe. The clues are all there. Materialist-reductionist science has to accept that near-death experiences, together with all their associated perceptions, can tell us so much about the universe.

All we need to do is take a leap into the unknown.

BIBLIOGRAPHY

(1997). *Uniform Determination of Death Act.* Uniforms Law Annotated (ULA), 12

Abanes, R. (1996). *Journey into the Light: Exploring Near-Death Experiences.* Grand Rapids: Baker Books.

Aboitiz, F. & Montiel, J. F. (2021, June 23). 'The Enigmatic Reissner's Fiber and the Origin of Chordates'. *Frontiers in Neuroanatomy,* pp. 1–8.

Agrillo, C. (2011). 'Near-Death Experience: Out-of-Body and Out-of-Brain?' *Review of General Psychology,* 1–10.

Alexander, E. (2012). *Proof of Heaven.* New York: Simon & Schuster.

Alexander, E. 'My Experience in a Coma'. Retrieved from ebenalexander.com: http://ebenalexander.com/about/my-experience-in-coma/

Allison, R. (1980). *Minds in Many Pieces.* New York: Rawson Wade.

Altschuler, E. & Ramachanddran, V. S. (2007). 'A Simple Method to stand outside oneself'. *Perception 36,* 623–624.

Aminoff, M., Scheinman, M. M., Griffin, J. C. & Herre, J. M. (1988). 'Electrocerebral accompaniments of syncope associated with malignant ventricular arrhythmias'. *Annals of Internal Medicine,* 108, 791–796.

Arstila, V. (2012). 'Time slows down during accidents'. *Frontiers of Psychology 3 (196).*

Aserinsky, E. & Kleitman, N. (1953). 'Regularly occurring periods of ocular motility and concomitant phenomena during sleep'. *Science 118,* 361–375.

Atherton, H. (1680). *The resurrection proved, or, The life to come demonstrated being a strange but true relation of what happened to Mrs Anna Atherton who lay in a trance 7 days: with her speech when she came to life / as it came from her brother Dr. Atherton.*

Atwater, P. (1992). 'Is There a Hell? Surprising observations about the near-death experience'. *Journal of Near-Death Studies 10,* 149–160.

Atwater, P. M. (1980). 'Coming back'. *Vital Signs, 1 (3), 6.*

Augustine, K. (2007). 'Does Paranormal Perception Occur in Near-Death Experiences?' *Journal of Near-Death Studies,* 203–236.

Auyong, D. B., Klein, S. M., Gan, T. J., Roche, A. M., Olson, D. & Habib, A. S. (2010). 'Processed electroencephalogram during donation after cardiac death'. *Anesthesia and Analgesia, 110(5),* 1428–1432.

Badham, P. (1997). 'Religious and near-death experience in relation to belief in a future life'. *Mortality. Vol 2,* No.1.

Badham, P. (2013). *Making Sense of Death and Immortality.* London: SPCK Publishing.

Badham, P. & Badham, L. (1982). *Immortality or Extinction.* London: SPCK.

Bailey, L. W. (2001). 'A "Little Death": The Near-Death-Death Experience and Tibetan Delogs'. *Journal of Near-Death Studies 19 (3),* 139–159.

Barker, S. A., Borjigin, J., Lomnicka, I. & Strassman, R. (2013). 'LC/MS/MS analysis of the endogenous dimethyltryptamine hallucinogens, their precursors, and major metabolites in rat pineal gland microdialysate'. *Biomed Chromatogr. 27,* 1690–1700.

Barrett, W. (1986). *Death-Bed Visions: Psychic Experiences of the Dying.* London: Aquarian Press.

Bear, D. M. (1979). 'Temporal lobe epilepsy: A syndrome of sensory-limbic hyperconnection'. *Cortex. 15,* 357–384.

Bear, D. & Fedio, P. (1977). 'Quantitative analysis of interictal behavior in temporal lobe epilepsy'. *Archives of Neurology, 34,* 454–467.

Beck, T. E. & Colli, J. E. (2003). 'A Quantum Biomechanical Basis for Near-Death Life Reviews'. *Journal of Near-Death Studies,* 169–189.

Becker, C. B. (1982). 'The failure of Saganomics: Why birth models cannot explain near-death phenomena'. *Anabiosis 2,* 102–109.

Bede. (1968). *A History of the English Church & People.* London: Penguin Classics.

Beecher, H. K. (1968). 'A definition of irreversible coma: report of the ad hoc Committee of the Harvard Medical School to examine the definition of brain death'. *JAMA 205,* 337–340.

Belanti, J., Perera, M. & Jagadheesan, K. (2008). 'Phenomenology of Near-death Experiences: A Cross-Cultural Perspective'. *Transcultural Psychiatry 45:1*, 121–133.

Berger, H. (1929). '*Über das Elektroenkephalogramm des Menschen*'. *Arch. Psychiatr. 87*, 527–570.

Bernat, J. L. (1984). 'The definition, criterion and statute of death'. *Seminars in Neurology 4*, 45–51.

Betti , L., Palego, L., Demontis, G. C., Miraglia, F. & Giannaccini , G. (2019, September 14). 'Hydroxyindole-O-methyltransferase (HIOMT) activity in the retina of melatonin-proficient mice'. *Heliyon 5 (9)*.

Birnholz, J. C. (1981). 'The development of human fetal eye movement patterns'. *Science, 213*, 679–681.

Blacker, C. (1975). *The Catalpa Bow: A Study of Shamanistic Practices in Japan*. London: George Allen & Unwin.

Blackmore, S. (1988, May 5). 'Visions from the dying brain'. *New Scientist*, 43–46.

Blackmore, S. (1993). *Dying to Live: Near-Death Experiences*. Buffalo: Prometheus Books.

Blackmore, S. (1996: 89). 'Near-Death Experiences'. *JR Soc Med*, 73–76.

Blackmore, S. (1998). 'Experiences of Anoxia'. *Journal of Near-Death Studies 17*, 111–120.

Blackmore, S. J. (1993). 'Near-death experiences in India: They have tunnels too'. *Journal of Near-Death Studies*, 205–217.

Blackmore, S. J. & Troscianko, T. S. (1989). 'The physiology of the tunnel'. *Journal of Near-Death Studies 8*, 15–28.

Blanke, O. (2004). 'Out-of-body experiences and their neural basis'. *BMJ 329*, 1414–1415.

Blanke, O. & Mohr, C. (2005). 'Out-of-body experience, heautoscopy, and autoscopic hallucinations of neurological origin: Implications for neurocognitive mechanisms of corporeal awareness and self consciousness'. *Brain Research Reviews 50*, 184–199.

Blanke, O., Landis, T., Spinelli, I. & Seeck, T. (2004). 'Out-of-body experience and autoscopy of neurological origin'. *Brain 127*, 243–258.

Blanke, O., Ortigue, S., Landis, O. & Seeck, T. (2002). 'Stimulating illusory own-body perceptions'. *Nature 419*, 269–270.

Blanke, O., Ortigue, S., Landis, T. & Seeck, M. (2002). 'Stimulating illusory own-body perceptions: The part of the brain that can induce out-of-body experiences has been located'. *Nature, 419*, 269–270.

Bókkon, I. (2008). 'Phosphene phenomenon: A new concept'. *Biosystems Vol 19 Issue 2*, 168–174.

Bókkon, I. & Vimal, R. L. (2009, September 4). 'Retinal phosphenes and discrete dark noises in rods: A new biophysical framework'. *Journal of Photochemistry and Photobiology*, pp. 255–259.

Bonenfant, R. (2001 (2)). 'A Child's Encounter with the Devil: An Unusual Near-Death Experience with Both Blissful and Frightening Elements'. *Journal of Near-Death Studies*, 87–100.

Bong-Han, K. (1962). 'Study on the reality of acupuncture meridian'. *Journal of Jo Sun Medicine 9*, 5–13.

Borjigin, J. (2013). 'Surge of neurophysiological coherence and connectivity in the dying brain'. *Proc Natl Acad Sci USA 110 (35)*, 14432–14437.

Borjigin, J., Wang, M. M. & Mashour, G. A. (2013, October 29). 'Reply to Chawla and Seneff: Near-death electrical brain activity in humans and animals requires additional studies'. *Proc Natl Acad Sci (PNAS) Vol 10. No 44*.

Bowker, J. (1991). *The Meaning of Death*. Cambridge: Cambridge University Press.

Braithwaite, J. J. (2008). 'Towards a cognitive neuroscience of the dying brain'. *The (UK) Skeptic*, 8–16.

Bremmer, J. N. (2002). *The rise and fall of the afterlife: The 1995 Read-Tuckwell Lectures at the University of Bristol*. New York: Routledge.

Brightman, M. W. & Reese, T. S. (1969). 'Junctions Between Intimately Apposed Cell Membranes in the Vertebrate Brain'. *Journal of Cell Biology, 40*, 648–677.

Brinkley, D. & Perry, P. (2008). *Saved By The Light*. HarperOne.

Britton, W. B. & Bootzin, R. R. (2004). 'Near-death experiences and the temporal lobe'. *Psychol Sci 15 (4)*.

Brugger, P., Regard, M. & Landis, T. (1997). 'Illusory reduplication of one's own body: phenomenology and classification of autoscopic phenomena'. *Cognitive Neuropsychiatry*.

Bukkyo Dendo Kyokai (1980). *The Teaching of Buddha*. Tokyo: Buddhist Promotion Foundation.

Bünning, S., & Blanke, O. (2005). S, Blanke O (2005) 'The out-of body experience: precipitating factors and neural correlates'. *Prog Brain Res 150*, 331–350.

Burt, C. (1968). 'Psychology and Psychical Research'. *Society for Psychical Research*, 79–80.

Carhart-Harris, R. L., Erritzoe, D., Williams, T., Stone, J. M., Reed, L. J., Colasanti, A., Nutt, D. (2012). 'Neural correlates of the psychedelic state as determined by fMRI studies with psilocybin'. *Proceedings of the National Academy of Sciences of the United States of America, 109 (6)*, 2138–2143.

Carr, D. (1981 February 14). 'Endorphins at the approach of death'. *Lancet*, 390.

Carr, D. B. (1982). 'Pathophysiology of stress-induced limbic lobe disfunction. A hypothesis relevant to NDEs'. *Anabiosis 2*, 75–89.

Cassol, H., Argembeau, A. D., Laureys, S. & Martial, C. (2019). 'Memories of near-death experiences: are they self-defining?' *Neuroscience of Consciousness*, 1–9.

Caton, R. (1875). 'Electrical currents of the brain'. *British Medical Journal 2* (765), 278.

Chalmers, D. J. (1995). 'Facing Up to the Problem of Consciousness'. *Journal of Consciousness Studies 2 (3)*, 200–219.

Chamberlain, D. (1998). *The Mind of Your Newborn Baby*. Berkely, CA: North Atlantic Books.

Chamberlain, D. B. (1990). *Babies Remember Birth: And Other Extraordinary Scientific Discoveries About the Mind and Personality of Your Newborn*. New York: Ballantine Books.

Chao, W., Bókkon, I., Dai, J. & Antal, I. (2011, January 19). 'Spontaneous and visible light-induced ultraweak photon emission from rat eyes'. *Brain Research*, 1–9.

Charland-Verville, V., Jourdan, J. P., Thonnard, M., Ledoux, D., Donneau, A.-F., Quertemont, E. & Laureys, F. (2014).

'Near-death experiences in non-life threatening events and coma of different etiologies'. *Human Neuroscience, 8*, 203.

Chawla, L. S., Junker, C., Jacobs, B., Seneff, M. G. & Akst, S. (2009). 'Surges of Electroencephalogram Activity at the Time of Death: A Case Series'. *Journal of Palliative Medicine No 12*, 1095–1100.

Chawla, L. S., Terek, M., Junker, C., Akst, S., Yoon, B., Brasha-Mitchell, E. & Seneff, M. (2017). 'Characterization of end-of-life electroencephalographic surges in critically ill patients'. *Death Studies*, 1–8.

Chawla, L. & Seneff, M. G. (2013). 'End-of-life electrical surges'. *Proc Natl Acad Sci*.

Cherkin, A. & Harroun, P. (1971). 'Anesthesia and Memory Processes'. *Anesthesiology*, 469–474.

Cheyne, J. A. & Girard, T. A. (2009). 'The body unbound: Vestibular–motor hallucinations and out-of-body experiences'. *Cortex. Vol 45, Issue 2*, 201–215.

Clute, H. L. & Levy, W. J. (1990). 'Electroencephalographic changes during brief cardiac arrest in humans'. *Anesthesiology*, 821–825.

Cohn-Sherbok, D. (1987). 'Death and Immortality in the Jewish Tradition'. In P. Badham, & L. Badham, *Death and Immortality in the Religions of the World*. London: Paragon.

Colli, J. E. (2001). 'Angels and aliens: Encounters with both near-death and UFOs'. *Presented at the International Association of Near-Death Studies International Conference*. Seattle.

Corazza, O. & Schifano, F. (2010). 'Near-death states reported in a sample of 50 misusers'. *Substance Use & Misuse, 45(6)*, 916–924.

Cornell-Bell, A. H., Finkbeiner, S. M., Cooper, M. S. & Smith, S. J. (1990). 'Glutamate induces calcium waves in cultured astrocytes: long-range glial signaling'. *Science 247*, 470–473.

Couliano, I. P. (1991). *Out Of This World: Otherworldly Journeys from Gilgamesh to Albert Einstein*. London: Shambhala.

Council, J. B. & Greyson, B. (1985). 'Near-death experiences and the "fantasy-prone" personality: Preliminary findings'. *Paper presented to the 93rd Annual Convention of the American Psychological Association*. Los Angeles.

Counts, D. A. (1983). 'Near-Death and Out-of-Body Experiences in a Melanesian Society'. *Anabiosis Vol 3. No 2*, 115–135.

Cozzi, N. V., Mavlyutov, N. V., Thompson, M. A., & Ruoho, A. E. (2011). 'Indolethylamine N-methyltransferase expression in primate nervous tissue', 840.19. *Soc. Neurosci. Abs., 37*. 840 19.

Craffert, P. C. (2015). 'When is an Out-of-Body Experience (Not) an Out-of-Body Experience? Reflections about Out-of-Body Phenomena in Neuroscientific Research'. *Journal of Cognition and Culture*, 13–31.

Craffert, P. F. (2019). 'Making Sense of Near-Death Experience Research: Circumstance Specific Alterations of Consciousness'. *Anthropology of Consciousness, Vol. 30, Issue 1*, 64–89.

Dachet, F., Brown, J. B. & Valyi-Nagy, T. (2021). 'Selective time-dependent changes in activity and cell-specific gene expression in human postmortem brain'. *Sci Rep 11*, 6078.

Dahaba, A. A. (2005). 'Different Conditions That Could Result in the Bispectral Index Indicating an Incorrect Hypnotic State'. *Anesth Analg 101*, 765–763.

Davis, A. K., Clifton, J. M., Weaver, E. G., Hurwitz, E. S., Johnson, M. W. & Griffiths, R. R. (2020, April 28). 'Survey of entity encounter experiences occasioned by inhaled N,N-dimethyltryptamine: Phenomenology, interpretation, and enduring effects'. *J. Psychopharmacol*, 1008–1020.

Davis, L. (1988). 'A Comparison of UFO and Near-Death Experiences as Vehicles for the Evolution of Human Consciousness'. *Journal of Near-Death Studies 6 (4)*, 240–257.

De Ridder, D., Van Laere, K., Dupont, K., Menovsky, T. & Van Der Heyning, P. (2007). 'Visualizing out-of-body experience in the brain'. *N. Engl J Med*, 1829–1833.

Dean, J. G., Liu, T., Huff, S., Sheler, B., Barker, S. A., Strassman, R. J., Borjigin, J. (2019). 'Biosynthesis and Extracellular Concentrations of N,N-dimethyltryptamine (DMT) in Mammalian Brain'. *Scientific Reports 9 (1)*.

Debruyne, H., Peremans, K. & Audenaert, K. (2011). 'Cotard's syndrome'. *Mind Brain 2*, 67–72.

DeHaan, S. & Fuchs, T. (2010). 'The Ghost in the Machine: Disembodiment in Schizophrenia – Two Case Studies'. *Psychopathology 43*, 327–333.

Deltgen, F. (1978). 'Culture, Drug and Personality'. *Ethnomedizin 5*.

Dewhurst, K., & Beard, A. W. (2003). 'Sudden religious conversions in temporal lobe epilepsy'. *Epilepsy & Behavior 4*, 78–87.

Diagnostic and statistical manual of mental disorders, 4th ed. (1994). Washington DC: American Psychiatric Association.

Dittrich, L. (2013, July 10). 'The Doctor Whose Story Debunked Proof of Heaven'. *Esquire*.

Dittrich, L. (2013, July 2013). 'The Prophet'. Retrieved from Esquire.com: https://www.esquire.com/entertainment/interviews/a23248/the-prophet/

Domino, E. F., Chodoff, P. & Corrsen, G. (1965). 'Pharmacologic effects of CI-581, a new dissociative anesthetic, in man'. *Clinical and Pharmacological Therapeutics 6*, 279–291.

Donner, K. (1954). *Among the Samojeds in Siberia*. New Haven.

Dossey, L. (1989). *Recovering the Soul: A Scientific and Spiritual Search*. New York: Bantam Books.

Drab, K. J. (1981). 'The tunnel experience: Reality or hallucination?' *Anabiosis: The Journal of Near-Death Studies, 1(2)*, 126–152.

Dreyfus-Brisac, C. (1964). 'The electroencephalogram of the premature infant and full-term newborn. Normal and abnormal development of waking and sleeping pattern'. In P. Kellaway & I. Peterson, *Neurological and Electroencephalographic Correlative Studies in Infancy* (186–207). London: Grune & Stratton.

Druss, R. G. & Kornfeld, D. S. (1967). 'The Survivors of Cardiac Arrest: A Psychiatric Study'. *JAMA. Vol 201. No 5*, 291–296.

Duncan, F. E., Que, E. L., Feinberg, E. C., O'Halloran, T. V. & Woodroff, T. K. (2016, April 26). 'The zinc spark is an inorganic signature of human egg activation'. *Sci Rep 6*.

Ehrsson, E. E. (2007). 'The Experimental Induction of Out-of-Body Experiences'. *Science 317*, 1048.

Eliade, M. (1989). *Shamanism: Archaic Techniques of Ecstasy*. London: Arkana.

Ellwood, G. F. (2000). 'Religious experience, religious worldviews, and near-death studies'. *Journal of Near-Death Studies 19*, 5–21.

Enami, M. (1954). 'Preoptico-subcommissural neurosecretory system in the eel'. *Endo crinologia Japonica, 1*, 133–145.

Engmann, B. (2014). *Near-Death Experiences: Heavenly Insights or Human Illusion?* Heidelberg/New York/London: Springer.

Evans-Wentz, W. (1957). *The Tibetan Book of the Dead or the After-Death Experiences on the Bardo Plane, according to Lama Kazi Dawa-Sumdip's English Rendering 1927*. Oxford: Oxford University Press.

Faguet, R. A. (1979). 'With the eyes of the mind: autoscopic phenomena in the hospital setting'. *Gen Hosp Psychiatry* 1, 311–314.

Fenwick, P. (1997). 'Is the Near-Death Experience Only N-Methyl-D-Aspartate Blocking?' *Journal of Near-Death Studies*, 43–53.

Fenwick, P. & Fenwick, E. (1995). *The Truth in the Light: An Investigation of Over 300 Near-Death Experiences*. London: Headline Book Publishing.

Fiore, E. (1988). *The Unquiet Dead*. New York: Ballantine.

Flammarion, C. (1922). *Death and its mystery. I. Before Death*. London: T. Fisher Unwin.

Flynn, C. P. (1982). 'Meanings and Implications of NDEr Transformations: Some Preliminary Findings and Implications'. *Anabiosis: The Journal of Near-Death Studies* 2, 3–13.

Foerster, O. & Penfield, W. (1930). 'The structural basis of traumatic epilepsy and results of radical operation'. *Brain 63*, 99–119.

Fontana y Col, A. E. (1974). '*Terapia antidepresiva con CI 581 (Ketamina)*'. *Acta Psiquiat. Psicol. America Latina; 1974* (20.32).

Fox, M. (2003). *Through The Valley of the Shadow of Death: Religion and Spirituality and the Near-Death Experience*. London: Routledge.

Fracasso, C., Aleyasin, A., Friedman, H. & Young, S. (2010). 'Near-death experiences among a sample of Iranian Muslims'. *Journal of Near-Death Studies 29*, 265–272.

French, C. C. (2001, December 15). 'Dying to know the truth: visions of a dying brain, or false memories?' *The Lancet*, 210–211.

Friendly, A. (1977). *Beaufort of the Admiralty: The life of Sir Francis Beaufort 1774–1857*. London: Hutchinson.

Gabbard, G. O. & Twemlow, S. W. (1989). 'Comments on "A Neurobiological Model for Near-Death Experiences"'. *Journal of Near-Death Studies*, 261–263.

Gabbard, G. O. & Twemlow, S. W. (1991). 'Do "Near-Death Experiences" Occur Only Near Death? Revisited'. *Journal of Near-Death Studies 10 (1)*, 41–47.

Gabbard, G. O., Twemlow, S. W. & Jones, F. C. (1981). 'Do "Near-Death Experiences" Occur Only Near Death?' *Journal of Nervous and Mental Disease, 169*, 374–377.

Gabbard, G. O., Twemlow, S. W. & Jones, F. C. (1982). 'The out-of-body experience: A phenomenological typology based on questionnaire responses'. *American Journal of Psychiatry, 139*, 450–455.

Gallimore, A. R. (2019). *Alien Information Theory: Psychedelic Drug Technologies and the Cosmic Game*. London: Strange World Press.

Gallup, G. & Proctor, W. (1982). *Adventures in Immortality*. New York: McGraw Hill.

Gambrell, M. (2005). 'Using the BIS monitor in palliative care: A case study'. *J Neurosci Nurs*, 140–143.

Gardiner, E. (1989). *Visions of Heaven and Hell before Dante*. New York: Italica.

Garrity, A. G., Pearlson, G. D., McKiernan, K., Lloyd, D., Kiehl, K. A. & Calhoun, V. D. (2007). 'Aberrant "default mode" functional connectivity in schizophrenia'. *Am J Psychiatry. 164*, 450–457.

Gayton, A. H. (1935). 'The Orpheus Myth in North America'. *Journal of American Folklore*, 263–293.

Geschwind, N. (1983). 'Interictal behavioral changes in epilepsy'. *Epilepsia, 24(I)*, 23–30.

Gilkey, J. C., Jaffe, L. F., Ridgeway, E. B. & Reynolds, G. T. (1978). 'A free calcium wave traverses the activating egg of the medaka, Oryzias latipes'. *Cell Biol 76,* 448–466.

Ginzberg, R. (1949). 'Three years with Hans Berger: A contribution to his biography'. *J.Hist. Med.Allied Sci,* 361–371.

Giovetti, P. (2007). *Near-death experiences. Testimonianze di esperienze in punto.* Rome: Edizioni Mediterranee.

Gnoli, G. (1965). *'Lo stato di maga'. AION IS,* 105–117.

Gnoli, G. *Ashavan: Contributo allo studio de llibro di Arda Wiraz.* Iranica.

Gomez-Jeria, J. S. & Lic, Q. (2006). 'A Near-Death Experience in Pu Songling's Strange Stores from Liaozai's Studio'. *Journal of Near-Death Studies,* 113–120.

Gray, J. (2004). *Consciousness: Creeping Up on the Hard Problem.* Oxford: Oxford University Press.

Green, C. (1968). *Out-of-the-body experiences.* London: Ballentine.

Greer, D. M., Shemie, S. D., Torrance, S., Varelas, P. & Goldenberg, F. D. (2020). 'Determination of brain death/death by neurologic criteria: the world brain death project'. *JAMA 324,* 1078–1091.

Greicius, M. D., Florew, B. H., Menon, V., Glover, V. H., Solvason, H. B., Kenna, H., Schatzberg, A. F. (2007). 'Resting-state functional connectivity in major depression: abnormally increased contributions from subgenual cingulate cortex and thalamus'. *Biol Psychiatry. 62,* 429–437.

Greicius, M. D., Srivastava, G., Reiss, G. & Menon, V. (2004). 'Default-mode network activity distinguishes Alzheimer's disease from healthy aging: evidence from functional MRI'. *Proc Natl Acad Sci USA. 101,* 4637–42.

Grey, M. (1985). *Return From Death: An Exploration of the Near-Death Experience.* London: Arkana.

Greyson, B. (1983). 'The Near-Death Experience Scale: Construction, reliability, and validity'. *Journal of Nervous and Mental Disease 171,* 369–750.

Greyson, B. (1985). 'A typology of near-death experiences'. *American Journal of Psychiatry 142,* 967–969.

Greyson, B. (1993). 'Near-Death Experiences and the Physio-Kundalini Syndrome'. *Journal of Religion and Health Vol 32, No 4,* 277–290.

Greyson, B. (1998). 'Biological Aspects of Near-Death Experiences'. *Perspectives in Biology and Medicine, Volume 42, Number 1,* 14–32.

Greyson, B. (2000). 'Near-Death Experiences'. In E. Cardena, S. J. Lynn & S. Krippner, *Varieties of Anomalous Experience: Examining the Scientific Evidence* (315–352). Washington DC: American Psychological Association.

Greyson, B. (2010). 'Implications of Near-Death Experiences for a Postmaterialist Psychology'. *Psychology of Religion and Spirituality,* 37–45.

Greyson, B. (2021). *After: A Doctor Explores What Near-Death Experiences Reveal About Life and Beyond.* New York: St Martin Essentials.

Greyson, B. & Holden, J. (2003). 'Incidence and correlates of near-death experiences in a cardiac care unit'. *Gen Hosp Psychiatry 25,* 269–276.

Greyson, B. & Ring, K. (2004). 'The Life Changes Inventory – Revised'. *Journal of Near-Death Studies 23 (1),* 41–54.

Greyson, B., & Stevenson, I. (1980). 'The phenomenology of near-death experiences'. *Am J Psychiatry 137,* 1193–1196.

Greyson, B., Kelly, E. F. & Ross Dunseath, W. J. (2013). 'Surge of neurophysiological activity in the dying brain'. *PNAS vol 110 No 47,* E4405.

Greyson, B., van Lommel, P. & Fenwick, P. (2022). 'Commentary: Enhanced Interplay of Neuronal Coherence and Coupling in the Dying Human Brain'. *Frontiers in Aging Neuroscience. Vol 14.*

Griffiths, R. (1926). *Hymns of the Rigveda.* Benares: Medical Hall Press.

Grof, S. (1975). *Realms of the Human Unconscious: Observations from LSD Psychotherapy.* New York: Viking.

Hampe, J. (1979). *To Die is Gain: The Experience of One's Own Death.* London: DLT.

Hansen, A. J. (1985). 'Effect of anoxia on ion distribution in the brain'. *Physiol Rev,* 101–148.

Harner, M. (1987). 'The ancient wisdom in shamanic cultures'. In S. Nicholson, *Shamanism* (3–16). Wheaton, IL: Quest Books.

Harris, S. (2012, October 12). *This Must Be Heaven*. Retrieved from samharris.org: https://www.samharris.org/blog/this-must-be-heaven

Hashami, A., Oroojan, A., Rassouli, M. & Ashrafizadeh, H. (2023). 'Explanation of near-death experiences: a systematic analysis of case reports and qualitative research'. *Frontiers of Psychology Vol 14 2031*, 1–39.

Heaney, J. (1984). *The Sacred and the Psychic: Parapsychology and Christian Theology*. New Jersey: Paulist Press.

Heim, A. (1992). *'Notizen uber den Tod durch Absturz'* ('Remarks on fatal falls'). In *Yearbook of the Swiss Alpine Club* (327–337). Zurich: Swiss Alpine Club.

Herzog, D. B. & Herrin, J. T. (1985). 'Near-Death experiences in the very young'. *Critical Care Medicine 13*, 1074–1075.

Hilgard, E. R. (1984). 'The Hidden Observer and Multiple Personality'. *International Journal of Clinical and Experimental Hypnosis 32:2*, 248–253.

Hobson, J. A., Hong, C. C., & Friston, K. J. (2014). 'Virtual-reality and consciousness interface in dreaming'. *Frontiers in Psychology*.

Hoffman, A. (1980). *LSD: My Problem Child*. New York: McGraw-Hill.

Holden, J. M. (2007). 'More Things in Heaven and Earth: A Response to "Near-Death Experiences with Hallucinatory Features"'. *Journal of Near-Death Studies*, 33–42.

Holden, J. M. (2009). 'Veridical perception in near-death experiences'. In J. M. Holden, B. Greyson & D. James, *The Handbook of Near-Death Experiences* (185–211). Santa Barbara: Praeger/ABC-CLIO.

Holden, J. M., Greyson, B. & James, D. (2009). *The Handbook of Near-Death – Thirty Years of Investigation*. Santa Barbara: Praeger ABC CLIO.

Hughes, J. R. (2008). 'Gamma, fast, and ultra-fast waves in the brain: Their relationships with epilepsy and behavior'. *Epilepsy and Behavior. Vol 13, Issue 1*, 25–31.

Ingerman, S. (1991). *Soul retrieval: Mending the fragmented self*. San Francisco: Harper.

Irwin, H. J. (1990). 'Fantasy Proneness and Paranormal Beliefs'. *Psychological Reports*, 655–658.

Irwin, H. J. (1993). 'The near-death as a dissociative phenomenon: An empirical assessment'. *Journal of Near-Death Studies 12*, 95–103.

Jaffe, L. F. (1980). 'Calcium explosions as triggers of development'. *Ann NY Acad Sci*.

Jansen, K. (1998). 'Ketamine – Near Death and Near Birth Experiences'.

Jansen, K. (2004). *Ketamine: Dreams and Realities*. Sarasota: Multidisciplinary Association for Psychedelic Studies.

Jansen, K. L. (1996). 'Neuroscience, Ketamine and the Near-Death Experience'. In L. Bailey, J. Yates & (Eds), *The Near-death experience*. London: Routledge.

Jansen, K. L. (1997). 'Response to commentaries on "The ketamine model of the near-death expererience"'. *Journal of Near-Death Studies, 16*, 79–95.

Jarrett, C. (2020). 'To Death and Back'. *BBC Science Focus Magazine – Extreme Science*, pp. 26–31.

John, E. R. (2001). 'A Field Theory of Consciousness'. *Consciousness and Cognition 10*, 184–213.

John, E. R., Prichep, L. S., Kox, W., Valdes-Sosa, P., Bosch-Bayard, J., Aubert, E., Guigino, L. D. (2001). 'Invariant Reversible QEEG Effects of Anesthetics'. *Consciousness and Cognition 10*, 165–183.

Jourdan, J. P. (1994). 'Near-Death and Transcendental Experiences'. *Near-Death and Transcendental Experiences*, 177–200.

Jouvet, M. & Michael, F. (1959). 'Electromyographic correlations of sleep in the chronic decorticate and mesencephalic cat'. *R.Seances.Soc.Biol. Fil, 153*, 422–425.

Judson, J. R. & Wiltshaw, E. (1983 Sept). 'A Near-death experience'. *Lancet*, 561–562.

Jung, C. J. (1969). 'Synchronicity: An acausal connecting principle'. In C. J. Jung, *The collected works of C. G. Jung, Vol. 8, 2nd ed.* (pp. 417–531). New Jersey: Princeton University Press.

Jung, C. J. (1989). *Memories, Dreams, Reflections*. New York: Vintage.

Kalweit, H. (1988). *Dreamtime and Inner Space*. London: Shambhala.

Kastrup, B. (2021). *A rational, empirical case for postmortem survival based solely on mainstream science*. Essentia Foundation.

Keene, M. F. & Hewer, E. E. (1935). 'The Sub-commissural organ and the mesocoelic recess in the human brain, together with a note on Reissner's Fiber'. *J Anat. 69 (pt 4)*, 501–507.

Keith, A. (1971). *The religion and philosophy of the Veda and Upanishads*. Westport, CT: Greenwood Press.

Kellehear, A. (1993). 'Culture, biology, and the near-death experience: A reappraisal'. *Journal of Nervous and Mental Disease 181 (3)*, 148–156.

Kellehear, A. (2001). 'An Hawaiian near-death experience'. *Journal of Near-Death Studies*, 31–35.

Kelly, E. W., Greyson, B. & Kelly, E. F. (2007). 'Unusual experiences near death and related phenomena'. In A. Gauld, M. Grosso & B. Greyson, *Irreducible Mind* (367–421). Lanham, MD: Rowman & Littlefield.

Kelly, E. W., Greyson, B. & Stevenson, I. (2000). 'Can experiences near death furnish evidence of life after death?' *Omega vol 40 (4)*, 513–519.

Kelly, E., Kelly, E. W., Crabtree, A., Gauld, A., Grosso, M. & Greyson, B. (2007). *Irreducible mind: toward a psychology for the 21st century*. New York: Rowman & Littlefield Publishers, Inc.

Kim, A. M., Bernhardt , M. L., Kong, B. Y., Ahn, R. W., Vogt, S., Woodroff, T. K. & O'Halloran, T. V. (2011, July 15). 'Zinc sparks are triggered by fertilization and facilitate cell cycle resumption in mammalian eggs'. *ACS Chem Biol. 15:6 (7)*, 716–723.

Klemenc-Ketis, Z., Kersnik, J. & Grmec, S. (2010). 'The effect of carbon dioxide on near-death experiences in out-of-hospital cardiac arrest survivors: a prospective observational study'. *Critical Care 14:R56*, 1–7.

Kohno, K. (1969). 'Electron microscope study of Reissner's fiber'. *Zellforsch 94*, 565–573.

Kongara, K., McIlhone, A., Kells, N. & Johnson, C. (2014). 'Electroencephalographic evaluation of decapitation of the anaesthetized rat'. *Lab. Anim. 48*, 15–19.

Koob, A. (2009, October 27). 'The Root of Thought: What Do Glial Cells Do?' *Scientific American, 27*.

Kreps, J. I. (2009). 'The search for Muslim near-death experiences'. *Journal of Near-Death Studies, 28*, 67–86.

Kvaerne, P. (2001). *The Bon Religion of Tibet: The Iconography of a Living Tradition* . London: Shambhala.

Lai, C. F., Kao, T. W., Wu, M. S., Chang, C. H., Lu, C. S., Yang, C. S., Chen, W. Y. (2007). 'Impact of near-death experiences on dialysis patients: a multi-center collaborative study'. *Amer. J. Kidney Dis. 50 (1)*, 124–132.

Lake, J. (2019). 'The near-death experience (NDE) as an inherited predisposition: Possible genetic, epigenetic, neural and symbolic mechanisms'. *Medical Hypothesis 126*, 135–148.

Landes, R. (1968). *Ojibwa Religion and the Midewiwin*. London: American University Press.

Lange, R., Greyson, B. & Houran, J. (2004). 'A Rasch Scaling Validation of a "Core" Near-Death Experience'. *British Journal of Psychology 95*, 161–77.

Lawson, A. H. (1994). 'Response to the Twemlow Paper'. *Journal of Near-Death Studies*, 245–265.

Leake, J. (2010, May 30). 'That's not the Afterlife – it's a brainstorm'. *Sunday Times*.

Leary, T., Metzner, R. & Alpert, R. (1964). *The Psychedelic Experience: A Manual Based on the Tibetan Book of the Dead*. New York: University Books.

Lee, B. C., Kim, S. & Soh, K. S. (2008). 'Novel anatomic structures in the brain and spinal cord of rabbit that may belong to the Bonghan system of potential acupuncture meridians'. *J Acupunct Meridian Stud*, 29–35.

Lee, H. S., Ghetti, A., Pinto-Duarte, A., Wang, X., Dziewczapolski, G., Galimi, F., Heinemann, S. F. (2014). 'Astrocytes contribute to gamma oscillations and recognition memory'. *Proc Natl Adad Sci USA*.

Lehmann, A. (1892). *Die Hauptgesetze des meschlichen Gefühlslebens (The principle laws of the human life of emotions)*. Leipzig: O.R. Reisland.

Lempert, T., Bauer, M. & Schmidt, D. (1994). 'Syncope and near-death experience'. *Lancet 344*, 829–830.

Lerma, J. (2009). *Learning from the light*. Career Press: Franklin Lakes, NJ.

Lester, D. (2005). *Is There Life After Death: An Examination of the Empirical Evidence*. London: McFarland & Company.

Li, D., Mabrouk, O. S., Liu, T., Tian, F., Xu, G., Choi, S. J., Borjigin, J. (2015, April 6). 'Asphyxia-activated cortico-cardiac signaling accelerates cardiac arrest'. *Neuroscience*.

Liberles, S. D. (2009). 'Trace amine-associated receptors are olfactory receptors in vertebrates'. *Annals of the New York Academy of Sciences 1170*, 168–172.

Liester, M. B. (2013). 'Near-Death Experiences and ayahuasca-induced experiences – Two unique pathways to a phenomonologically similar state of consciousness'. *Journal of Transpersonal Psychology Vol 45. No 1*, 24–48.

Lippman, P. W. (1953). 'Hallucinations of physical duality in migraine'. *Journal of Nervous and Mental Disease*, 345–350.

Long, J. & Holden, J. M. (2007). 'Does the Arousal System Contribute to Near-Death And Out-of-Body Experiences? A Summary and Response'. *Journal of Near Death Studies 25 (3)*, 135–169.

Long, J. M., Long, J. & MacLurg, J. (2006). 'Out-of-Body Experiences: All in the Brain?' *Journal of Near-Death Studies*, 99–107.

Luke, D. (2012). 'Psychoactive substances and paranormal phenomenon: A comprehensive Review'. *International Journal of Transpersonal Studies. Vol 31 Issue 1*, 97–156.

Malarky, K. (2010). *The Boy Who Came Back From Heaven*. Carol Stream: Tyndale House.

Manford, M. & Anderman, F. (1998). 'Complex visual hallucinations: Clinical and neurobiological insights'. *Brain, 121*, 1819–1840.

Marsh, M. N. (2010). Out-of-Body and Near-Death Experiences: *Brain-State or Glimpses of Immortality?* Oxford: Oxford University Press.

Marsh, M. N. (2016). 'The Near-Death Experience: A Reality Check?' *Humanities 5 (2)*.

Martial, C., Cassol, H., Charland-Verville, V., Merckelbach, H. & Laureys, S. (2018, June 7). 'Fantasy Proneness Correlates With the Intensity of Near-Death Experience'. *Front. Psychiatry. Vol 9*.

Martial, C., Cassola, H., Charland-Verville, V., Pallavicini, C., Sanz, C., Zamberlan, F., Tagliazucchi, E. (2019). 'Neurochemical models of near-death experiences: A large-scale study based on the semantic similarity of written reports'. *Consciousness and Cognition 69*, 52–69.

Martial, C., Mensen, A., Charland-Verville, V., Vanhaudenhuyse, A., Rentmeister, D., Ali Bahri , M., Faymonville, M.-E. (2019, October 1). 'Neurophenomenology of near-death expererience memory in hypnotic recall: a within-subject EEG study'. *Nature Research*.

Maslow, A. A. (1943). 'A Theory of Human Motivation'. *Psychological Review*, 370–396.

Maslow, A. H. (1971). *The Farther Reaches of Human Nature*. New York: Viking Compass.

Maslow, A. H. (1973). *Psychologie des Seins : ein Entwurf*. Munich: Kindler.

Maslow, A. H. (1994). *Religions, Values, and Peak-Experiences*. London: Penguin.

Masumian, F. (2002). *Life after death: A study of afterlife in world religions*. Los Angeles: Kalimat Press.

Masumian, F. (2009). 'World Religions and Near-Death Experiences'. In J. M. Holden, B. Greyson & D. James, *The Handbook of Near-Death Experiences: Thirty Years of Investigation* (159–183). Santa Barbara: Praeger.

Mavromatis, A. (2010). *Hypnagogia: The Unique State of Consciousness Between Wakefulness and Sleep*. London: Thyrsos Press.

Mayer, R. S. (1988). *Through divided minds: Probing the mysteries of multiple personalities*. New York: Doubleday.

Mayer, R. S. (1991). *Satan's children: Case Studies in Multiple Personality*. New York: G.P. Putnam's Sons.

Mays, R. (2013, August 12). *Esquire Article on Eban Alexander Distorts the facts*. Retrieved from IANDS.org: https://www.iands.org/ndes/more-info/ndes-in-the-news/970-esquire-article-on-eben-alexander-distorts-the-facts.html

Mays, R. G. & Mays, S. B. (2015). 'Explaining Near-Death Experiences: Physical or Non-Physical Causation?' *Journal of Near-Death Studies*, 125–149.

Mazzi, C., Mancini, F. & Savazzi, S. (2014). 'Can IPS reach visual awareness without V1? Evidence from TMS in healthy subjects and hemianopic patients'. *Neuropsychologia 64*, 134–144.

McDougall, D. (1907). 'The Soul: Hypothesis Concerning Soul Substance Together with Experimental Evidence of the Existence of Such Substance'. *American Medicine*, 240–243.

McGill, M. L., Devinsky, O., Kelly, C., Milham, M., Castellanos, F. X., Quinn, B. T., Thesen, T. (2012). 'Default mode network abnormalities in idiopathic generalized epilepsy'. *Epilepsy & Behavior. Vol 23, 3*, 353–359.

McGinn, C. (1989). 'Can we solve the mind-brain problem?' *Mind, 98*, 349–366.

McKay, R. & Cipolotti, L. (2007). 'Attributional style in a case of Cotard delusion'. *Conscious. Cogn. 16*, 349–359.

Meduna, L. (1950). *Carbon Dioxide Therapy*. Springfield: Charles Thomas.

Metzinger, T. (2009). *The Ego Tunnel: The Science of the Mind and the Myth of The Self*. New York: Basic Books.

Meynert, T. (1892). '*Zur Mechanik des Gehirnbaues*' ('On the mechanism of the brain'). In W. Braumuller, *Sammlung von populaer-wissenschaftlichen Vortraegen über den Bau und die Leistungen des Gehirns (Collection of popular-scientific lectures on the form and function of the brain)*. Vienna.

Michael, P. (2023). 'The Death Trip: A Case Study of Psilocybin's Simulation of the Phenomonology and Long-Term Changes of the Near-Death Experience'. In A. Tollan, *Breaking Convention: A Seismic Shift in Psychedelia* (5–22). London: Strange Attractor Press.

Michael, P., Luke, D. & Robinson, O. (2021, December 16). 'An Encounter with the Other: A Thematic and Content Analysis of DMT Experiences From a Naturalistic Field Study'. *Frontiers of Psychology*, 1–20.

Michael, P., Luke, D. & Robinson, O. (2023, June 29). 'This is your brain on death: a comparative analysis of a near-death experience and subsequent 5-Methoxy-DMT experience'. *Frontiers in Psychology. Vol 14.*, 1–17.

Mikorey, M. (1960). 'Das Zeitparadoxon der Lebensbilderschau in Katastrophensituationen'. *Zentralbl Neural Psychiatr 159:4*.

Miller, F. G. & Truog, R. (2012). *Death, Dying, and Organ Transplantation*. Oxford: Oxford University Press.

Minsky, M. (1988). *The Society of Mind*. New York: Simon and Schuster.

Mobbs, D. & Watt, C. (2011). 'There is nothing paranormal about near-death experiences'. *Trends Cogn. Sci. 15*, 447–449.

Moody, R. (1975). *Life After Life*. Covington Ga: Mockingbird.

Moody, R., & Perry, P. (1993). *Reunions: Visionary Encounters with Departed Ones*. London: Little, Brown & Company.

Moorjani, A. (2012). *Dying to be Me*. Carlsbad: Hay House.

Morris, L. L. & Knafi, K. (2003). 'The Nature and meaning of the near-death experience for patients and critical care nurses'. *Journal of Near-Death Studies 21 (3)*, 139–167.

Morse, M. (1985). 'Near-death experiences in a pediatric population'. *American Journal of Diseases of Children*, 596–600.

Morse, M. L. (1994). 'Near-death experiences and Death-Related Visions in Children'. *Current Problems in Pediatrics*, 55–83.

Morse, M. L., Castillo, P., Venecia, D., Milstein, J. & Tyler, D. (1986). 'Childhood near-death experiences'. *American Journal of Diseases of Children, 140*, 1110–1114.

Morse, M. L., Venecia, D. & Milstein, J. (1989). 'Near-death experiences: A Neurophysiologic Explanatory Model'. *Journal of Near-Death Studies*, 45–53.

Morse, M. & Perry, P. (1992). *Transformed by the Light*. New York: Villard.

Murphy, T. (2001). 'Near-Death Experiences in Thailand'. *Journal of Near-Death Studies 19 (3)*, 101–108.

Murphy, T. (2001). 'The Structure and Function of Near-Death Experiences: An Algorithmic Reincarnation Hypothesis'. *Journal of Near-Death Studies 20 (2)*, 101–118.

Muthukumaraswamy, S. D. (2013). 'High-frequency brain activity and muscle artifacts in MEG/EEG: a review and recommendations'. *Front. Hum. Neurosci. 7.*

Nagel, T. (1974). 'What is it like to be a bat?' *Philosophical Review 4*, 435–450.

Nahm, M. (2009). 'Four Ostensible Near-Death Experiences of Roman Times with Peculiar Features: Mistake Cases, Correction Cases, Xenoglossy, and a Prediction'. *Journal of Near-Death Studies 27 (4)*, 211– 222.

Nahm, M. & Nicolay, J. (2010). 'Essential Features of Eight Published Muslim Near-Death Experiences: An Addendum to Joel Ibrahim Kreps'. *Journal of Near-Death Studies 29 (1)*, 255–263.

Nair-Collins, M. (2022, Winter). 'Expanding the Social Status of "Corpse" to the Severely Comatose: Henry Beecher and the Harvard Brain Death Committee'. *Perspectives in Biology and Medicine, vol. 65 no. 1*, 41–58.

Neihardt, J. (1974). *Black Elk Speaks*. London: Abacus.

Nelson, K. (2015, March-April). 'Near-Death Experiences: Neuroscience Perspectives on Near-Death Experiences'. *Mo Med 112(2)*, 92–96.

Nelson, K. R., Mattingly, M. & Schmitt, F. A. (2007). 'Out-of-body experience and arousal'. *Neurology*, 794–795.

Noyes, R. & Kletti, R. (1972). 'The experience of dying from falls'. *Omega, 3*, 45–52.

Noyes, R. & Kletti, R. (1976). 'Depersonalization in the face of life-threatening danger: a description'. *Psychiatry 39*, 19–27.

Noyes, R. & Kletti, R. (1976). 'Depersonalization in the face of life-threatening danger: an interpretation'. *Omega*, 103–114.

Noyes, R. & Kletti, R. (1977). 'Panoramic memory: A response to the threat of death'. *Omega 8*, 181–194.

Noyes, R. & Slyman, D. (1979). 'The subjective response to life-threatening danger'. *Omega; 9*, 313–321.

Oderberg, D. S. (October 2019). 'Death, unity and the brain'. *Theoretical Medicine and Bioethics.*

Ogston, A. (1919). *Reminiscences of Three Campaigns*. London: Hodder and Stoughton.

Ohayon, M. M. (2000). 'Prevalence of hallucinations and their pathological associations in the general population'. *Psychiatry Research 97*, 153–164.

Osis, K. & Haraldsson, E. (1977). *At The Hour of Death*. New York: Avon.

Owens, J. E., Cook, E. W. & Stevenson, I. (1990). 'Features of "near-death experience" in relation to whether or not patients were dead'. *The Lancet 336*, 1175–1177.

Palhano-Fontes, F., Andrade, K. C., Tofoli, L. F., Santos, A. C., Crippa, J. A., Hallak, J. E., Araujo, D. B. (2015, February 18). 'The psychedelic state induced by ayahuasca modulates the activity and connectivity of the default mode network'. *PLoS One.*

Palmer, J. A. (1978). 'The Out-of-Body Experience'. *Parapsychology Review 9(5)*, 19–22.

Pandarakalam, J. P. (1990). 'Enigma of the near-death experience'. *Indian Journal of Psychological Medicine 13 (1)*, 131–136.

Pani, P., Giarroccoa, F., Brunamonti, E. & Stefano, M. (2018, September 5–7 September). 'Persistence of cortical neuronal activity in the dying brain'. *Resucitation*, 5–7.

Parnia, S. (2013). *The Lazarus Effect: The Science that is Rewriting the Boundaries Between Life and Death*. Rider.

Parnia, S., Waller, D. G., Yeates, R. & Fenwick, P. (2001). 'A qualitative and quantitative study of the incidence, features and aetiology of near-death experiences in cardiac arrest survivors'. *Resucitation 48*, 149–156.

Pasricha, S. (1995). 'Near-Death Experiences in South India: A Systematic Study'. *Journal of Scientific Exploration Vol 9, No 1*, 79–88.

Pasricha, S. & Stevenson, I. (1986). 'Near-death experience in India'. *Journal of Nervous and Mental Disease*, 165–170.

Peake, A. (2005). 'Cheating the Ferryman: A New Paradigm of Existence?' *Journal of Near-Death Studies. Vol 23 No 2*, 67–99.

Peake, A. (2008). *The Daemon: A Guide to Your Extraordinary Secret Self.* London: Arcturus.

Peake, A. (2016). *Opening The Doors of Perception.* London: Watkins.

Peake, A. (2019). *The Hidden Universe: An Investigation into Non-Human Intelligences.* London: Watkins.

Peake, A. (2022). *Cheating The Ferryman: The Revolutionary Science of Life After Death.* London: Arcturus.

Penfield, W. (1951). 'Memory Mechanisms'. *Seventy-Sixth Annual Meeting of the American Neurological Association* (pp. 178–198). Atlantic City: McGill University.

Penfield, W. (1972). 'The Electrode, the Brain and the Mind'. *Z. Neurol 201*, pp. 297–309.

Penfield, W., & Erickson, T. C. (1941). *Epilepsy and Cerebral Location.* Charles C Thomas.

Persinger, M. A. (1989). 'Modern neuroscience and near-death experiences: Expectancies and implications. Comments on "A neurobiological model for near-death experiences"'. *Journal of Near-Death Studies 7*, 233–239.

Persinger, M. A. & Makarec, K. (1987). 'Temporal lobe epileptic signs and correlative behaviors displayed by normal populations'. *Journal of General Psychology, 114*, 179–195.

Plato. (1955). *The Republic (tr. H.D.P. Lee) Pt. 11.* London: Penguin.

Plutarch. (1984). *Moralia (vol. 7). (P. H. De Lacy & B. Einarson, trans.).* London: William Heinemann.

Popper, K. & Eccles, J. C. (1893). *The Self and its Brain: An Argument for Interactionism.* New York: Routledge.

President's Commission for the Study of Ethical Problems in Medicine and Biomedical and Biobehavioral Research. (1981). *Defining Death: A Report on the Medical, Legal and Ethical Issues in the Determination of Death.* Washington DC: US GPO.

Punzak, D. (2017). *A Spiritual Hypothesis: An Enquiry Into Abnormal and Paranormal Behavior.* Bloomington: Author House.

Purkayastha, M. & Mukherjee, K. K. (2012). 'Three cases of near-death expererience: Is it physiology, physics or philosophy?' *Ann Neurosci. 19 (3)*, 104–06.

Radin, D. (2006). *Entangled Minds: Extrasensory Experiences in a Quantum Reality.* New York: Paraview Pocket Books.

Randles, J. (1988). *Alien Abductions.* New Brunswick, N.J.: Inner Light Publications.

Randles, J. (1997). *Alien Contact: The First Fifty Years.* New York: Barnes & Noble.

Rawlings, M. (1979). *Beyond Death's Door.* London: Thomas Nelson & Sons.

Reichel-Dolmatoff, G. (1971). *Amazonian Cosmos. The Sexual and Religious Symbolism of the Tukano Indians.* Chicago: University of Chicago Press.

Revonsuo, A. (2010). *Consciousness: The Science of Subjectivity.* Hove, New York: Psychology Press.

Ridge, M. (2005). 'Review of "Consciousness: Creeping Up On The Hard Problem" by Jeffrey Gray'. *Mind, Vol 114*, 417– 421.

Ring, K. (1980). *Life at Death: A Scientific Investigation of the Near-Death Experience.* New York: Coward, McCann & Geoghegan.

Ring, K. (1984). *Heading Toward Omega: In Search of the Meaning of the Near-Death Experience.* New York: William Morrow.

Ring, K. (1992). *The Omega Project: Near-Death Experiences, UFO Encounters, and Mind at Large.* New York: Kindle Edition.

Ring, K. (2011). *The Omega Project: Near-Death Experiences, UFO Encounters, and Mind at Large.* New York: William Morrow & Co.

Ring, K. & Cooper, S. (1997). 'Near death and out-of-body experiences in the blind: a study of apparently eyeless vision'. *Journal of Near-Death Studies*, 101–147.

Ring, K. & Elsaesser-Valarino, E. (2006). *Lessons from the Light: What We Can Learn from the Near-Death Experience.* Needham: Moment Press.

Ring, K. & Lawrence, M. (1993). 'Further evidence for veridical perception during near-death experiences'. *Journal of Near-Death Studies*, 223–229.

Ring, K. & Rosing, C. J. (1990). 'The Omega Project: An Empirical Study of the NDE-Prone Personality'. *Journal of Near-Death Studies 8 (4)*, 211–239.

Ritchie, G. (1998). *Ordered To Return: My Life After Dying*. Hampton Roads: Hampton Roads Publishing.

Ritchie, G. & Sherrill, E. (1978). *Return from Tomorrow*. Grand Rapids: Chosen Books Publishing.

Robertson, J. A. (1999). 'The dead donor rule'. *Hastings Center Report 29(6)*, 6–14.

Rosen, D. H. (1975). 'A Follow-up Study of Persons Who Survived Jumping from the Golden Gate and San Francisco-Oakland Bay Bridges'. *West J Med 122*, 289–294.

Ross, C. (1989). *Multiple personality disorder: Diagnosis, clinical features, and treatment*. New York: John Wiley.

Ruoho, A. E. (2009, February 13). 'The Hallucinogen N,N-Dimethyltryptamine (DMT) Is an Endogenous Sigma-1 Receptor Regulator (2009)'. *Science*, 934–937.

Saavedra-Aguilar, J. C. & Gomez-Jeria , J. S. (1989). 'A neurobiological model of near-death experiences'. *Journal of Near-Death Studies*, 205–222.

Sabom, M. (1982). *Recollections of Death: A Medical Investigation*. New York: Harper & Row.

Sabom, M. (1998). *Light & Death: One Doctor's Fascinating Account of Near-Death Experiences*. Grand Rapids: Zondervan.

Sacks, O. (2007). *Musicophilia: Tales of Music and the Brain*. London: Picador Classic.

Sacks, O. (2012, December 12). 'Seeing God in the Third Millennium'. *The Atlantic*.

Sagan, C. (1979). *Broca's Brain – Reflections on the Romance of Science*. New York: Random House.

Salisbury, F. B. (1967). 'The Scientist and the UFO'. *BioScience*, 15–24.

Sartori, P. (2008). *The near-death experiences of hospitalized intensive care patients: A five-year clinical study*. Lewiston: Edward Mellen Press.

Sartori, P., Badham, P. & Fenwick, P. (2006). 'A Prospectively Studied Near-Death Experience with Corroborated Out-of-Body Perceptions and Unexplained Healing'. *Journal of Near-Death Studies 25 (2)*, 69–84.

Scholem, G. (1977). *Zohar: The Book of Splendour*. London: Rider.

Schwaninger, J., Eisenberg, P. R., Schectman, K. B. & Weiss, A. N. (2002). 'A prospective analysis of near-death experiences in cardiac arrest patients'. *Journal of Near-Death Studies 20*, 215–232.

Schwartzkrion, P. A. (1997). 'Origins of the Epileptic State'. *Epilepsia 38 (8)*, 853–858.

Sealy, W. C. (1989). 'Hypothermia: Its possible role in cardiac surgery'. *Annals of Thoracic Surgery 47*, 170–172.

Serdahely, W. (1995). 'Variations from the Prototypic Near-Death Experience: The "Individually Tailored" Hypothesis'. *Journal of Near-Death Studies. 13(3)*, 185–196.

Serdahely, W. J. (1990). 'Pediatric near-death experiences'. *Journal of Near-Death Studies, 9*, 33–39.

Serdahely, W. J. (1992). 'Similarities Between Near-Death Experiences and Multiple Personality Disorder'. *Journal of Near-Death Studies 11 (1)*, 19–38.

Serdahely, W. J. & Walker, B. A. (1990). 'A Near-Death Experience at Birth'. *Death Studies 14*, 177–183.

Shamdasani, S. (2003). *Jung and the Making of Modern Psychology: The Dream of a Science*. Cambridge: Cambridge University Press.

Shiels, D. (1978). 'A cross-cultural study of beliefs in out-of-the-body experiences'. *Journal of the Society for Psychical Research. Vol. 49, no 775*, 697.

Shirokogoroff, S. M. (1923). 'General Theory of Shamanism among the Tungus'. *JRAS, North-China Branch*, 246–249.

Shlobin, N. A., Aru, J., Vicente, R. & Zemmar, A. (2023). 'What happens in the brain when we die? Deciphering the neurophysiology of the final moments in life'. *Frontiers in Aging Neuroscience Vol 15*.

Shulgin, A. & Shulgin, A. (1997). *TIHKAL*. Berkeley: Transform Press.

Shushan, G. (2009). *Conceptions of the Afterlife in Early Civilizations*. New York: Continuum International Publishing Group.

Shushan, G. (2011). 'Afterlife Conceptions in the Vedas'. *Religion Compass 5/6*, 202–213.

Siclari, F., Baird, B., Perogamvros, L., Bernardi, G., LaRocque, J. J., Riedner, B., Tononi, G. (2017). 'The neural correlates of dreaming'. *Nat. Neurosci. 20*, 872–878.

Siegel, R. K. (1977, October). 'Hallucinations'. *Scientific American*, 132–140.

Smit, R. H. & Rivas, T. (2010). 'Rejoinder to "Response to 'Corroboration of the Dentures Anecdote Involving Veridical Perception in a Near-Death'"'. *Journal of Near-Death Studies, 28(4)*, 193–205.

Soh, K. (2004). 'Bonghan duct and acupuncture meridian as optical channel of biophotons'. *Journal of the of the Korean Physical Society*, 1196–1198.

Spetzler, R. F., Hadley, M. N., Rigamonti, D., Carter, L. P., Raduzens, P. A., Shedd, S. A. & Wilkinson, E. (1988). 'Aneurysms of the basilar artery treated with circulatory arrest, hypothermia, and barbiturate cerebral protection'. *Journal of Neurosurgery 68*, 868–879.

St Clair, M. (1997). *Beyond the Light: Files of Near-Death Experiences*. New York: Barnes & Noble.

Stafford, L. B. (2004). 'Jung's Synchronistic Interpretation of the Near-Death Experience: An Unnecessary Mystification'. *Journal of Near-Death Studies 22 (4)*, 261–268.

Stetson, C., Cui, X., Montigue, P. R. & Eagleman, D. M. (2006). 'Motor-sensory recalibration leads to an illusory reversal of action and sensation'. *Neuron (51)*, 651–659.

Stetson, C., Fiesta, M. P. & Eagleman, D. M. (2007). 'Does time really slow down during a frightening event?' *PLoS ONE 2*.

Stevenson, I. & Cook, E. W. (1995). 'Involuntary memories during severe physical illness or injury'. *Journal of Nervous and Mental Disease, 183*, 452–458.

Stevenson, I. & Greyson, B. (1979). 'Near-death experiences: relevance to the question of survival after death'. *JAMA 242*, 254–267.

Stevenson, I., Cook, E. W. & McClean-Rice, N. (1990). 'Are persons reporting "near-death experiences" really near death? A study of medical records'. *Omega – Journal of Death and Dying 20*, 45–54.

Storm, H. (2005). *My Descent Into Death: A Second Chance at Life*. New York: Harmony.

Strassman, R. (2001). *DMT: The Spirit Molecule: A Doctor's Revolutionary Research into the Biology of Near-Death and Mystical Experiences (2001)*. Rochester, Vermont: Inner Traditions Bear and Company.

Strassman, R. J. (1997). 'Endogenous ketamine-like compounds and the NDE: If so, so what?' *Journal of Near-Death Studies 16 (1)*, 27–41.

Sutherland, C. (1992). *Reborn in the Light: Life After Near-Death Experiences*. New York: Bantam.

Tanous, A. (1976). *Beyond Coincidence*. New York: Doubleday.

Tart, C. (1968). 'A Psychophysiological Study of Out-of-Body Experiences in a Selected Subject'. *Journal of the American Society for Psychical Research 62 (1)*, 3–27.

Tart, C. C. (1998). 'Six Studies of Out-of-Body Experiences'. *Journal of Near-Death Studies 06:17*, 73–99.

Tart, C. T. (1970). 'Self Report Scales of Hypnotic Depth'. *International Journal of Clinical and Experimental Hypnosis 18:2*, 105–125.

Teasdale, G. & Jennett, B. (1974). 'Assessment of coma and impaired consciousness. A practical scale'. *The Lancet 2*, 81–84.

Tellegen, A. & Atkinson, G. (1974). 'Openness to absorbing and self-altering experiences ("absorption"), a trait related to hypnotic susceptibility'. *J Abnorm Psychol 83*, 268–277.

Thornton, C. & Sharpe, R. M. (1998). 'Evoked responses in anaesthesia'. *British Journal of Anaesthesia*, 771–781.

Tian, L., Jiang, T., Wang, Y., Zang, Y., He, Y., Liang, M., Zhuo, Y. (2006). 'Altered resting-state functional connectivity patterns of anterior cingulate cortex in adolescents with attention deficit hyperactivity disorder'. *Neurosci Lett. 400*, 39–43.

Tien, A. Y. (1991, December 26). 'Distributions of hallucinations in the population'. *Soc Psychiatry Psychiatr Epidemiol*, 287–292.

Timmermann, C., Roseman, L., Williams, L., Erritzoe, D., Martial, C., Cassol, H., Carhart-Harris, R. (2018, August 15). 'DMT Models the Near-Death Experience'. *Front Psychol.*

Tong, F. (2003). 'Out-of-Body Experiences – From Penfield to present'. *Trends in Cognitive Science*, 104–106.

Toren, I., Aberg, K. C. & Paz, R. (2020). 'Prediction errors bidirectionally bias time perception'. *Nature Neuroscience, 23*, 1198–1202.

Tranströmer, T. (2006). *The Great Enigma: New Collected Poems.* New York: New Direction Books.

Truzzi, M. (1978). 'On the Extraordinary: An Attempt at Clarification'. *Zetetic Scholar Vol 1, No 1*, 11.

Twemlow, S. W., Gabbard, G. O. & Coyne, L. (1982). 'A multivariate method for the classification of preexisting near-death conditions'. *Anabiosis 2*, 132–139.

van der Helm, E., Yao, J., Dutt, S., Rao, V., Saletin, J. M. & Walker, M. P. (2011). 'REM sleep depotentiates amygdala activity to previous emotional experience'. *Current Biology 21 (23)*, 2029–2032.

van der Sluijs, M. (2009). 'Three Ancient Reports of Near-Death Experiences: Bremmer Revisited'. *Journal of Near-Death Studies*, 223–252.

Van Eimeren, T., Monchi, O., Ballanger, B. & Strafella, A. P. (2009). 'Dysfunction of the default mode network in Parkinson disease: a functional magnetic resonance imaging study'. *Arch Neurol. 66*, 877–883.

van Lommel, P. (2007). *Eindeloos bewustzijn; een wetenschappelijke visie op de BijnaDood Ervaring.* Kampen: Ten Have.

van Lommel, P. (2010). *Consciousness Beyond Life.* San Francisco: Harper One.

van Lommel, P. (2011). *Beyond Life: The Science of Near-Death Experiences.* London: Harper Collins.

van Lommel, P., van Wees, R., Meyers, V. & Elfferich, I. (2001). 'Near-death

expererience in survivors of cardiac arrest'. *The Lancet*, 2039–2045.

van Rijn, C. M., Krijnen, H., Menting-Hermeling, S. & Coenen, A. M. (2011). 'Decapitation in rats: latency to unconsciousness and the "wave of death"'. *PLoS One 6:e16514.*

Vanhaudenhuyse, A., Thonnard, M. & Laureys, S. (2009). 'Towards a Neuro-scientific Explanation of Near-death Experiences?' In J. L. Vincent, *Intensive Care Medicine* (961–968). New York: Springer.

Velmans, M. (2005). 'Book Review: Consciousness: Creeping Up On The Hard Problem' by J. Gray. *Applied Cognitive Psychology 19*, 529–530.

Vicente, R., Rizzuto, M., Sarica, C., Kazuaki, Y., Sadr, M., Tarun, K., Zemmar, A. (2022). 'Enhanced Interplay of Neuronal Coherence and Coupling in the Dying Human Brain'. *Frontiers in Aging Neuroscience 14.*

Volk, S. (2011). *Fringe-ology: How I Tried to Explain Away the Unexplainable – And Couldn't.* London: Harper Collins.

Vollenweider, F., Leenders, K. L., Scharfetter, C., Maguire, P., Stadelmann, O. & Angst, J. (1997). 'Positron Emission Tomography and Fluorodeoxyglucose Studies of Metabolic Hyperfrontality and Psychopathology in the Psilocybin Model of Psychosis'. *Neuropsychopharmacology 16*, 357–372.

Vriens, E. M., Bakker, E. M., DeVries, J. W., Wieneke, G. H. & van Huffelin, A. C. (1996). 'The impact of repeated short episodes of circulatory arrest on cerebral function'. *Electroencephalography and Clinical Neurophysiology, 98*, 236–242.

Wade, J. (1996). *Changes of mind: A holonomic theory of the evolution of consciousness.* New York: State University of New York Press.

Walters, F., Chui, V., Atkinson, A. & Blom, J. D. (2018). 'Severe sleep deprivation causes hallucinations and a gradual progression toward psychosis with increasing time awake'. *Frontiers in Psychiatry*, 1–13.

Walton, T. (1996). *Fire in the Sky*. New York: Marloe & Company.

Wasson, R. G. (1986). 'Persephone's Quest'. In R. G. Wasson, S. Kramrisch, J. Ott & C. A. Ruck, *Persephone's Quest: Entheogens and the Origins of Religion*. New Haven: Yale University Press.

Watson-Franke, M.-B. (1975). '*Guajiro-Schamanen (Kolumbien und Venezuela)*'. *Anthropos 70*, 194–207.

Wettach, G. E. (2000). 'The Near-death experience as a Product of Isolated Subcortical Brain Function'. *Journal of Near-Death Studies*, 71–90.

Whinnery, J. (1997). 'Psychophysiologic correlates of unconsciousness and near-death experiences'. *Journal of Near-Death Studies 15*, 231–258.

Wile, L. (2018, September 3). 'A Neurocosmological Neurotheology Organized around Reissner's Fiber'. *Annals of Behavioral Neuroscience*, 56–65.

Wile, L. (2019). 'Reissner's Fiber's Strange Evolutionary Loops'. *NeuroQuantology*. *Vol 17. Issue 11*, 1–8.

Wile, L. (2022). 'The Heavenly Passage Known in the West as Reissner's Fiber'. *Religions 13 248*, 1–8.

Wile, L. C. (1994). 'Near-Death Experiences: A Speculative Neural Model'. *Journal of Near-Death Studies 12 (3)*, 133–142.

Williams, H. L., Conway, M. A. & Cohen, G. (2008). 'Autobiographical Memory'. In G. Cohen & M. A. Conway, *Memory in the Real World* (21–90). Hove: Psychology Press.

Wilson, S. C., & Barber, T. X. (1983). 'The fantasy-prone personality: Implications for understanding imagery, hypnosis, and parapsychological phenomena'. In A. Sheikh & (Ed), *Imagery: Current theory, research, and application* (340–387). New York: John Wiley.

Wittmann, M., Neumaier, L., Evrard, R., Weibel, A. & Schmied-Knittel, I. (2017). 'Subjective time distortion during near-death experiences: an analysis of reports'. *Zeitschrift für Anomalistik. Band 17*, 309–320.

Woerlee, G. M. (2004, May–June). 'Darkness, Tunnels, and Light'. *The Skeptical Enquirer*, 28–32.

Woerlee, G. M. (2007). *The Unholy Legacy of Abraham*. Leicester: Matador.

Woerlee, G. M. (2010). 'Response to "Corroboration of the Dentures Anecdote Involving Veridical Perception in a Near-Death Experience"'. *Journal of Near-Death Studies 28 (4)*, 181–191.

Woerlee, G. M. (2011). 'Could Pam Reynolds Hear? A New Investigation into the Possibility of Hearing During this Famous Near-Death Experience'. *Journal of Near-Death Studies*, 3–25.

Woolger, R. J. & Shingen, T. 'Beyond Death: Transition and the Afterlife'. Royal College of Psychiatrists.

Wutzler, A., Mavrogiorgou, P., Winter, C. & Juckel, G. (2011). 'Elevation of brain serotonin during dying'. *Neuroscience Letters*, 20–21.

Zaleski, C. (1987). *Otherworld Journeys: Accounts of Near-Death Experience in Medieval and Modern Times*. Oxford: Oxford University Press.

Zhi-ying , F. & Jian-xun, L. (1992). 'Near-Death Experiences Among Survivors of the 1976 Tangshan Earthquake'. *Journal of Near-Death Studies 11 (1)*, 39–48.

INDEX